Pre-Intermedia

Teacher's Book

New Headway English Course

John and Liz Soars
Mike Sayer

OXFORD
UNIVERSITY PRESS

Great Clarendon Street, Oxford OX2 6DP

Oxford University Press is a department of the University of Oxford. It furthers the University's objective of excellence in research, scholarship, and education by publishing worldwide in

Oxford New York

Athens Auckland Bangkok Bogotá Buenos Aires Calcutta Cape Town Chennai Dar es Salaam Delhi Florence Hong Kong Istanbul Karachi Kuala Lumpur Madrid Melbourne Mexico City Mumbai Nairobi Paris São Paulo Shanghai Singapore Taipei Tokyo Toronto Warsaw

with associated companies in Berlin Ibadan

Oxford and Oxford English are registered trade marks of Oxford University Press in the UK and in certain other countries

First published 2000

ISBN 0 19 436671 5

Printed in Portugal

Acknowledgements

The authors and publisher are grateful to those who have given permission to reproduce the following extracts and adaptations of copyright material:

Sailing by Sutherland © 1972 by kind permission of Universal/Island Music.
Killing Me Softly With His Song © 1974 by Fox & Gimbel. Onward Music Ltd. 11 Uxbridge Street, London W8 7TQ.
Sittin' On The Dock Of The Bay Words and Music by Otis Redding and Steve Cropper © 1968 East Memphis Music Corp/Cottilion Music Inc/Irving Music Inc, USA. (75%) Warner/Chappell Music Limited, London W6 8BS (25%) Rondor Music (London) Ltd, London SW6 4TW. Reproduced by permission of International Music Publications Ltd.
I'll Be There For You by Phil Solen, Marta Kauffman, David Crane, Michael Skloff, Allee Willis and Danny Wilde © 1995 WB Music Corp/ Warner-Tamerlane Publishing Corp, USA Warner/Chappell Music Limited, London W6 8BS. Reproduced by permission of International Music Publications Ltd.

Illustrations by:
Neil Gower: pp117, 120, 129
Tech Graphics Dept. OUP: pp54, 77
Harry Venning: p130

Photography by:
Stockbyte: p124
Telegraph Colour Library: p126

Contents

New Headway Pre-Intermediate

Introduction

New Headway Pre-Intermediate

Why a new version of *Headway Pre-Intermediate?*

A main reason for producing new versions of *Headway Elementary* and *Headway Pre-Intermediate* was to bring them into line with *New Headway Intermediate* and *New Headway Upper-Intermediate.* Having rewritten the two higher level books, it became increasingly apparent that it was necessary to ring some changes with the two lower levels. We felt that the time had come to give them a much fresher and lighter feel, but at the same time we didn't want to lose those elements that have proved successful with so many teachers. We believe that at lower levels the content and approach of language teaching is inevitably more restricted, and so a lot about the books remains the same.

What remains the same?

The basic *Headway* methodology is the same. Proven traditional approaches are used alongside those which have been developed and researched more recently.

The grammatical syllabus is largely unchanged because the requirements of lower level students are usually more predictable than at later levels.

There is a great variety of practice activities. Some of these have been amended rather than replaced. Nevertheless there are still many new ones.

Vocabulary is not only integrated throughout but also developed in its own section.

Skills work is integrated and balanced. It all comes from authentic sources but has been simplified and adapted to suit the level.

There is an *Everyday English* section.

What are the differences?

The design is completely new, and this represents a break in what a *Headway* Student's Book traditionally looked like. It is cleaner and fresher, and activities are easier to follow. There is more space on a page, and some of the exercises and activities are shorter.

The vast majority of the texts are new. We took this opportunity to freshen up the topics. Teachers very easily get fed up with using the same texts year after year. Sometimes we have found a parallel text on the same topic, but more often we have selected a new topic and a new text.

There are several new features, such as the *Starter* at the beginning of a unit, and the *Grammar Spot.*

Many of the vocabulary exercises are different, new or amended, as are the topics of the *Everyday English* section.

STARTER

This is designed to be a warmer to the lesson. It is a short student-centred activity and always has direct relevance to the language to be introduced in the unit. The aim is to focus students on the topic or key language point of the unit. It also enables the teacher to find out how well the students can use the language of the unit.

GRAMMAR SPOT

This is a mix of explanation, questions, and self-check tasks to reinforce the grammar being taught. There is a page reference given to the fuller Grammar Reference at the back of the book.

What's in the Teacher's Book?

- **Full teaching notes**, answers, and possible problems
- ***Don't forget!* section** which refers to relevant exercises in the Workbook, the video, and to the Word list.
- **Tapescripts** in the main body of the teaching notes
- **Word list**
  There is a list of words that appear unit by unit in *New Headway Pre-Intermediate.* Photocopy the Word list for each unit as you go through the book and give a copy to each of your students. It is probably best given towards the end of each unit as an aid to revision.
  Encourage students to write in the translation if they feel it is necessary. Most of the new words are here, but if we feel a word isn't very useful or very common, we have omitted it. Some very useful words are repeated if they appear in a later unit; it is a good idea to revise them.
- **Extra ideas and songs section** with notes on how to use them for use after Units 1–4, 5–8, 9–12, and 13–14. You will find the songs on the recording at the end of each section, i.e. at the end of Units 4, 8, 12, and 14.
- **Stop and check tests**
  There are four Stop and check revision tests which cover Units 1–4, 5–8, 9–12, and 13–14. These can either be set in class, or given for homework (preferably over a weekend) and then discussed in the next lesson. Students can work in small groups to try to agree on the correct answer, then you can go over it with the whole class, reminding students of the language items covered. It is important that, in the translation sentences which come at the end of each Stop and check test, students translate the ideas and concepts, and not word by word.
- **Progress tests**
  There are three Progress tests which cover Units 1–5, 6–10, and 11–14.

What's in the Workbook?

The Workbook is an important component of the course. It revises the grammatical input of the Student's Book and contains the writing syllabus. Many of the exercises are on the Student's Workbook recording, for use in class or at home.

What's in the Teacher's Resource Book?

The Teacher's Resource Book is a new feature for *Headway.* It contains photocopiable games and activities to supplement the main course material.

VIDEO

A *Headway Pre-Intermediate Video*, Video Guide, and Activity Book are available as an optional accompaniment to the course. The video is linked to the syllabus and consists of mini-documentaries on topics that reflect those in the Student's Book, and situational language such as in a shop and in a pub.

Finally!

There is a lot that is new in the new editions, but there are many aspects that you will be familiar with. We actually try to guide students to an understanding of new language, rather than just have examples of it on the page. We attach great importance to practice activities, both controlled and free, personalized and impersonal. The skills work comes from a wide range of material – newspapers, magazines, biographies, short stories, radio programmes, songs – and features both British and American English. We hope you and your students enjoy using the books, and have success with them whether using *Headway* for the first time or having learned to trust its approach from previous use.

Tenses • Questions
Using a bilingual dictionary
Social expressions 1

Getting to know you

Introduction to the unit

You are probably beginning a new class with a group of students you don't know. Students might know each other, or they might not. Your main aim over the first few lessons together is to try to make the group gel. You need to establish a good classroom atmosphere, where everyone feels comfortable. Hopefully you will all not only work hard, but have fun at the same time.

Another of your aims will be to check out your students' language abilities. How good are they at using the tense system? Do they confuse the Present Simple and Continuous? (Probably.) Can they form questions in English? (Probably not.) What's their vocabulary like? Is there a disparity in their skills abilities? Can they speak English better than write it? Do they panic when listening to a recording? All this information will allow you to get to know them, and also help you to plan your lessons.

The theme of this unit is communication. The Starter and opening 'Two Students' sections revise present and past tenses and question forms, and students are encouraged to ask questions to get to know each other in the *Practice* section.

The *Reading and speaking* section contains a text about how people communicate, and the *Listening and speaking* section involves listening to two neighbours describe their relationship.

There are opportunities for students to roleplay polite conversations and practise social expressions.

Language aims

Grammar – tenses There is revision of the Present Simple and Continuous, the Past Simple, the *going to* future, the modal verb *can*, and the full verb *have*. (*Have* appears with the *do/does/did* forms. *Have got* and *have* are contrasted in Unit 2.) Students should be familiar with these tenses and verb forms, but they will no doubt still make many mistakes.

This unit provides general revision of these verb forms and their meanings, and gives you the opportunity to assess your new students' strengths and weaknesses. All the verb forms are dealt with in greater depth in later units of *New Headway Pre-Intermediate.*

Question forms The secondary grammatical aim of Unit 1 is revision of question forms. These often present learners of English with problems.

Common mistakes:

**Where you live?*	**What you do last night?*
**Where do he live?*	**What did you last night?*
**Do you can speak French?*	**Where you went?*

Another problem for learners is voice range. English has a very wide voice range, and this is apparent in question formation.

Where do you live?

Do you like learning English?

Students often have a very flat intonation, and they need to be encouraged to make their voice rise and fall as necessary.

Vocabulary In the *Vocabulary* section, students are helped to use a bilingual dictionary effectively, both L1 to English and English to L1.

Everyday English Common social expressions are introduced and practised through dialogues.

Notes on the unit

STARTER (SB p6)

1 Ask students to work in pairs to match the questions with the answers.

Answers

Where were you born?	In Thailand.
What do you do?	I'm a teacher.
Are you married?	No, I'm single.
Why are you learning English?	Because I need it for my job.
When did you start learning English?	A year ago.
How often do you have English classes?	Three times a week.

2 Students ask and answer the questions in pairs.

TWO STUDENTS (SB p6)

Tenses and questions

1 Ask students to look at the photograph of Maurizio and think of questions to ask him, for example: *Where are you from?* Write a few suggestions on the board.

T 1.1 Tell students to listen to Maurizio and read the text at the same time. Ask if they found the answers to any of their questions and check any words they didn't understand. Then ask students to work in pairs to complete the text with the verbs in the box.

Answers and tapescript
My name's Maurizio Celi. I (1) **come** from Bologna, a city in the north of Italy. I'm a student at the University of Bologna.
I (2) **'m studying** modern languages – English and Russian.
I also know a little Spanish, so I (3) **can speak** four languages.
I (4) **'m enjoying** the course a lot, but it's really hard work.
The course (5) **started** three years ago.
I (6) **live** at home with my parents and my sister. My brother (7) **went** to work in the United States last year.
After I graduate, I (8) **'m going to work** as a translator. I hope so, anyway.

In the feedback, ask students to tell you whether each verb has present, past, or future meaning, but don't get into detail about use at this stage.

2 Ask students to look at the picture of Carly. Ask questions.
Examples
Where is she? (At home.)
What's she doing? (She's studying.)
How old is she? (About thirty-five.)
Is she studying at university? (Perhaps. We don't know.)

Ask students to work in pairs to complete the questions about Carly. Monitor and note the sort of problems your students have with question formation.

POSSIBLE PROBLEMS
- Students omit *does* and *did* in the Present and Past Simple.
- They confuse the Present Continuous and the Present Simple (*What does she studying?).
- They treat the modal verb *can* as though it were a full verb (*How many languages does she can speak?).
- They forget *is* in the *going to* question. (*What she going to do after the course?)

Answers
2 **Where does she** live?
3 **Who does she** live with?
4 What **is she** studying?
5 **Is she** enjoying the course?
6 How many **languages does she** speak?
7 **When** did her course start?
8 What **is she going to do** after she graduates?

When students have finished, ask individuals for the completed questions. When each question form has been established, give a model yourself and drill each question, chorally if you like, but certainly individually, for pronunciation. Remember that English uses a wider voice range than many other languages, and question-word questions should start with the voice high and then fall.

Where does she come from?

T 1.2 Ask students to listen to Carly, then to work in pairs to write the answers to the questions.

Answers and tapescript
1 She comes from Australia.
2 She lives near London.
3 She lives with her husband and three children.
4 She's studying art.
5 Yes, she is.
6 Two.
7 A year ago.
8 She's going to look for a job in an art gallery or museum.

T 1.2
Hi. My name's Carly and I come from Australia. But I live near London now with my husband Dave and our three children. I came to Britain fifteen years ago when I got married.
I'm a student with the Open University. This means I watch special programmes on the television and work at home. I send my work to my course teacher every week. I'm studying art and the course is really interesting. At the moment, I'm reading about Italian painters in Italian, which is difficult because I only speak a little Italian!
My course started a year ago and it's three years long. After I graduate, I'm going to look for a job in an art gallery or museum.

3 Ask students to work in pairs to complete the questions.

Answers
2 **Do you have** a job?
3 What **are you doing** at the moment?
4 **When did you come** to England?
5 **What's your husband's** name?
6 **What does your husband do?**

Again, drill these questions around the class, focusing on the way the tone of voice starts high then falls.

GRAMMAR SPOT (SB p7)

The *Grammar Spot* in each unit aims to get students to think analytically about the language, so don't rush it. Ask students to discuss grammar questions in pairs before feeding back to the whole class as this encourages peer teaching and builds students' confidence. If you are teaching a monolingual class, and your students find it easier or more rewarding to answer in L1, encourage them to do so.

1 If you didn't focus on this earlier, ask students to work in pairs to find examples of verb forms with present, past and future meaning in the text about Maurizio and Carly. However, don't go into any detail about form and use of past and future tenses here as they will be dealt with in later units.

2 Ask students to discuss the two questions about present tenses in pairs or threes then discuss their answers as a class.

Answers
The two verb forms are the Present Simple and the Present Continuous.
They are formed differently. The third person of the Present Simple ends in *-s*. The Present Continuous is formed with the verb *to be* + *-ing*.
More importantly, they mean different things. The Present Simple is used to express an action which is always true, or true for a long time. The Present Continuous is used to express an activity happening now, or around now.

3 Ask students to work in pairs to match the question words and answers. Do the first as an example. This activity gets students to think about the meaning of the question words. In the feedback, you could get students to guess what the whole question might be.

Answers

What . . . ?	A sandwich.
Who . . . ?	Jack.
Where . . . ?	In New York.
When . . . ?	Last night.
Why . . . ?	Because I wanted to.
How many . . . ?	Four.
How much . . . ?	$5.
How . . . ?	By bus.
Whose . . . ?	It's mine.
Which . . . ?	The black one.

Ask students to read Grammar Reference 1.1 and 1.2 on p129 for homework.

PRACTICE (SB p8)

Talking about you

1 Ask students to work in pairs and give them a few minutes to think about how to form the questions, then get them to take turns to ask and answer with their partner. It might be a good idea to do this activity as a mingle, especially if students don't know each other very well. If your students do already know each other well, distribute pictures of people cut out of magazines, and they can assume these new identities.

Monitor as students are asking and answering questions, helping and correcting as necessary.

As a follow-up, get students to ask you the questions. Or, alternatively, give students three or four minutes in pairs to think of some different questions to ask you. If they know you very well already, you could use a picture of someone else. Hold it up and say *This is me. Think of some questions to ask me.*

Correct any mistakes very carefully. You want to have genuine communication at this point, but you also want well-formed questions with good pronunciation.

2 Focus students on the questions, and read them out, modelling good pronunciation. Alternatively, ask each question to an individual in the class, thus modelling pronunciation and getting students to think about how to respond. Notice that the questions test two present tenses, the Past Simple, and the Present Continuous to refer to a future arrangement. Divide students into small groups to ask and answer the questions. Monitor, help and correct any errors.

3 Ask students to write a paragraph about themselves using the text about Maurizio as a model. You could set this as homework.

Getting information

4 In this information gap activity students must ask each other questions to find out about Joy Darling, a postwoman. In an activity of this kind the more preparation and setting up you do, the more likely that students will do it accurately and well.

Lead in by focusing students on the photograph of Joy and asking them questions about it.

Where's Joy? (In the street.)
What's she doing? (She's delivering letters.)
Does she wear a uniform? (Yes, she does.)
Does she drive a van for work? (Yes, she does.)

Photocopy the information cards on p117 of the Teacher's Book. Give half the class Student A cards, and half the class Student B cards. Ask them to read their information and check any words they don't know.

Then ask them to work with a partner with the same card to prepare questions using the question word prompts. Monitor and help them prepare. When they are ready, change the pairs so that one Student A is with a Student B. Model the activity briefly by asking one or two questions, then let students ask and answer each other's questions to complete their information.

COMPLETE TEXT

Joy Darling started working as a postwoman thirty years ago, when she was 22. She drives a van because she delivers letters to a lot of small villages.

She gets up at 3.30 in the morning and starts work at 5.00. Every day she drives about 150 miles. She finishes work at 2.00 in the afternoon.

After work she goes home and has lunch with her husband, Jim. He has a part-time job. He works in a shop. They like gardening, so they spend the afternoon outside in their garden.

They have two children, who both live in California. Last year Joy and Jim went to Los Angeles and visited their children and four grandchildren. They stayed for a month.

They're going to Australia next month because some friends are having a big party. It's their friends' wedding anniversary, and they want everyone to be there.

Check it

5 Students work in pairs to decide which is the correct verb form. As you get the answers, ask *Why?* each time to reinforce the rules about the Present Simple and Continuous, Past Simple, and the *going to* future.

Answers

1 **comes** (because this is a fact which is always true)
2 **speaks** (same reason)
3 **is wearing** (because this is happening now)
4 **Do you like** (because this is always true and *like* is a state verb)
5 **went** (because this is in the past)
6 **is going to study** (because this is in the future – an intention)

ADDITIONAL MATERIAL

Workbook Unit 1

These exercises could be done in class to give further practice, for homework, or in a later class as revision.

Exercises 1–3 Recognizing tenses

Exercises 4–10 Question forms

VOCABULARY (SB p9)

Using a bilingual dictionary

Bilingual dictionaries are very useful when students are beginning to learn a language, but they need to be used with caution. They vary greatly in amount of detail and accuracy of information. The better ones will separate out different meanings, and give plenty of example sentences. Problems arise especially when students look up a word in the L1 to English section and find perhaps three or four words in English to choose from. They need to look at the information very carefully to know which one is correct in context.

In these exercises, students are asked to look at their own dictionary to see how much information it gives. They then practise using both halves of their dictionary, first English to L1 then L1 to English.

1 Ask students to look at the dictionary extract. If they are used to using dictionaries to look words up in their own language, they should be able to do it for a foreign language quite easily. However, the reverse is also the case. If students aren't used to using dictionaries in L1, basic skills such as alphabetical order and the standard conventions of dictionary entries (how information is presented; the order of information; symbols) will need to be practised.

2 Ask students to work in pairs and decide if the words in the box are nouns, verbs, adjectives, adverbs, prepositions, or past tenses.

Answers

bread	*n*	never	*adv*
hot	*adj*	went	*pt*
write	*v*	on	*prep*
quickly	*adv*	came	*pt*
beautiful	*adj*	eat	*v*
in	*prep*	letter	*n*

3 Ask students if they can think of any words in English with two meanings. Then focus them on the table and point out the two different meanings of *book*. Ask students to work in pairs then ask them to use dictionaries to look up the other words in the table and write sentences to show the two meanings of each word. Monitor and help.

T 1.3 Ask students to compare their sentences with the sample answers on the recording.

Sample answers and tapescript

1 I'm reading a good **book**.
I **booked** a room at a hotel.
2 What **kind** of music do you like?
My mother's a very **kind** person.
3 **Can** you swim?
I'd like a **can** of Coke.
4 What does this **mean**?
Some people are very **mean**. They don't like spending their money.
5 I live in a **flat**.
Holland is a **flat** country.
6 Do you want to **play** football?
We saw a **play** at the theatre.
7 The **train**'s coming.
Athletes have to **train** very hard.
8 The phone's **ringing**.
What a lovely **ring** you're wearing!

4 This final activity allows students to decide for themselves which words they would like to look up. You might decide to do it at the beginning of the next lesson as a quick revision of dictionary use.

SUGGESTION

Instead of getting students to look around the room, bring in as many everyday objects as you can. When students have found the word in the dictionaries, put the object on the floor. Carry on until all (or most) of the objects are on the floor. Point to an object and ask for the word to be repeated. Correct any mistakes. Ask a student to come out to the front and point at an object and invite a student to repeat.

What follows is a memory game. Remove one object from the floor. Students must remember what the object was, so that when you point to the empty space on the floor, they can still tell you the word. Carry on removing objects until about a third remain on the floor. After that, it becomes very difficult to remember exactly what was where!

ADDITIONAL MATERIAL

Workbook Unit 1
Exercise 11 is a vocabulary exercise on jobs in which students will need to use dictionaries to find suffixes and where the stress is.

READING (SB p10)

Communication

A NOTE ON COMMUNICATION

This may be the first time that you are doing a fluency-based lesson with this class, and your aims in such lessons are obviously different from accuracy-based ones. Your aim now is to promote natural language use, with students trying to understand and trying to make themselves understood with all the language they possess. The extent to which your students are used to the demands of such lessons will vary, depending on their previous language-learning experience.
It can be frustrating for students at this level to do fluency work, because their lack of language prevents them from understanding and saying all that they would like. However, if the right topics are found, it can be extremely beneficial and enjoyable for students to realize that they can operate as real language users.

In the pre- and post-reading tasks in this section, students get to talk about how people and animals communicate. Let this discussion go on as long as everyone seems interested. You might find that by the time you get to the 'What do you think?' questions, students are tired, having worked hard at the speaking activity and the reading comprehension.

1 Ask students to work in pairs (or groups of three or four) to write down as many different ways of communicating as they can. Use the cartoons to start them off. Monitor and help with vocabulary. In the feedback, list some of their ideas on the board.
Some suggestions:
Using a phone
Writing and posting a letter
Sending an e-mail
Using the Internet
Sending a fax
TV and radio
Smoke signals
Sign language
Braille
Morse code

2 Write the following list of 'ideas to communicate' on the board and mime one or two to get the students started, (for example, lifting an imaginary cup of coffee to your lips, pointing to your watch). Then put the students in pairs to mime the ideas to each other. Alternatively, you could make this an information gap activity, by giving each student a different list of ideas on a handout which they have to mime to their partner.
Do you want a cup of coffee?
What time is it?
I'm tired.

Have you got any money?
I like your haircut.
I'll phone you at 7.
Can you swim?
I've got a headache.
I'm cold/hot.
This food is too hot.
I can't carry this bag.
What's that awful smell?

3 Focus students on the headings and check that they understand them, then ask students to read the article and match the headings to the paragraphs. Tell them not to worry about words in the text they don't know at this stage. Ask students to check their answers in pairs before feedback.

Answers

Paragraph 1	How we communicate
Paragraph 2	Differences between people and animals
Paragraph 3	A history of communication
Paragraph 4	Communication today

4 Ask students to match the pictures and ancient societies.

Answers

Picture a	Rome
Picture b	Greece
Picture c	14th century Europe
Picture d	Egypt

5 Focus the class on the comprehension questions and check that there are no problems with understanding, then ask students to work in pairs or small groups to look back at the text and answer the questions.

Answers

1 Bees/dance
Elephants/make sounds humans can't hear
Whales/sing songs
Monkeys/use their faces to show emotions
2 Humans have language. They can write poetry, tell jokes, make promises, explain, persuade, tell the truth, tell lies.
3 Radio, film, television, and the Internet.
4 **Good**: you can give and get information quickly
Bad: it is difficult to know what information is important

A NOTE ON THE VOCABULARY

Reading texts are an excellent source of new vocabulary because they introduce words in natural contexts which allow students to guess what words might mean. There are a number of different ways of dealing with the unknown vocabulary in this text and other texts in the coursebook. Here are two suggestions:

1 After they have read the text, ask students to underline words they don't know then try to guess what they mean. You could get them to check with a partner before checking their guesses in a dictionary.
2 If you know your students and their first language well, you could predict words they don't know then give students synonyms or definitions and ask them to find matching words in the text, for example *Find a word that means the largest animal in the sea.*

Discourage students from using dictionaries too many times as they read. They may lose the thread of the article if they spend too much time looking up words.

What do you think?

Discuss these questions as a class. Question 3 will bring out any current news about information technology. Notice that the question (and probably the answer) uses the Present Continuous.

LISTENING AND SPEAKING (SB p12)

Neighbours

This is the first of several jigsaw activities in *New Headway Pre-Intermediate.* If a jigsaw goes well, students have to speak a lot, listen a lot, (perhaps) read a lot, and write. So it is a multi-skills lesson with a built in information gap – Group A doesn't know what Group B knows (and vice versa), and they have to work together to find the missing information. The only drawback of such activities is that with jigsaw listening (not so much reading), ideally you need two rooms, as students can't concentrate on their own recording if they are all together. Hopefully, this drawback is compensated for by the involvement of students.

1 Check that students understand 'ideal neighbours' then elicit what they think makes a good neighbour. Get as many ideas as you can.

Ask students to work individually to complete the questionnaire then compare their answers with their partner. Try to encourage lots of discussion in the feedback.

2 Discuss the quotation and the questions in small groups or as a class.

3 **T 1.4** and **T 1.5** Focus students on the photograph of Mrs Snell and Steve and point out that they are neighbours. Ask students if they think they might be good neighbours, and if not, why not? Divide students into two groups, with a tape recorder and the right tape.

Tapescripts

T 1.4 Mrs Snell

I've got a new neighbour. He moved in a few weeks ago. He's got a job, because I see him leaving the house every morning and then coming home in the evening. He's a builder, I think. He wears jeans and a T-shirt, so it can't be a very good job. Sometimes he comes home late.

I've never spoken to him. When he sees me, he says hello, but I don't answer back because nobody has introduced us. How can I speak to him?

His girlfriend is living with him. I know it's not unusual these days, but I still don't like it, boys and girls living together and not married. It's such a small flat. I don't know how two people can live there.

He had a party last week. Forty people! The noise! It went on until two in the morning. He said sorry the next day, but it was a bit late by then. I didn't sleep all night.

Oh, there's the door. I can see him now. He's going out with his girlfriend. I wonder what they're doing tonight. Having a good time. Going to the pub, probably.

T 1.5 Steve

I moved into this flat a few weeks ago, and I'm really enjoying living here. There's only one bedroom, and at the moment my sister is staying with me because she's looking for a job.

I work in advertising. It's hard work, and the hours are really long, but I like it. And it's well paid. The office is really relaxed. No one wears a suit or a tie.

The only thing I don't like about this flat is one of the neighbours, Mrs Snell, I think her name is. She's really strange. She never speaks to anyone. I always say hello to her, and 'Are you all right?' and 'What a lovely day today!', but she never says a word. Maybe she doesn't like young people.

I had a party a few days ago. It really wasn't very noisy. About ten of us were here until 11.00 and then we went out to a club. When I saw Mrs Snell the next day, I said I hoped there wasn't too much noise, but as usual she didn't say anything. Funny lady.

This evening my sister and I are going to visit a friend of ours who's in hospital, and then we're going out for a Chinese meal.

4 Tell them to listen to the recording several times and to answer the questions. You should go between the two groups, making sure that they are all right, and helping where necessary. Tell them that they can't answer *all* the questions and that the questions are not in the same order as the text.

When both groups are ready, bring the class back together, and ask students to find a partner from the other group. If you have an odd number of students, you will need a group of three. Be careful that the class doesn't collapse into chaos at this point! Students need to find a partner and sit down together *as quickly as possible*!

When students have shared all their information, go through the answers briefly as a class.

Answers

1 He moved in a few weeks ago.
2 No, it isn't.
3 She thinks he's a builder. In fact, he works in advertising. It is a good job.
4 Yes, he does.
5 He wears jeans and a T-shirt.
6 She thinks it's his girlfriend, but in fact it's his sister.
7 He says 11 o'clock. She says 2 o'clock.
8 He says about 10. She says forty.
9 She thinks he's going to the pub, but in fact he's going to see a friend in hospital, then he's going for a Chinese meal.
10 She finds it difficult to talk to someone without being introduced. Perhaps she's shy. She is certainly suspicious of young people.

Roleplay

The aim of this activity is to give students some fluency practice. Don't worry about mistakes. It is more important that students are able to express themselves as fully as possible.

Divide students into threes. Ask them to decide whether they want to be Steve, Mrs Snell, or the other neighbour. When they have selected their roles, give them some time to look at the answers to the questions in 4, or to look at the tapescripts on p118, and to prepare what they are going to say.

When they are ready, model the activity by taking the role of the neighbour and acting out the start of the conversation with a couple of confident students. Monitor the groups as they do the roleplay, and prompt students if they run out of things to say.

What do you think?

Discuss this as a class. Note that *generation gap* means a difference in attitude, or a lack of understanding, between young people and older people (OALD).

Give students a little time to write their lists then put them in small groups to discuss their ideas.

EVERYDAY ENGLISH (SB p13)

Social expressions 1

1 Ask students to look at the pictures. Where do they think the people are? What's the relationship between them? Ask students what they think the people are saying to each other. Point out that we say certain things at certain times. Try to elicit other typical expressions.
Ask students to match the expressions and responses. Do one as an example. This exercise is more difficult than it at first appears. Some students will finish it very quickly, but will probably have made several mistakes. Monitor closely, look at their work and say how many they have right and wrong, without saying which ones, and ask them to look again.

T 1.6 Listen to the recording to check the answers.

Answers and tapescript
'How are you?' 'Fine, thanks.' (Two friends greeting each other informally.)
'Hello, Jane!' 'Hi, Peter!'
'How do you do?' 'How do you do?' (Formal. Said when you meet somebody for the first time, especially in a business situation.)
'See you tomorrow!' 'Bye!' (Neutral)
'Good night!' 'Sleep well!' (Said as people go to bed.)
'Good morning!' 'Good morning!' (Formal: said, for example, at work.)
'Hello, I'm Ela Paul.' 'Pleased to meet you, Ela.' (Informal. Said when you meet somebody for the first time.)
'Cheers!' 'Cheers!' (When you're having an alcoholic drink.)
'Excuse me!' 'Yes. Can I help you?' (In a shop, for example, to get someone's attention.)
'Bless you!' 'Thanks.' (When someone sneezes.)
'Have a good weekend!' 'Same to you!' (Said on a Friday afternoon or evening.)
'Thank you very much indeed.' 'Not at all. Don't mention it.' (Formal. Informally, we might say *That's OK.*)
'Make yourself at home.' 'That's very kind. Thank you.' (Said when a guest comes to your home.)

Ask students to tell you in what situations the dialogues are taking place.

Play the recording again and get students to repeat each expression as a class. Alternatively, you could model the expressions getting individuals in the class to repeat, focusing on correct intonation, which is very important here.

2 Ask students to work in pairs to test whether they can use the expressions.

3 Students work in pairs again to prepare two short dialogues. Introduce this activity by building up a dialogue as a model on the board first, and getting students to think where their dialogue is to take place before they start writing. Monitor and help.

Listen to a few of the dialogues, and feed back on any errors, focusing on students' intonation.

Don't forget!

Workbook Unit 1
Exercise 12 Writing an informal letter

SUGGESTION
In the Teacher's Book we sometimes suggest when the writing activities could be done, but generally we leave it up to you to decide.

It can be productive to use a code when you are correcting written work so that you direct students to the nature of the mistake, and then they have to try to correct it. This is not always possible – the mistake might be way beyond what they could be expected to understand. Be selective in what you ask students to self-correct.

You might like to use the following symbols:

G	Grammar	/	This word isn't necessary.
P	Punctuation	^	A word is missing
WO	Word order	T	Tense
WW	Wrong word	Sp	Spelling
Prep	Preposition		

It is a useful, although difficult, skill to teach students to proof-read their written work before handing it in. Here are two suggestions.

1 Make a list of some of your students' mistakes from a written homework. Write them on the board. Students must first identify the nature of the mistake using one of the above symbols, then actually correct it.

2 When you collect in written work, you can occasionally redistribute it straight away, making sure that a student doesn't get his/her own work back. In pairs, and in pencil, students try to find and correct mistakes. Do this just for ten minutes. Students tend to get very critical, and start finding mistakes where there aren't any!

Pronunciation book Unit 1

Word list
Photocopy the Word list for Unit 1 (TB p152) for your students and ask them to write in the translations, learn them at home, and/or write some of the words into their vocabulary notebook.

Present tenses • *have/have got*
Collocation – daily life
Making conversation

The way we live

Introduction to the unit

The theme of this unit is the way we live. The opening 'People and places' section has reading and listening texts containing facts and figures about different English-speaking countries. The *Practice* section provides the opportunity to practise Present tenses and *have/have got* in the context of lifestyles. The *Reading and listening* section contains readings about how other nationalities find life in the United States, the *Vocabulary* section collocates nouns and verbs around the topic of daily life, and the *Listening and speaking* section contains a radio programme in which two couples talk about their partner's annoying habits.

There are opportunities throughout the unit for students to talk about their own way of life and about their own country.

Language aims

Grammar – Present tenses Present tenses are revised in terms of form and use, with particular attention given to forming Present Simple questions and short answers using the auxiliary *do/does*. It is assumed that students will have a certain familiarity with both the Present Simple and the Present Continuous, although of course mistakes will still be made.

have/have got The verb *have* for possession is used as part of the practice for the Present Simple. However, it is also contrasted with *have got* for possession in both form and use.

Students at this level are often familiar with *have got* from their beginners' and elementary courses, but they are a little confused about its relation to the full verb *to have* both in its form, particularly in questions and negatives, and in its use. In fact, they are often interchangeable, but generally speaking *have got* is more informal.

Vocabulary The first vocabulary activity is a matching exercise which gets students to collocate verbs with noun phrases, and the second is an exercise which gets them to order these phrases under the topic headings of different rooms. The lexical area is 'Daily life', chosen because it fits well with the theme of the unit, allowing students to talk about what they do in their homes.

There is a personalized practice activity in which students are asked to describe their favourite room to their partner.

Everyday English This provides practice in making a conversation. It introduces and practises phrases students can use to start a conversation and keep it going.

Notes on the unit

STARTER (SB p14)

As a lead-in, ask students to name as many English-speaking countries as they can. This should be done *quickly*. You could make it into a little competition. Set a time limit and see who can write down the most in that time.

Ask students to work in pairs to look at the flags in their book, discuss which country they think they belong to and write the name of the country beneath the flag.

Answers

1 Australia	3 South Africa	5 The United States
2 New Zealand	4 Scotland	6 Canada

Check answers with the whole class before the next exercise.

PEOPLE AND PLACES (SB p14)

Present tenses and *have/have got*

1 Tell students that they are going to read three short texts with some facts about three of the countries. Tell them not to worry about the missing words.

Ask them to work in pairs to read, then discuss which of the six countries they think is being described. This can generate quite a lot of discussion, as some countries are easier to identify than others, so you may have to encourage them to do it by a process of elimination.

If there are any vocabulary problems, deal with them quickly yourself rather than asking students to use dictionaries. You do not want the activity to last too long, because the main aim of the reading here is to provide a context for the grammar.

In the feedback, encourage some full-class discussion about which country is being described by each text. Ask questions such as:

What did you decide? Why? How did you decide? Which facts helped you to decide?

Answers
a Australia b Canada c South Africa

Focus students on the missing words from each text, and ask them to work in pairs to put them in the correct gap. Do the first as an example.

Answers
a huge immigrants enjoy exports
b only variety has favourite
c black climate grows elephants

2 **T 2.1** Tell students that they are going to hear three people describing the other three countries. Ask them to match a flag and photograph with each description, then discuss which of the countries they think are being described with their partner. Again, before you give the answers, encourage some whole class discussion.

Answers and tapescript
d **New Zealand**
Well, my country's got a population of . . . er . . . about three and a half million, so it's not a big place. Most of the people are from Europe, but about twelve per cent are Maori . . . they were the original inhabitants. A lot of people live in bungalows, which are small houses on one floor, and have a pet. It's a very beautiful country. It's got a lot of mountains, and people love the countryside. Oh, and we're very good at rugby and cricket.
e **Scotland**
My country is the northern part of a bigger country, but we've got our own parliament. There are just over 5 million of us. We've got a lot of mountains, and there are also lots of rivers, lakes, and islands. People come to my country to fish. Our salmon is famous all over the world. And we also produce a very famous drink called whisky.
f **the United States**
I come from a big country. It has a lot of wide open spaces. We have a population of . . . almost 300 million, and these people have come from all over the world. We have big, cosmopolitan cities, but a lot of people live on farms, ranches, and in small towns. We like baseball and football – our kind of football. And we love to eat . . . hamburgers with fries, and apple pie and ice-cream.

3 Ask students to close their books and try to remember three facts about each country.

GRAMMAR SPOT (SB p15)

This lesson reaches its main aim at this point. Focus the attention of the whole class on these questions so that your students are clear about the grammatical aims of the lesson.

Answers

1 The tense used is the Present Simple (not the Present Continuous) because present habits and permanent/general truths are described.

2 *She has three children* refers to all time.
She's having a shower refers to now.

3 *Have* is used in texts a–c because they are giving formal and factual information in writing, and *have* is used in more formal writing.
Have got is used in texts d and e. It is more likely to be used when speaking informally.

Refer students to Grammar Reference 2.1–2.4 on p130.

4 The aim here is not only to personalize the activity and have a short discussion about students' own countries, but also for you, the teacher, to be noting how well students are using present tenses and *have/have got.*

In a monolingual class, get students to work briefly in pairs to come up with a few sentences. In a class with a variety of nationalities, you might want to get students to work individually to think of a few things to say before discussing it as a class.

PRACTICE (SB p16)

This section aims to provide controlled oral and written practice of the grammar.

Talking about you

1 Note that the forms of *have* and *have got* are different. *Have* behaves like a full verb in the Present Simple with the auxiliary *do/does* in questions, negatives, and short answers. *Have got* uses *has/have* as the auxiliary in questions, negatives and short answers.

T 2.2 Play the recording and ask students to repeat the different forms, paying attention to the pronunciation, particularly the stress and rising intonation in the questions and the falling intonation in the answers.

Have you got a car? *Yes, I have.*

2 Ask students to work in pairs. Tell them to use the prompts to ask and answer questions. Model the activity with a confident student.

This practice is personalized but still controlled. It is important that you go round the class to help and correct where necessary.

Tell students to take it in turns first to ask and then to answer the questions. They can choose whether they use *have* or *have got* in the question, but the answer must match.

POSSIBLE PROBLEMS

- Students omit the auxiliary *do/does* and/or *got*:
  **Have you a car?*
  **I haven't a computer.*
  (Although these forms are possible, they are stylized and archaic, and it would be unwise to present students with three forms of *have*.)
- They mix the two forms:
  **I don't have got a computer.*
  Have you got a car? **Yes, I do.*
- They are reluctant to use the more natural short answers:
  Have you got a car? **Yes, I've got a car.* (rather than just *Yes, I have.*)
  Do you have a computer? **No, I don't have a computer.* (rather than just *No, I don't.*)

A nice way to end the activity and draw the full class together again is to ask one or two members of the class to tell the others about their partner. This also provides practice of the third person after the first and second person practice in the pairwork.

Teacher *Thomas, tell us about Maria.*
Thomas *Maria has a camera and a stereo but she doesn't have a computer or a bicycle*, etc.

Getting information

3 This exercise is a controlled information gap activity which brings together practice of the Present Simple and *have/have got*. It also reminds students of the difference between the uses of the Present Simple and Present Continuous.

Before the lesson, remember to make photocopies of the chart on p118 of the Teacher's Book for half the students in your class.

Tell students you are going to give them charts with different information. They will have to ask questions to find their partner's information. Put them in pairs and make it clear which student is A and which is B, then ask students to work together to prepare their questions fully. This should preferably be done orally, but some weaker students might feel happier doing it in writing too.

Possible answers
Where does he/she come from?
Is he/she married?
Does he/she have any children?
Has he/she got any brothers or sisters?
How many children/sisters/brothers has he/she got/does he/she have?
What does he/she do?
What does he/she do in his/her free time?
Where does he/she go on holiday?
What's he/she doing at the moment?

T 2.3 Play the recording so that students can check their questions and repeat for pronunciation before they start the next part of the activity.

Tapescript
Where does he come from?
Is she married?
Does she have any brothers and sisters?
Has he got any children?
How many brothers and sisters has she got?
What does he do?
What does she do in her free time?
Where do they go on holiday?
What's she doing at the moment?

4 Hand out the charts and tell students to ask and answer questions to complete their missing information. Model the first couple of questions with a confident student to get them started.

While students are asking and answering questions to complete their charts you should go round the pairs to help and check.

When the charts are completed ask one or two individuals to tell the whole class about someone in the charts. For example:

Teacher *Juan, tell us about Mike.*
Juan *Well, he comes from Vancouver. He isn't married. He's got a sister and he works for a computer company. He likes skiing and going to* ... etc.

You could also encourage a little bit of discussion at this point by asking students if the people in the charts are typical of their country in relation to the information in the texts on p14.

5 Students question each other about their own free time and holidays. This is to give some personalized practice of the Present Simple in first and second persons for those students who might benefit from further practice. Give students time to prepare questions based on the prompts in the Student's Book, then ask them to stand up, walk around and ask their questions to two or three students they don't know very well. Monitor and listen for errors.

Check it

6 The aim of this activity is to check that students have grasped the differences between the Present Simple and the Present Continuous, and *have* and *have got*, in terms of form and meaning. Ask students to work individually or in pairs. Putting students in pairs to do this exercise enables them to help and teach each other.

Answers
1 Where do you go on holiday?
2 Do you have any children?
3 ... I come from Germany.
4 ... Everyone is dancing.
5 I don't have a mobile phone.
6 ... but he doesn't wear a uniform.
7 ... 'He's sitting by the window.'
8 I like black coffee.

Go through the answers as a class. Ask them why they have reached their decisions, and in this way you will revise the rules. Alternatively, you may wish to set this activity for homework.

Ask students to read Grammar Reference 2.3 on p130 of the Student's Book for homework.

ADDITIONAL MATERIAL

Workbook Unit 2
These exercises could be done in class to give further practice, for homework, or in a later class as revision.
Exercises 1–5 Present Simple
Exercises 6–8 Present Simple or Continuous?
Exercises 9 and 10 *have/have got*

VOCABULARY (SB p17)

Daily life

In this sort of activity your students will see the advantages of recording vocabulary in related groups. Encourage your students to keep their own special notebook for vocabulary.

As you go through the units of *New Headway Pre-Intermediate*, get students to check the photocopied Word list for each unit.

1 Begin by telling students to look at the first box of verbs and nouns. Ask them if they can match any verb with a noun. If necessary, do one or two as an example. Tell them to work in pairs to match verbs and nouns in the rest of the boxes. You could circulate and help at this stage, but don't be tempted to give the answers.

T 2.4 When students have finished, play the recording so that they can listen and check their answers.

Answers and tapescript
have breakfast
wash my hair
watch a film on TV
talk to my friends

make a cup of tea
listen to music
relax on the sofa
do my homework

have a shower
clear up the mess
do the washing-up
have or put posters on the wall

cook a meal
go to the toilet
put on make-up
read magazines

Go through the answers with the whole class and deal with any problems with meaning and pronunciation.

2 Tell students to match the activities from exercise 1 with the correct room. You could elicit one or two examples under the heading *Kitchen* to start them off. Ask students to work in pairs and to write the phrases on the lines. Circulate and help. When students have finished, go through the answers as a class.

Sample answers
Kitchen: have breakfast, make a cup of tea, do the washing-up, cook a meal
Living room: watch a film on TV, talk to my friends, relax on the sofa, read magazines
Bathroom: wash my hair, have a shower, go to the toilet, put on make-up
Bedroom: listen to music, do my homework, clear up the mess, have/put posters on the wall

3 The aim of exercises 3 and 4 is to practise the vocabulary in a personalized way.

Model the activity by telling students which is your favourite room and telling them two or three things you do in that room using the vocabulary from exercise 1. Then get students to look at the example in the book. Give them a few minutes to choose their favourite room and think about what they are going to say.

4 Put students in pairs or groups. Ask them to describe their favourite room to their partner or group, without saying which room it is. Their partner or group guess the room. The main aim here is fluency, but you could circulate and make sure students are using the vocabulary accurately.

Alternatively, you could set this for homework and your students could describe the room to each other at the beginning of the next lesson.

ADDITIONAL MATERIAL

Workbook Unit 2

Exercise 11 is a vocabulary activity which introduces more household items with pictures, and gives further practice in dictionary work.

SUGGESTION

Remember to encourage students to keep a vocabulary notebook and remind them to add words to this whenever they do a vocabulary exercise such as this one.

READING AND SPEAKING (SB p18)

Living in the USA

This is a fluency activity, in the form of a jigsaw reading. The class divides into three groups and each group reads a different article about someone from another country who went to live in the United States.

After the reading, students from the different groups get together to swap information about the person in their article. This should result in some natural speaking practice where students' main attention is on the completion of the reading task. The selection of the articles means that students will need to use (naturally and without noticing it) some of the grammar taught in this unit – Present Simple and *have/have got.*

1 Ask students to close their eyes for a few minutes and think of the United States, then write down the first five things about the United States that come into their heads. Two examples are given in the Student's Book to help trigger ideas and signal that this activity is meant to be fun.

Divide the class into three groups for the jigsaw activity at this point.

Ask students to compare their lists with the other students in their group. Go round as they compare, and draw the attention of the whole class to any things that you think are interesting or funny. Encourage others in the class to comment, thereby generating a short discussion if you can. Keep asking them to tell you *why* they thought of the things.

2 Read the opening paragraph of the article, *Living in the USA*, as a class. Check that students understand *immigrants* and *descendants.* You could get some quick predictions from students by asking them how they think new immigrants find the US when they first arrive. Students read about their person.

3 Focus students on the comprehension questions. Each group has the same four questions to answer after the reading.

You should also ask them if the person in their article mentions any things about the United States that they discussed in exercise 1.

Answers

Roberto Solano

1 He came to the US 10 years ago because he wanted to be successful.
2 He runs a soccer store.
3 He likes living in the US because you can be what you want.
4 It was difficult because he didn't speak the language and it was cold. He missed the sunshine, the food, and his girlfriend.

Endre Boros

1 He came to the US 13 years ago because he was offered an opportunity (a job) for two years.
2 He is a mathematician at a university.
3 He likes the friendly people, the fact that there are people from all over the world, and the independence. He feels in control.
4 He felt everything was so big.

Yuet Tung

1 She came to the US eight years ago to study fine art.
2 She works for a publisher.
3 She likes the huge stores, the space, the friendly people, and the international food.
4 She hated driving.

4 Get the groups to re-form, this time with at least one A, one B, and one C in each group. Students have to tell each other about the person in their article before they go on to read the other articles and, as a group, answer more detailed questions on all three people.

5 Ask students to read the other two extracts. If they have any vocabulary problems they ask the student who has

already studied that article to help them. This is for speed, and to encourage a feeling of co-operation in the group. Dictionary work would slow things down at this stage.

Tell the group to discuss the questions all together.

POSSIBLE PROBLEM

If students become very involved in activities they sometimes start talking in L1.

If this happens just occasionally in a group don't worry, but if L1 takes over you could remind them to speak in English as best they can, because it's good practice.

You are not going to be correcting them much in this activity, as its aim is fluency, not accuracy.

Answers

1 They are all married, they like the United States and the friendly people, they have successful careers and work hard, they drive a lot.
2 Yes.
3 Roberto.
4 No, Yuet Tung doesn't.
5 Roberto and Endre.
6 The independence, the opportunity to be in control of your own life and to do well in life.
7 **Roberto**: Nothing directly, but he missed the sunshine, the food, and his girlfriend.
Endre: In Hungary they only use the car at weekends.
Yuet Tung: In Hong Kong everyone uses public transportation, because it's good and cheap.
8 Yes.
9 The car is part of their life. Nobody walks.

You could circulate during this activity, but if students are working well in their group, let them get on with the activity and discussion. Feed back the answers as a class at the end.

What do you think?

This activity is to round off the lesson and make the discussion more personal to students.

They could form groups or pairs again to get some ideas, but there probably won't be much time for a long discussion. You could also ask *What five things do you think foreign people think of first about your country?* thus bringing the lesson full circle!

LISTENING AND SPEAKING (SB p20)

You drive me mad (but I love you)!

The main aim of this activity is to develop your students' ability to listen for gist and for specific information.

However, the context also revises and extends students' ability to use the Present Simple with frequency adverbs to describe annoying habits. Try not to over-correct students, as a key aim should be general fluency.

1 Check that students understand the expression *he/she drives me mad* perhaps by modelling some real or imaginary examples of annoying behaviour from your family.

For example: *My mother drives me mad when she doesn't listen to a word I say.*

My brother/sister drives me mad when he/she takes my CDs without telling me.

Ask one or two students to give you an example, then focus students on exercise 1 and ask them to write as many sentences about people in their life as they can. Give them a time limit as you do not want them to take too long on this activity. When they have finished, ask students to work in pairs and ask them to tell each other their sentences. Monitor carefully, then draw the class together and have a short class feedback.

2 Model the activity by telling students about the annoying habits of someone you know, then focus the class on exercise 2. Give students time to prepare then put them in pairs or small groups to discuss. Go round and listen and show interest but don't be too quick to correct mistakes.

3 Read through the introduction with students then ask them to look at the cartoons and say what annoying habits are being represented.

Sample answers

1 can never find anything
2 never finishes a job/is untidy
3 is always on the phone
4 watches TV all the time
5 drives badly
6 dresses badly
7 takes a long time to get ready
8 can never make his mind up

Note that these are only suggestions. Get students to speculate as much as possible.

T 2.5 Ask students to listen to the recording and write the name of the person being described under each picture. Let them check their answers in pairs then feed back as a class.

Answers and tapescript

1 Alison 2 Dave 3 Carol 4 Mike
5 Carol 6 Dave 7 Alison 8 Mike

P = Presenter C = Carol M = Mike D = Dave A = Alison

P Hello and welcome to the programme. Today we're going to hear just what couples really think of each other. What drives you mad about your partner? Here's Carol, talking about her husband, Mike.

C Well, there are a lot of arguments about television in our house. He gets the remote control and he's always changing channels, so I never see what I want to. All he wants to watch is football, football, football. When I try to talk to him, he doesn't listen because he's watching the TV. And . . . something else . . . he never remembers anything – birthdays, when we're going out – nothing. I have to do it all. I decide where we're going on holiday, what car to buy. He can't make a decision to save his life.

P So there we have Carol's opinion. What does Mike say about her?

M When we're out in the car and she's driving, she doesn't change gears. She's talking about somebody or other, and not thinking about driving at all. I want to shout at her 'Change gear now!' but I don't. When I want to watch something on television, like . . . the news, she always wants to watch a soap or a film. And another thing. She's always on the phone. She spends hours talking to our daughter, and do you know where she lives? Just round the corner.

P But what do they think of their marriage? Here's Carol.

C Well, I can't change him now, so I'll just have to put up with him.

P And Mike?

M We've been married for twenty-five years, and she's the only one for me!

P And now we have another couple, Dave and Alison. Oh, and by the way, Dave's an electrician.

A What drives me absolutely mad is that he starts a job and never finishes it. At work he's so professional, but at home, if I want a light in the bedroom changed, it takes him months. And he's so untidy. He just drops things on the floor. I keep saying that I don't want to be his mother as well as his wife. When we go out, he looks so scruffy, even when I'm all dressed up. His clothes are so old-fashioned. He never throws anything away.

P Oh, dear. Now what does Dave have to say about Alison?

D Well, she's never ready on time. She always finds something to do that means we're always late, wherever we go. She's usually doing her hair or her make-up while I'm saying 'Come on, love, it's time to go.' And she loses things. She forgets where she parked the car, she leaves the car keys in the most stupid places. But what is most annoying about Alison is that she's always right!

P And their final opinions about each other?

A He's great. He's good fun, and he's one in a million.

D See? As I said, she's always right!

P So, there we are. My thanks to Carol and Mike, and Dave and Alison.

4 Ask students to correct the false sentences in pairs. Do the first as an example. You may need to play the recording a second time at this stage.

Answers

1 False. Carol says Mike always watches television, and Mike says Carol always watches television.
2 True. In Carol's opinion.
3 True. In Carol's opinion.
4 False. He doesn't shout but he wants to.
5 True. In Alison's opinion.
6 False. He is very professional.
7 False. She doesn't want to tidy up after him as if she was his mother.
8 False. She loses things, forgets things, and leaves things in stupid places.

Go through the answers as a class. Allow some discussion as there may be more than one interpretation of some of the answers.

What do you think?

The aim of this activity is to provide some light-hearted free speaking in which students are encouraged to express their own opinion. It could be done as a class. Alternatively, you could divide students into small groups to discuss the questions, then take a few comments from each group at the end.

EVERYDAY ENGLISH (SB p21)

Making conversation

The aim of this section is to get students to think about the techniques involved in starting and keeping a conversation going, and to introduce and practise some phrases which might help them.

1 **T 2.6** You could lead in by eliciting from students ways of having a successful conversation and listing these suggestions on the board. Alternatively, ask students to tell you what problems they have when having a conversation in English, and list the problems on the board.

Focus students on the instruction in the Student's Book and ask students to listen and say which dialogue is more successful and why.

Answer and tapescript

The second dialogue is more successful because Jean-Paul asks questions, shows interest, and adds comments of his own.

T 2.6

J = James M = Maria

J Hello. What's your name?

M Maria.

J I'm . . . James. I'm a teacher. And . . . where are you from?

M Rome.

J Er ... What ... what do you do?
M I'm a student.
J Mm. And ... how long have you been here in London, Maria?
M Two months.
J Are you having a good time?
M Mm ... Yes.
(Pause)
J Can I get you a coffee?
M No.
J Are you missing your family at all?
M No.
J Have you got any brothers or sisters?
M Yes.
J Er ... Oh! Er ... What do they do?
M They are students, too.
J Oh well, I've got a class now. Goodbye, Maria.
M Ciao.

S = Sylvia J-P = Jean-Paul
S Hello. What's your name?
J-P Jean-Paul. And what's your name?
S Sylvia. Where are you from, Jean-Paul?
J-P I come from Paris, the most romantic city in the whole world. And you, Sylvia, where do you come from?
S I come from Scotland. What do you do in Paris?
J-P I'm an architect.
S Oh, really?
J-P Yeah. I design beautiful buildings for people with lots of money. I'm very expensive.
S How interesting.
J-P And how long have you been a teacher, Sylvie?
S Actually, my name's Sylvia.
J-P I am so sorry. Sylvie is the French name. Sylvia, sorry.
S Don't worry. I like it. I've been working here for five years.
J-P And do you enjoy it?
S Yes, very much. You meet a lot of people from all sorts of different countries. I like that very much. Are you enjoying it here?
J-P Very, very much. I'm learning a lot of English, I'm making a lot of friends, and even the food's not bad! Well, I'm not dead yet, and I've been here for five weeks. Sylvia, can I get you a coffee?
S I've got a few minutes before my next class, so that would be lovely. Thank you very much ...
J-P Why don't we ...

2 Ask students to read the dialogues in the tapescript on p119 in pairs, and compare them, noting the ways in which Jean-Paul keeps the conversation going. Get feedback from the class and compare what students have noted with the suggestions or problems listed on the board.

As a class, discuss the list of things that help a conversation. See if students can add to the list.

3 Ask students to work in pairs to match a line in A with a reply in B and a comment in C. Do the first one as an example and check vocabulary if necessary before students start. Monitor and help.

T 2.7 Listen to the recording to check answers and focus on pronunciation.

Answers and tapescript
1 'What a lovely day it is today!' 'Yes. Beautiful, isn't it?'
2 'It's very wet today.' 'Mm. Horrible. Makes you feel miserable, doesn't it?'
3 'How are you today?' 'I'm very well, thanks. How about you?'
4 'Did you have a nice weekend?' 'Yes, it was lovely. We had a pub lunch and went for a walk.'
5 'How are you finding living in London?' 'I'm enjoying it. It was a bit strange at first, but I'm getting used to it.'
6 'Did you have a good journey?' 'Yes, no problems. The plane was a bit late, but it didn't matter.'
7 'Did you watch the football yesterday?' 'No, I missed it. Was it a good game?'
8 'What a lovely coat you're wearing!' 'Thank you. I got it in Paris last year.'
9 'If you have any problems, just ask me for help.' 'Thank you very much. That's very kind of you.'

Point out the exaggerated intonation pattern of some of the phrases and remind students that you can sound bored and uninterested if you don't vary your tone when speaking.

What a lovely day it is today!

Yes. Beautiful, isn't it?

Ask students to practise the dialogues in pairs. Monitor closely and encourage students to put some feeling into their intonation.

NOTE
The aim of exercises 4 and 5 is to provide some light-hearted practice in keeping a conversation going. It is a good idea to join in the mingle yourself, as this way you can provide a clear and consistent model of how to use the small talk, and a good intonation pattern to sound interested.

4 Ask students to work individually to prepare questions based on the four subjects in the Student's Book. Monitor and help.

5 Point out the example in the Student's Book and ask students to invent a new name and background. When they are ready, set the scene (a party) and ask students to stand up. Model an example conversation with a good student to show the others what to do, then tell them to start. Join in yourself, and encourage students to talk to as many people as possible and to keep conversations going for as long as possible.

Don't forget!

Workbook Unit 2
Exercises 12 and 13 Writing: linking words *and, so, but, however,* and *because* are practised. Then students are asked to write about their own lifestyle and the lifestyle of someone in their family.

Pronunciation book Unit 2

Word list
Photocopy the Word list for Unit 2 (TB p153) for your students, and ask them to write in the translations, learn them at home, and/or write some of the words into their vocabulary notebook.

Video
Situation (Section 1) *The Station*
This supplements Units 1 and 2 of the Student's Book. It features David and his Italian friend, Paola, who appeared in *Headway Elementary* video. David goes to the station to meet Paola off the train. Students practise greeting people and the language of stations.

Past tenses
Word formation
Time expressions

It all went wrong

Introduction to the unit

The theme of this unit is telling stories. The Past Simple and Past Continuous tenses are revised and practised in the context of newspaper stories about unusual crimes. In the *Listening and reading* section, students are invited to listen to a radio play then read a short story about a perfect crime.

Students have the opportunity to practise past tenses by means of personalized pairwork activities, writing a news report, and telling stories round the class.

Language aims

Grammar – Past Simple Students will already have a certain familiarity with the Past Simple, and may be able to use it quite accurately on a basic level.

POSSIBLE PROBLEMS

- Many regular verbs will be known, but you can expect problems with the pronunciation of *-ed* at the end, for example:

helped	*/helped/		/helpt/
saved	*/seɪved/	instead of	/seɪvd/
watched	*/wɔʃt/		/wɒtʃt/

  It is worth doing some work on this problem, but don't expect students to master it easily! It takes a long time to get right. Exercise 1 in Unit 3 of *Headway Pre-Intermediate Pronunciation* practises these endings.
  Students will also know some irregular verbs, such as *came, went, saw, met,* and *took*, but there are unfortunately still quite a few of them to learn! Remind students that there is a list of irregular verbs on p143 of the Student's Book. You could ask them to learn five new irregular verbs every week. Do a little test on them from time to time.

- The use of *did* causes problems. Students forget to use it. For example:
  **What time you get up?*
  **Where you went last night?*
  **I no see you yesterday.*
  **You have a good time at the party?*

- Learners try to form a past tense of *have* with *got*, which is uncommon in English.
  **I had got a cold yesterday.*
  English prefers forms with just *had*.

Past Continuous The Past Continuous could well be new to students at this level. In this unit it is contrasted with the Past Simple, and in this context, the difference between the two tenses is clear. However, the fundamental use of the Past Continuous to describe background events and temporary situations in the past is quite a difficult one to grasp. Learners find it hard to see the difference between sentences such as:
It rained yesterday.
It was raining when I got up.
I wore my best suit to the wedding.
She was wearing a beautiful red dress.

The Past Continuous is not dealt with in great depth in this unit. At this stage, it is enough to lay a foundation, so that students will learn to recognize the tense as they see it in context, and gradually begin to produce it.

While is often used with verb forms in the Past Continuous. *While I was having lunch, James arrived.*

Learners often confuse *while* and *during*. Exercise 11 in Unit 3 of the Workbook deals with this.

Vocabulary The *Vocabulary* section contains several exercises on word building. Students are encouraged to build their vocabulary and their awareness of how English works by looking at how suffixes and prefixes can change verbs to nouns, nouns to adjectives, and positives to negatives.

Everyday English The *Everyday English* section deals with time expressions – saying dates, and phrases with and without prepositions. But these areas cause problems of form, because there are so many 'bits' to get right.

Notes on the unit

STARTER (SB p22)

In this Starter activity students' knowledge of basic irregular past tenses is checked.

Ask students to work in pairs to fill the gaps then feed back as a class, drilling any past tenses that students find difficult to pronounce. If necessary, refer students to the list of irregular verbs on p143 of the book.

Answers

1 be	5 say	9 get
2 see	6 have	10 can
3 go	7 take	11 make
4 tell	8 give	12 do

Alternatively, you could test students' ability to use past tenses by asking them some questions about last night or last weekend.

What did you do last night? Where did you go?
Did you go to the cinema? What did you see?
What time did you go to bed?

Listen carefully to their replies to see how well they are using the Past Simple. You could ask them *What tense were all my questions?* to see if they know the name of the tense.

THE BURGLARS' FRIEND (SB p22)

Past Simple

1 Ask students to look at the picture and the headline to the newspaper article. Ask questions to set the situation and get students to predict the story. Pre-teach any key vocabulary, such as *burglar, purse, drawer, pocket money*.

T 3.1 Focus students on the gist question *Why was Russell the burglars' friend?* and ask them to read and listen to the story. Ask them if they predicted the story correctly.

2 Check that students can recognize irregular past forms by asking them to find some in the text and match them to the infinitives in the exercise. Encourage them to work in pairs or to work individually and check with a partner.

Answers

wake	woke	leave	left
hear	heard	hold	held
find	found	think	thought
keep	kept	catch	caught

In the feedback, model or drill the past forms for pronunciation.

3 **T 3.2** Tell students that they are going to listen to some sentences about the story which are incorrect. They must listen and correct the mistakes. Read the example very carefully, and point out that they have to write two sentences, one negative and one positive, then play the recording. You may need to pause after each sentence to give students time to write. After the first playing, ask students to work in pairs to compare information, then play the recording again if necessary, and students work in pairs again to check.

Tapescript

1 Russell woke up at two o'clock.
2 He woke up because he was thirsty.
3 He heard a noise in the kitchen.
4 He found three men.
5 Russell's mother kept her purse in her handbag.
6 They left at five o'clock.
7 When they left, Russell watched TV.
8 The police caught the burglars the next day.

When getting the feedback to this exercise, insist on good pronunciation. This requires a wide voice range to express surprise and strong stress to show contrast.

He didn't wake up at 2 o'clock.

He woke up at 3 o'clock.

Answers

2 He didn't wake up because he was thirsty. He woke up to go to the toilet.
3 He didn't hear a noise in the kitchen. He heard a noise in the living room.
4 He didn't find three men. He found two men.
5 She didn't keep her purse in her handbag. She kept it in a drawer.
6 They didn't leave at five o'clock. They left at four o'clock.

7 He didn't watch TV. He went back to bed.
8 They didn't catch the burglars the next day. They caught them last week.

4 Ask students to work in pairs to make the questions. They should write them down. Monitor and help. In the feedback, insist on correctly formed questions, and make sure the question starts with the voice high.

Why did he wake up?

Sample answers
2 Where were his parents?
3 Why did he go downstairs?
4 How many men were there?
5 What did they tell him?
6 Where did his mother keep her purse?
7 How much pocket money did he give them?
8 When did they leave?
9 When did they find out about the burglary?
10 When did the police catch the two burglars?

GRAMMAR SPOT (SB p23)

Ask students to work in pairs or threes to answer the grammar questions.

Answers

1 The Past Simple, because it is a newspaper report of an incident that happened in the past.
The question is formed with *did* + infinitive (students will probably use the term infinitive instead of base form).
The negative is formed with *didn't* + infinitive.

2 a asked /t/
showed /d/
wanted /ɪd/
walked /t/
started /ɪd/
b tried /d/
carried /ɪd/
c liked /t/
believed /d/
used /d/
d stopped /t/
planned /d/

T 3.3 Ask students to listen and repeat the past forms. Drill the words for the pronunciation of *-ed*.

3 Regular past tenses are formed by adding *-ed*.
If the verb ends in consonant + *y*, change the *-y* to *-ied*.
We double the final consonant when the verb ends consonant – vowel – consonant.

Refer students to the list of irregular verbs on p143, and Grammar Reference 3.1 on p131.

PRACTICE (SB p23)

Making connections

The aim of this activity is to give students further accuracy practice in producing past forms, and to check their ability to use the connectors, *so, because, and,* and *but.*

1 Focus students on the box and the example, then ask them as a class to connect *feel ill* with a phrase in the right-hand column. When they have got the idea, ask students to work in pairs to produce as many sentences as they can. This could be done as a written exercise or, if you think your students can manage it, it could be done as an oral exercise in pairs. Monitor, help and correct, paying particular attention to the pronunciation of past forms.

T 3.4 Students listen and check their answers.

Sample answers and tapescript
1 I broke a cup, but I mended it with glue.
2 I felt ill, so I went to bed.
3 I made a sandwich because I was hungry.
4 I had a shower and washed my hair.
5 I lost my passport, but then I found it at the back of a drawer.
6 I called the police because I heard a strange noise.
7 I ran out of coffee, so I bought some more.
8 I forgot her birthday, so I said sorry.
9 The phone rang, so I answered it.
10 I told a joke, but nobody laughed.

POSSIBLE PROBLEM
Students may not be sure about how to use the connectors, particularly *so*. You may wish to check students' ability to use them before starting the exercise by writing some examples on the board and asking check questions. For example:

	but I mended it with glue.
I broke a cup,	*so I bought another one.*
	and I broke a plate.
	because I dropped it.

Which sentence shows a contrast? *… but …*
Which sentence adds extra information? *… and …*
Which sentence shows a consequence? *… so …*
Which sentence says why you did something? *… because …*

Talking about you

The aim here is to round off the lesson with a personalized free speaking activity using the Past Simple.

2 Ask students to work in pairs to talk about what they did last night, last weekend, etc. Monitor the groups carefully. There will no doubt be mistakes of form and

pronunciation, but you can't correct them all, so be selective! As you go round the groups, you could write down some mistakes, and after you have conducted the feedback you could write them on the board for the class to correct.

ADDITIONAL IDEA

This is a variation on a drill to practise the question and the Past Simple. Find pictures of people doing everyday things such as going for a walk, watching TV, playing tennis, fishing, swimming, reading, writing a letter, playing a piano, etc. You need quite a few, about ten. Ask the class to stand up in a circle if you have a small class, or several circles if you have a large class. Give Student A a picture of, say, someone playing tennis. Ask the student *What did you do yesterday?* Student A says *I played tennis.* Student A gives the picture to Student B, and asks *What did you do yesterday?* Student B says *I played tennis*, and hands the card to Student C. B asks C *What did you do yesterday?* etc. You, meanwhile, give another card to Student A and ask *What did you do yesterday?*, etc. All the pictures are passed round in a circle.

Ask students to read Grammar Reference 3.2 on p132 at home.

ADDITIONAL MATERIAL

Workbook Unit 3
These exercises could be done in class to give further practice, for homework, or in a later class as revision.
Exercises 1–6 Past Simple

NEWSPAPER STORIES (SB p24)

Past Continuous

This might be the first time that your students have been formally introduced to the Past Continuous. In the exercises in this unit, there is more emphasis on recognition than production. This is for the reasons mentioned in the introduction to this unit.

The presentation consists of two articles, which have had phrases using the Past Continuous taken out. Students must decide which phrases with the Past Continuous go with which story, and then where exactly in each story they should go. The idea implicit here is to show students that the main events of a story are expressed by the Past Simple – the stories make perfect sense without the phrases containing the Past Continuous. The Past Continuous phrases give background information and description.

1 Tell students they are going to read two articles about unusual crimes. Ask them to look at the first headline and guess what it might be about, then read the article quickly to see if they were right. In the feedback, check any difficult vocabulary.

Focus students on the infinitives above article **a** then ask them to change them to past forms and put them in the gaps.

Answers
1 stole 2 said 3 gave 4 had 5 could

Repeat the procedure for article **b**.

Answers
1 went 2 left 3 broke 4 heard 5 came

2 Read the instructions for this exercise and focus students on the sentences. As an example, ask students to tell you where the first sentence goes, then ask them to work in pairs or small groups to decide which article the other phrases go with, and then where exactly they go in the story.

T 3.5 Students listen and check their answers. At this stage, they could practise reading out the sentences, paying attention to the weak stress in *was* /wəz/ and *were* /wə/.

Answers and tapescript
Hands up, I've got a burger!
Last Tuesday a man armed with just a hot hamburger in a bag stole $1,000 from a bank in Danville, California.
Police Detective Bill McGinnis said that the robber, **who was wearing a mask**, entered the Mount Diablo National Bank at about 1.30 p.m. and gave the teller a note demanding $1,000. He claimed that he had a bomb in the bag. The teller said she could smell a distinct odour of hamburger coming from the bag. Even so, she handed the money to the man. **As he was running out of the bank**, he dropped the bag with the hamburger. He escaped in a car **that was waiting for him outside**.
Teenage party ends in tears
When Jack and Kelly Harman went away on holiday, they left their teenage daughter alone in the house. Zoë, aged 16, wanted to stay at home **because she was revising for exams**. Her parents said she could have some friends to stay. However, Zoë decided to have a party. **Everyone was having a good time when suddenly** things started to go wrong. Forty uninvited guests arrived, **and some of them were carrying knives**. They broke furniture, smashed windows, and stole jewellery.
When Mr and Mrs Harman heard the news, they came home immediately.

GRAMMAR SPOT (SB p24)

Answers

1 The tense used is the Past Continuous. The Past Continuous is used to give background information and description. (The Past Simple is used to tell the story.)

2 We make questions by inverting the subject with *was* or *were*.
Was she making coffee?
We make negatives by adding *not* or *n't* after *was* or *were*. We usually use *n't* when speaking.
She wasn't making coffee.

3 In the first sentence she made the coffee *after* we arrived, possibly as a result of our arrival.
When we arrived,

Past ——X—X—— Present
she made some coffee.

In the second sentence, she started making coffee *before* we arrived and the making of the coffee was in progress when we arrived.

When we arrived,

Past ——X—— Present
|- - - - - - - - - - - - - - - - - -|
she was making some coffee.

Refer students to Grammar Reference 3.2 and 3.3 on p132.

ADDITIONAL IDEA
Students have read examples of the Past Continuous, but they haven't repeated any yet. Write these sentences on the board:

Zoë was revising for her exams.
Everyone was having a good time.
A car was waiting for him.
He was wearing a mask.
Some boys were carrying knives.

Ask students *How is this tense formed?* (*was/were + -ing*). Point out that *was* and *were* are weak /wəz/ and /wə/. Give models of the sentences yourself, and then drill them around the class.

PRACTICE (SB p25)

SUGGESTION
Before going on to the Practice exercises, you might decide that your students would like some more information about this (new) tense. You could read Grammar Reference 3.2 and 3.3 on p132. In Unit 3 of the Workbook, exercise 7 is a mechanical drill to practise forming the Past Continuous. Once they have done it, your students might feel more confident about doing the following exercises. Don't be surprised if there are quite a few mistakes with the Past Continuous. You have just introduced students to a new tense, and it will take time for them to see how it operates. Let students have the rules reinforced as they see the correct answers in exercises 1 and 2, and be prepared to re-teach if necessary.

Discussing grammar

1 Students work in pairs to decide which is the correct verb form and underline it.

Answers
1 saw
2 was shopping, lost
3 stopped, was driving
4 did you cut
5 was cooking, dropped
6 arrived, was having
7 Did you have

2 Students work in pairs to put the verbs in the correct form.

Answers
1 was going, met
2 didn't want, was raining
3 was listening, rang
4 picked
5 said, were watching

Getting information

Make photocopies of enough information cards for all students in your class before the lesson. The information cards are in the Teacher's Book on p119.

3 Read the instructions as a class, then ask students to work in pairs and hand out the information cards. It is often a good idea to hand out the same information card to each pair, get them to read it, then get them to work in pairs to prepare questions from the cues. When they are ready, change the pairs so that there is one Student A with each Student B. Model the activity with a good student, then monitor and listen for errors, particularly with question formation, as they do the activity.

COMPLETE TEXT

Mr and Mrs Harman arrived home at 10.30 in the evening. Zoë was staying with friends. She felt terrible because her parents would be furious with her.

Her parents started to clean the house. Then they phoned Zoë and told her to come home immediately.

Zoë got back home at two in the morning. She said she was very sorry and she promised that she would never have another party.

ADDITIONAL IDEA

Students work in groups of four to write a news story. Don't underestimate how long activities such as this take if they are to be done thoroughly. Allow 20–30 minutes. You could start by discussing some possible news stories as a class, and ask students to give you some details.

Groups sometimes take a while to get started. They have to decide on a story, decide who's going to write, and decide what the wrong information is, so be prepared to give them a gentle nudge to keep the lesson moving.

fortunately/unfortunately

The aim of the following exercises is to introduce the words *fortunately* and *unfortunately* and then to give students lots of practice in using the Past Simple tense by means of a fun whole class activity. It should be lots of fun, but don't forget to monitor and feed back on errors involving the use of the past tense.

4 Focus students on the story and model it, paying particular attention to your intonation, rising on *fortunately*, falling on *unfortunately*.

fortunately *unfortunately*

Gesture to a student to continue the story by adding the next sentence, beginning *Fortunately*. Then gesture to another student to continue, and so on around the class. You could correct any errors at the end.

5 Put students in a circle if possible, and start one of the stories by reading out the first sentence. As the story goes around the class, note down any errors to feed back at the end. Alternatively, put students in groups of four to do the activity and monitor the groups, or even start two different stories, going round the group in opposite directions.

ADDITIONAL MATERIAL

Workbook Unit 3
Exercises 7 and 8 the Past Continuous
Exercise 9 Past Simple or Continuous?

LISTENING AND READING (SB p26)

A radio drama

In this activity, students listen to a radio play then read a short story, both of which tell the same dramatic story of a perfect crime. Students have the pictures to help them to understand.

1 **T 3.6** Read the introduction as a class, then ask students to describe what they can see in the pictures, in pairs or open class. Pre-teach some of the vocabulary items, for example, *ice statue, hit, wedding anniversary*.

Ask students to say why they think this is a perfect crime, then play the recording. As they listen, ask students to look at the pictures and find out why it *is* a perfect crime. In the feedback, if they don't know the answer, don't tell them yet.

Tapescript
A radio drama – The perfect crime
A = Alice H = Henry P = Detective Parry
T = Sergeant Taylor F1 and F2 = Friends

Alice Jackson is a happily married woman. She loves her baby son, and she adores her husband, Henry. Tonight is her tenth wedding anniversary, and some friends are coming round to have a drink. Everything seems perfect . . . but . . . Alice's life is going to change.

A Hello, darling. Have some beer.
H Sit down. I've got something to say . . . I'm sorry. I know it's a bad time to tell you. It's our anniversary. But it's just that Kathy and I are in love. Bobby won't miss me, he's too young.
A I'll get ready for the party . . .
H What on earth . . . ?
A Hello, police please. Hello, is that the police? Come quickly. It's my husband. Something awful has happened to him.
P Detective Parry, Mrs Jackson. Where is he?
A In the kitchen. Is he all right?
P He's dead.
A No, no, not Henry! My Henry! Oh Henry!'
P What happened?
A I was putting the baby to bed upstairs. And I just came downstairs and found him lying on the kitchen floor.
T Burglars.
P Sit down, Mrs Jackson. Sergeant Taylor, get Mrs Jackson a drink. A brandy with some ice. Phew! It's hot in this room. I hope you understand, Mrs Jackson, that we have to search the house immediately. We must find the murder weapon.
A Yes, yes. Of course.
P What was that?
T It's this statue, sir. It's melting.
T Phew! Can I have a glass of water, Mrs Jackson? It's so hot in here.
P I think we all need one. And with ice.
F1 Poor Alice!

F2 Poor Henry! I don't believe it. What a shock for you!
A Oh thank you, thank you. Please . . . stay and have a drink. Help yourselves.
F1 I wonder what the burglar hit him with.
F2 Who knows? Mmm.

2 Ask students to work in pairs to answer the questions. You may need to play the recording again. In the feedback, let students speculate as there may be more than one interpretation of what they have heard.

Answers
1 Alice waiting for Henry to come home for their tenth wedding anniversary party.
Alice hitting Henry with the ice statue.
The party.
2 She was in love with him.
3 He told her he was in love with Kathy.
4 Kathy is the woman Henry is in love with. Bobby is Alice and Henry's baby son.
5 She said, 'I'll get ready for the party.' She was so shocked that she didn't know how to react. All she could do was to pretend that everything was normal.
6 She hit him with something.
7 She hit him on the head with the ice statue.
8 She said she was putting the baby to bed, came downstairs, and found him dead. The police thought it was burglars.
9 The room was so hot.

3 Tell students that they are now going to *read* the story of the perfect crime. Ask them what information they would like to learn from the story which they don't yet know, or ask them to write questions in the past tense which they would like to find the answers to. When they have finished reading, put them in pairs to discuss their findings before getting feedback.

SUGGESTION
You may wish to read the text out loud, while students follow it in their book. This allows you to bring the text to life through expression, and also briskly to explain words such as *adored*, *kiss*, *screamed*, and *comfort* through tone of voice or mime. It can improve students' reading speed, because they have to keep up as you read without worrying about words they don't know.

4 Focus students on the sentences and do the first as an example, then ask students to work in pairs to correct the false sentences. Correct students' misuse of past tenses in the feedback.

Answers
1 False. She loved him.
2 True. But also because she had a beautiful baby, a lovely home, and a husband she adored.
3 True.
4 True.
5 False. She didn't think for very long.
6 False. She wanted to melt the ice statue.
7 True.
8 False. It melted.

What do you think?

Ask students to work in pairs or threes to discuss the questions, then open it up as a whole class discussion.

Sample answers
1 At the beginning she was smiling because she had the perfect marriage. At the end she was smiling because she had committed the perfect crime.
2 It was the only way she could react to his news. No doubt she was shocked and angry: he destroyed her perfect marriage.
3 You will need to explain 'to get away with a crime'. It means to escape punishment. It was a very clever crime; she probably did get away with it.

Language work

5 Students work in pairs to write the past forms of the verbs, referring back to the text if necessary.

Answers

adored	phoned
opened	screamed
turned	took
walked	picked
hit	tried
fell	sobbed

Speaking

6 Students should now be ready to retell the story in some detail. Let them first do this in pairs to practise. Monitor them carefully, correcting the most important mistakes. This exercise is midway between a fluency and an accuracy-based activity. You want students to speak at length, but you also want the past tense usage to be correct.

When students are ready, ask one or two of them to tell the story to the rest of the class. You could begin the next class by asking a different student to retell the story. It only takes a few minutes, and you can revise the vocabulary and past tenses.

VOCABULARY (SB p28)

Nouns, verbs, and adjectives

1 Introduce students to the idea of word building with suffixes by writing a verb and a noun on the board, for example, *invite* and *care*, and asking students to change them to a noun and an adjective respectively, *invi'tation* and *'careful*.

Then focus students on the suffixes in the box and put them in pairs to complete the charts and mark the stress. Monitor and help.

In the feedback, model and drill the words to show the pronunciation and stress.

Answers

Noun	Verb
dis'cussion	dis'cuss
'government	'govern
invi'tation	**in'vite**
de'velopment	de'velop
expla'nation	ex'plain
edu'cation	**'educate**
de'cision	de'cide
en'joyment	en'joy
organi'zation	'organize
im'provement	**im'prove**
em'ployment	em'ploy

Noun	Adjective
'science	**scien'tific**
friend	**'friendly**
'happiness	'happy
'difference	'different
'danger	**'dangerous**
use	**'useful/less**
help	**'helpful/less**
speci'ality	'special
care	**'careful/less**
noise	**'noisy**
'industry	**in'dustrial**
am'bition	**am'bitious**

2 Ask students to work in pairs to complete the sentences. Do the first as an example. Students may wish to use dictionaries here. However, try to get them to guess which words to use by looking at the context of each sentence. In the feedback, check the meaning of any words students are still not sure about.

Answers

1 improved	5 useful	9 dangerous
2 ambitions	6 friendly	10 speciality
3 decision	7 organization	11 invite
4 differences	8 explanation	12 industrial

Making negatives

3 Look at the prefixes as a class and give students a couple of examples, such as *unusual* and *undress*, to show how they work. Elicit as many other examples as students can think of.

Ask students to work in pairs to complete the sentences. Do the first as an example.

Answers

1 untidy	5 unpacked	9 illegal
2 impossible	6 unemployed	10 unfair
3 dislike	7 disagree	
4 impolite	8 disappeared	

EVERYDAY ENGLISH (SB p29)

Time expressions

1 Ask students what today's date is, and practise saying it in the two ways.

the first of August   *August the first*

Point out that in American English the date is usually written with the month, not the day, expressed first. It is usually said *August first.*

Ask students to practise saying the dates and years in pairs. Before they listen to the recording, let students concentrate on getting the *form* of the dates and years right.

T 3.7 Listen to the recording. Stop the recording after each date, and drill it round the class. Concentrate now on correct form *and* pronunciation. It is very important that dates are said with strong and weak stresses.

● ●   ● ●   ●   ●
The sixteenth of July nineteen eighty-five

Tapescript

the eighth of January, nineteen ninety-eight
January the eighth, nineteen ninety-eight

the sixteenth of July, nineteen eighty-five
July the sixteenth, nineteen eighty five

the twenty-fifth of November, two thousand and two
November the twenty-fifth, two thousand and two

POSSIBLE PROBLEMS

- Students forget to say the definite article.
  **I came here on fifth August.*
- Students might not know all the ordinal numbers, especially *first*, *second*, *third*, and *twenty-first*, *twenty-second*, etc. You might want to practise these first. The pronunciation of some ordinal numbers is difficult because of consonant clusters.
  fifth   sixth   twelfth

Focus students on the dates written in American English, and ask if they can say what the difference is (the month is written before the day).

T 3.8 Play the recording to listen and check.

Tapescript
January eighth, nineteen ninety-eight
July sixteenth, nineteen eighty-five
November twenty-fifth, two thousand and two

2 Practise the dates as a class or in pairs. Encourage students to attempt the correct stress and intonation.

T 3.9 Play the recording for students to check whether they said the dates correctly.

Tapescript
June the fourth
the fifth of August
the thirty-first of July
March the first
February the third
the twenty-first of January, nineteen eighty-eight
December the second, nineteen ninety-six
the fifth of April, nineteen eighty
June the eleventh, nineteen sixty-five
the eighteenth of October, two thousand
January the thirty-first, two thousand and five

3 Students work in pairs to put *at*, *in*, *on*, or no preposition in the gaps. Monitor unobtrusively to find out how well students do the exercise, then tell them the answers.

Answers

at six o'clock	**on** Saturday	**in** 1995
– last night	**in** December	**at** the weekend (***on*** in US English)
on Monday morning	**in** summer	– two weeks ago
in the evening	– yesterday evening	**on** January 18

Tell students that we always use *at* with times, for example, *at 6 o'clock*. Ask students to work in pairs to work out other rules. In the feedback, list the rules on the board and refer students to Grammar Reference 3.4 on p132.

Rules

at	**in**	**on**	**no preposition**
times	months	days	last night/week, etc.
	years	dates	Monday morning, etc.
	seasons		today/yesterday
			two weeks ago, etc.

4 It might be interesting to answer the first question as a class, partly so that you can check students' answers, and partly because people are usually very interested to hear what time of day other people were born.

Model the other questions around the class, and drill them for pronunciation if necessary. Then put students in pairs or groups of three to ask each other the questions. Monitor and check that students are using dates correctly. Do a brief feedback, and correct any errors.

ADDITIONAL MATERIAL

Workbook Unit 3
Exercise 6 Past time expressions

Pronunciation book Unit 3

Don't forget!

Workbook Unit 3
Exercise 10 is a vocabulary exercise on *have* + noun.
Exercises 11 and 12 are two exercises on writing. Students are asked to write a story.

Word list
Photocopy the Word list for Unit 3 (TB p154) for your students, and ask them to write in the translations, learn them at home, and/or write some of the words into their vocabulary notebook.

Video
Report (Section 2) ***Sherlock Holmes*** A short documentary about Sherlock Holmes and his creator, Sir Arthur Conan Doyle.

much/many • *some/any*
a few, a little, a lot of • Articles
Shopping • Prices

Let's go shopping!

Introduction to the unit

The theme of this unit is shopping. In the opening section, 'The Weekend Shop', expressions of quantity are introduced in the context of two friends discussing their weekend shopping list. In a separate presentation section, a text about a shopkeeper, there is some work on the use of articles in English. The *Reading* is about the most popular shopping street in the world, Nowy Świat in Warsaw, and the *Vocabulary and listening* consists of four dialogues set in different shops.

Language aims

Expressions of quantity It is assumed that students will have some knowledge of expressions of quantity, but that the intricacies of this area (particularly in relation to count and uncount nouns) will mean that mistakes will still be common.

The point is also made that the rules about the use of *something/anything*, etc. are the same as for *some* and *any*. These are also practised.

Articles It is expected that students will not have actually studied articles in English to any great extent. However, they will probably be aware that the use of articles varies between languages. Those students whose L1 has no articles, such as Japanese and Arabic, find their use particularly difficult. Don't expect your students to have a deep understanding of article usage at the end of this unit. There are too many rules and exceptions. Hopefully they will know a little more.

Vocabulary Vocabulary is introduced around the topic of things we buy in a brainstorming activity before the main listening texts.

Everyday English Prices and the functional language of shopping are chosen to fit the theme of the unit. These are practised in a variety of everyday shopping situations.

Notes on the unit

STARTER (SB p30)

The aim of the alphabet game is to see how well your students understand the idea of count and uncount nouns. It also brings out a lot of vocabulary, revises past tenses from the previous unit, and it is fun.

Focus students on the examples in the book then model the first sentence. Nominate a student to read the second sentence and so on until they have got the idea. If you have a small class get them to sit in a circle to do this activity. Try to model and insist on good stress and a good rhythm.

● ● ● ●
Yesterday I went shopping and I bought an apple and some bread.

Don't let this activity go on too long. As you get towards halfway through the alphabet, students' memories will be tested. Be prepared to give lots of prompts, so you can get on to the main part of the lesson.

THE WEEKEND SHOP (SB p30)

Quantity

You could personalize the lead-in by writing *The shopping list* on the board and eliciting from students what they or their family usually buy every week.

1 Set the scene by reading the introduction and asking students to look at the photograph of Sarah and Vicky. Ask students some questions.

Where are they?
What are they doing?

Focus students on the shopping list and check any unknown words. You may also wish to check the meaning of a pint of milk and a dozen eggs. (1.76 pints /paɪnts/ = 1 litre, dozen /ˈdʌzən/ = 12)

T 4.1 Ask students to listen to the conversation between Sarah and Vicky without reading and tick the things on the shopping list that they mention.

Answers
milk eggs potatoes butter

Ask them to listen and read the second time, and to look at Vicky's questions. Then put students in pairs to discuss the questions in the *Grammar Spot*. In the feedback, you could check students' understanding by asking individuals check questions.

Sergio, can we count cheese?
Maria, can we count sausages?

Alternatively, you could ask students to list on the board the things that are countable and uncountable.

Countable	**Uncountable**
eggs	milk
potatoes	butter
tomatoes	cheese
sausages	Coke
crisps	wine
	bread

Point out that plural count nouns usually end with *-s* or *-es*. Students often find the word *crisps* difficult to pronounce because of the consonant cluster *sps*.

GRAMMAR SPOT (SB p30)

We can't count milk but we can count eggs.

We say *How much* when the noun is uncountable.

We say *How many* when the noun is countable, (*one, two, three*, etc.).

2 This exercise aims to check students have grasped the use of *how much* and *how many* before going on to study more expressions.

Focus students on the quantity expressions in the box and check their understanding of the vocabulary by asking them to match the expressions in the box with the items on the shopping list.

Answers

a bottle of red	wine
just one white loaf	bread
200g of Cheddar	cheese
four packets	crisps
six cans	Coke
six pork ones	sausages
four big ones	potatoes

Students continue the conversation in pairs. Monitor and correct. Encourage good pronunciation of the questions, particularly the intonation.

How much milk do we need? And how many eggs?

3 **T 4.2** Students read and listen to the rest of the conversation between Sarah and Vicky. Ask a few questions afterwards to check that students have followed the conversation, and to see how well they can use expressions like *a few*, *a little*, and *not many*.

For example:
How much orange juice have they got?
How many vegetables have they got?

GRAMMAR SPOT (SB p31)

1 Ask students to work in pairs to find seven count nouns and four uncount nouns in the conversation.

Answers
Count nouns: apples, grapes, vegetables, carrots, onions, crisps, nephews.
Uncount nouns: coffee, tea, orange juice, money.

2 The aim of this activity is for students to discover for themselves from context the sometimes confusing rules of use involved with count and uncount nouns. This exercise is not easy. Be prepared to give lots of help.

Students work in pairs to complete the table by finding examples of use in the conversation.

Answers

We use ...	with CNs	with UNs	in positive sentences	in questions	in negative sentences
some	✓	✓	✓	✓ (sometimes)	
any	✓	✓		✓	✓
much		✓		✓	✓
many	✓			✓	✓
a lot of	✓	✓	✓	✓	✓
a few	✓		✓		
a little		✓	✓		

You might want to check students' ability to use this language by doing exercises 1 to 4 in the *Practice* section at this stage.

3 Focus students on the table and ask them to find two examples of the phrases in the conversation. The use of the phrases is checked in exercise 5 of the following *Practice* section.

Answers
V Do we need anything else?
V ... did somebody finish it?

Refer students to Grammar Reference 4.1 on p133.

PRACTICE (SB p31)

Discussing grammar

1–3 Encourage your students to do these quite quickly. Ask them to do the five sentences in exercise 1 on their own as quickly as possible, then check with a partner. Do the same for 2 and 3, then go through all the answers together as a class. Point out that in exercise 2 *a lot/lots of* could be used in all the sentences except for number 5, and check students understand that it can only be replaced by *many* and *much* in questions and negatives.

Answers
1 1 any 2 any 3 some 4 some 5 any
2 1 much 2 many 3 much 4 many 5 many
3 1 a few 2 a lot/lots of 3 a little 4 a lot/lots of 5 a few 6 a little

Questions and answers

4 Ask students to look at the picture of Sarah and Vicky's bathroom and tell you what they can see. Try to elicit as much vocabulary as you can and drill it for pronunciation. Make sure students understand all the words they need first before they do the activity. Model the activity by asking two or three students questions, making sure your intonation pattern is clear and your voice rises at the end.

Have they got much make-up?

Is there any soap?

Have they got many towels?

Once students have got the idea, put them in pairs to ask and answer questions. Monitor closely and listen for errors and examples of good language use. Correct errors in a brief feedback.

Sample answers
Is there any shampoo?
Yes, but not much.
Have they got many towels?
Yes, a few.
Are there any toothbrushes?
Yes, there are two.
Have they got any toothpaste?
Yes, but not much.
Is there any toilet paper?
Yes, a little.
Are there any hairbrushes?
I can't see any.
Have they got any bottles of perfume?
Lots.

something/someone/somewhere

5 Do the first question as an example. Students work in pairs to complete the rest.

T 4.3 Students listen and check their answers.

Answers and tapescript
1 'Did you meet **anyone** nice at the party?'
'Yes. I met **someone** who knows you!'
2 'Ouch! There's **something** in my eye!'
'Let me look. No, I can't see **anything**.'
3 'Let's go **somewhere** hot for our holidays.'
'But we can't go **anywhere** that's too expensive.'
4 'I'm so unhappy. **Nobody** loves me.'
'I know **somebody** who loves you. Me.'
5 I lost my glasses. I looked **everywhere**, but I couldn't find them.
6 'Did you buy **anything** at the shops?'
'No, **nothing**. I didn't have any money.'
7 I'm bored. I want **something** interesting to read, or **someone** interesting to talk to, or **somewhere** interesting to go.
8 It was a great party. **Everyone** loved it.

Town survey

6 The aim of this activity is to provide some personalized fluency work for students. It is an opportunity for the

teacher to find out whether they can use *some*, *any*, etc. appropriately in a fluency situation.

Focus students on the two lists of good and bad things. Then put them in small groups of three or four to make their own lists. Nominate one person in each group to be the 'secretary' to write down the other students' suggestions. Monitor, prompt, and help with vocabulary. At the end, write a definitive list on the board and correct any errors or point out examples of good language use.

ADDITIONAL MATERIAL

Workbook Unit 4
These exercises could be done in class to give further practice, for homework, or in a later class as revision.
Exercises 1 and 2 Count and uncount nouns
Exercises 3–6 Expressions of quantity

SUGGESTION
At this point it might be a good idea to do the *Reading* section (*The best shopping street in the world*, p34) before you do the next grammar presentation. Your students might like the variety.

MY UNCLE'S A SHOPKEEPER (SB p33)

Articles

T 4.4 Ask students to look at the picture of the shopkeeper, and read and listen to the text about him. The vocabulary is simple and should cause no problems. However, you may wish to use the picture to check that students understand *shopkeeper* and *village*.

GRAMMAR SPOT (SB p33)

1 Ask students to read the text again more carefully and find all the definite and indefinite articles. They may need a quick reminder that this means *the* and *a/an*!

Answers
My uncle's **a** shopkeeper. He has **a** shop in **an** old village by **the** River Thames near Oxford. **The** shop sells **a** lot of things – bread, milk, fruit, vegetables, newspapers – almost everything! It is also **the** village post office. **The** children in **the** village always stop to spend **a** few pence on sweets or ice-cream on their way home from school. My uncle doesn't often leave **the** village. He hasn't got **a** car, so once **a** month he goes by bus to Oxford and has lunch at **the** Grand Hotel with some friends. He is one of **the** happiest men I know.

2 Point out that there is no article in front of *Oxford*. Ask students to find other nouns in the text where there is no article.

Answers
Oxford, bread, milk, fruit, vegetables, newspapers, sweets, ice-cream, home, school, bus, lunch.

Before they turn to the Grammar Reference section you could ask them a few general questions about articles.

Sample questions

Can you give any rules about the use of articles in English with examples from the text?
Do you know of any differences between the use of articles in English and in your own language?

At this stage you could ask students to turn to Grammar Reference 4.2 on p133 and find rules for some of the examples in the text.

Answers
(The words are in the order they appear in the text.)
a shopkeeper (because it is a profession)
a shop/ an old village (because they are referred to for the first time)
the River Thames (the name of a river)
Oxford (the name of a city)
The shop (the speaker and listener know the shop already)
a lot of things (an expression of quantity)
bread, milk, fruit (uncountable nouns)
vegetables, newspapers (countable plural nouns)
the village post office (there is only one)
The children (we understand it means the children of the village, and there is only one group of these)
the village (the speaker and listener know the village already)
a few pence (an expression of quantity)
sweets (countable plural noun)
ice-cream (uncountable noun)
home from school (because no article is used before home)
the village (the speaker and listener know the village already)
a car (because it is referred to for the first time)
once a month (an expression of quantity)
by bus (because no article is used before some forms of transport)
has lunch (because no article is used before meals)
the Grand Hotel (the name of a hotel)
one of the happiest men (we usually use *the* with a superlative because it is the only one)

Ask students to check their lists with a partner first, then conduct a feedback session with the whole class.

PRACTICE (SB p33)

Discussing grammar

Ask students to work in pairs to do these two exercises. They can refer to their lists of rules.

1 Students identify the mistake in each sentence and discuss why it is wrong.

Answers
1 He's **a** postman, so he has breakfast at 4 a.m.
2 Love is more important than money.
3 I come to school by bus.
4 I'm reading **a** good book at the moment.
5 'Where's Jack?' 'In **the** kitchen.'
6 I live in **the** centre of town, near the hospital.
7 My parents bought **a** lovely house in the country.
8 I don't eat bread because I don't like it.

2 Students complete the sentences with *a/an*, *the*, or no article.

Answers
1 I have two children, **a** boy and **a** girl. **The** boy is twenty-two and **the** girl is nineteen.
2 Mike is **a** soldier in **the** Army, and Chloë is at university.
3 My wife goes to work by train. She's **an** accountant. I don't have **a** job. I stay at home and look after **the** children.
4 What **a** lovely day! Why don't we go for **a** picnic in **the** park?
5 'What did you have for lunch?' 'Just **a** sandwich.'

Go through the exercises with the whole class. Ask them why they have reached their decisions, and in this way you will revise the rules.

ADDITIONAL MATERIAL

Workbook Unit 4
Exercises 7–9 Articles – (Exercise 8 would be suitable as a quick warmer at the start of almost any lesson.)
Exercise 10 Spelling of plural nouns (this would also be a good warmer.)

READING (SB p34)

The best shopping street in the world

You should try to create as much interest as possible in the subject of a text students are about to read. Consequently, it is often a good idea to start the lesson by personalizing the topic in some way. You could start this lesson with a picture of a famous shop or shopping street in your students' own country and ask them to tell you about it. You could write the names of famous shops that they will know on the board and ask students where they are and what you can buy there. You could also use the questions in the follow-up *What do you think?* section at the beginning of the lesson, instead of at the end.

1 Put students in pairs or groups of three to do the matching task. They should be able to guess most of the answers, but don't give them too long if they look blank. In the feedback, personalize it a little by asking if anyone has visited any of these stores, or bought anything from them.

Answers

Street	Town	Store	Product
Oxford Street	London	Marks & Spencer	underwear and jumpers
Champs Elysées	Paris	Guerlain	perfume
Fifth Avenue	New York	Tiffany's	jewellery
Via Montenapoleone	Milan	Gucci	leather goods

2 Ask students to look at the headline and read the opening paragraph as a class. Find out if any students know anything about NowyŚwiat, (pronounced /nɔvi ʃvɪət/).

Students then work in pairs to think about what they would like to know about the street and to prepare questions. You could suggest one or two to start them off.

What sort of shops are there?
How many people go there to do their shopping?

Make sure students have got at least four or five questions before reading. You could write some of the best questions on the board.

3 Ask students to read the article and answer as many of their questions as they can. They should try not to worry about words they don't know. In the feedback, let students tell you what answers they found to their questions. The best summary is:

Nowy Świat is the best shopping street in the world because ***the shops sell quality goods that you can't buy anywhere else.***

4 Read through the comprehension questions with students and check any difficult vocabulary. Get them to check their answers in pairs before feedback.

Answers
1 From a recent survey.
2 There are a lot of reasons, including: wide pavements, attractive buildings, exclusive cafés and restaurants, no billboards or neon lights, no loud music or tourists.
3 Nowy Świat: the shopping street, *Café Blikle*: an exclusive café, wide pavements with chic shops.
4 Because people think Polish shops have nothing to sell.
5 They are not mass produced.

6 You can buy almost everything: hand-made suits, French baby clothes, antiques, leather goods, folk art, books, records, clothes.
You can't buy mass-produced goods that you normally find in big department stores.
7 Hand-made suits, French baby clothes and antiques are expensive.
Items from *Pantera*, the leather goods shop, *Cepelia*, the folk art shop, and other shops and small boutiques are not expensive.
8 It is fashionable, lively, and the food is delicious.
9 They are unique.

Language work

The aim of this activity is to revise expressions of quantity.

Model the activity by giving students one or two example sentences.

In Nowy Świat, there are a lot of small shops.
There aren't any huge department stores.

Then, either put students in small groups and give them four or five minutes to say as many sentences as they can to each other, or, if they need more time to think, put them in pairs to write sentences and feed back open class.

What do you think?

This is a personalized fluency discussion which aims to revise vocabulary and get students talking.

Write a few famous brand names on the board, then put students in small groups to make a longer list. In the feedback, see if the class can agree on which three are the most famous.

Discuss the other questions as a class or in groups.

ADDITIONAL MATERIAL

Workbook Unit 4
Exercise 11 Clothes

NOTE
Don't forget to encourage your students to keep adding words to their own vocabulary notebooks and/or find the words in the Word list and write in the translation.

Also you could, by this stage of your course, have regular short vocabulary tests/competitions. Ask students to study the Word lists for the first four units. You could test vocabulary via pictures, definitions, and translation. This could be done in teams and students could sometimes devise their own tests for each other to increase motivation.

VOCABULARY AND LISTENING (SB p36)

Buying things

1 Ask students what they can buy or do in a clothes shop. Write some of their ideas on the board, then put them in pairs or threes to do the rest of the exercise. Give students a time limit so that they do this quite quickly, then feed back with the whole class.

Sample answers

a clothes shop	buy a shirt, jumper, etc., try on clothes, etc.
a chemist's	buy medicine, aspirin, soap, etc.
a café	buy a coffee or tea, eat a sandwich or cakes, drink beer or wine, read a paper, talk to friends, etc.
a bank	put money in, take money out, exchange money or traveller's cheques, etc.
a newsagent's	buy a newspaper or magazine, buy sweets, cigarettes or a lottery ticket, etc.

2 **T 4.5** The aim of this first listening activity is to improve students' ability to listen for gist, using contextual and lexical clues to work out the situation. Read through the questions together then play the recording. Pause after each conversation and ask students to discuss their answers in pairs before getting feedback.

Answers
Conversation 1
1 a clothes shop 2 a jumper 3 Yes 4 £39.99
Conversation 2
1 a newsagent's 2 *Vogue* – a magazine, 3 Yes
Conversation 3
1 a chemist's 2 tablets and tissues 3 Yes
Conversation 4
1 a café 2 an espresso and a doughnut (but changes to carrot cake) 3 Yes 4 £4.85

3 Students work in pairs to complete the conversations. You may need to play the recording again, pausing to give students time to write down their answers. Let students check their answers by referring to the tapescript on p120.

Answers and tapescript
T 4.5
1 **A** Hello. Can I help you?
B **I'm just looking**, thanks.
...
B I'm looking for a jumper **like this, but in blue**. Have you got **one**?
A I'll just have a look. **What size** are you?
B Medium.
A Here you are.

B That's great. **Can I try it on?**
A Of course. The changing rooms are over there.
...
B I like it.
A It **fits you very well**.
B How much is it?
A £39.99.
B OK. **I'll have it**.
A How would you like to pay?
B **Cash**.

2 A **Could you** help me? I'm looking for this month's edition of *Vogue*. Can you tell me **where it is**?
B Over there. Middle shelf. Next to *She*.

3 A Hello. I **wonder if you could** help me. I've got a bad cold and a sore throat. Can you **give me something for it**?
B OK. You can take these three times a day.
A Thank you. **Could I have** some tissues **as well**, please?
B Sure. **Anything else**?
A No, that's all, thanks.

4 A Good morning. Can I have a **black coffee**, please?
B Espresso?
A Yes, please. Oh, and a doughnut, please.
B **I'm afraid** there aren't **any left**. We've got some delicious carrot cake, and chocolate cake.
A OK. Carrot cake, then.
B Certainly. Is **that all**?
A Yes, thanks.
B **That'll be £1.85**, please.
A Thank you.

EVERYDAY ENGLISH (SB p37)

Prices and shopping

1 Focus students on the prices in the boxes. Drill them round the class for pronunciation.

T 4.6 Play the recording and ask students to write the numbers they hear. Put them in pairs to check their answers. Then get a full-class feedback on where each dialogue takes place.

Answers and tapescript
1 £2.80 (in a post office)
2 £28.50 (in a clothes shop)
3 £1.82 (in a baker's)
4 $12.20
5 $15,000
6 £1/2 million (£500,000)
7 £5.99 (in a bookshop)
8 $160

T 4.6
1 A A book of ten first class stamps, please.
B Two pounds eighty, please.
2 A How much is this jumper?
B Twenty-eight pounds fifty.
3 A A white loaf and three rolls, please.
B That'll be one pound eighty-two p.
4 A How much do I owe you?
B Twelve dollars and twenty cents.
5 A How much was your car?
B Fifteen thousand dollars.
6 A What a fantastic house!
B Darling! It cost half a million pounds!
7 A Just this book, please.
B Five pounds ninety-nine, then.
8 A How much was the check for?
B A hundred and sixty dollars.

2 Invite students to say the exchange rate between £ sterling/US dollars and their currency. This activity provides some controlled practice of prices. Model the question, *How much is ... ?*, then put students in pairs to ask each other. Monitor and check that they are saying prices correctly.

3 Check the vocabulary, then give students a few minutes to prepare and practise the dialogues in their pairs. Go round and help with their pronunciation. You could ask one or two pairs to act out some conversations in front of the class.

Don't forget!

Workbook Unit 4
Exercise 12 Filling in forms

Pronunciation book Unit 4

Word list
Photocopy the Word list for Unit 4 (TB p155) for your students, and ask them to write in the translations, learn them at home, and/or write some of the words into their vocabulary notebook.

Video
Situation (Section 3) ***Car Hire*** This is a short situation in which Paola hires a car.

EXTRA IDEAS UNITS 1–4
On p120 of the Teacher's Book there is a song, *Sailing*, and suggested activities to exploit it. If you have time and feel that your students would benefit from it, photocopy the song and use it in class. You will find the song after Unit 4 on the Class Cassette/CD. The answers to the activities are on p147 of the Teacher's Book.

Stop and check 1 (TB p130)
A suggestion for approaching the *Stop and check* tests is in the introduction on p5 of the Teacher's Book.

5 Verb patterns 1 • Future forms
Hot verbs
How do you feel?

What do you want to do?

Introduction to the unit

The title of this unit is 'What do you want to do?' In the opening 'Hopes and ambitions' section, various verb patterns within the context of hopes, ambitions, and plans are introduced and practised. In a second grammatical focus, *going to* is contrasted with *will*. There is a reading text about Hollywood kids, growing up in Los Angeles, and the *Listening* activity exploits the song *You've got a friend* by Carole King. The *Vocabulary* section looks at the Hot verbs *have*, *go*, and *come*.

Language aims

Grammar – verb patterns Students might well have come across several of the verb patterns in this unit, either formally or informally, but they will probably not have seen them presented under the heading *verb patterns*. It is worth explaining what a pattern is, i.e. something that repeats itself.

POSSIBLE PROBLEMS

- Mistakes of form are common with verb patterns, and it is this area that is specifically practised in the *Grammar Spot* and first practice activity.
  **I'm going work as a designer.*
  **She hopes finding a job soon.*
  **He want have a restaurant.*
- Two possible patterns with *like* are also presented, and these cause problems of form and use. With the two forms being similar, they are easily mixed up, but learners also find the conceptual difference of 'general versus specific preference' difficult to grasp.

  Common mistakes
  **I like play football.*
  **I'd like having a drink.*
  Common mistakes of use
  **I'm thirsty. I like a Coke.*
  **Do you like to come to the cinema tonight?*

In this unit, we suggest that for a general preference, *like* + *-ing* is used. Students might come across *like* + the infinitive to express this use.

I like to relax at the weekend.

The verb patterns presented in this unit are such high frequency items (with the exception of *hope*), that once you have presented them, they will automatically be revised and practised in many classroom activities. If mistakes occur in subsequent lessons, remind students of the rules.

going to* and *will *Going to* is contrasted with *will* in this unit, by only one use of each verb form. Both items are traditionally taught in a first year book, so the forms will not be new. *Will* to express a spontaneous offer was practised in the *Everyday English* section of Unit 4. In this unit it is seen with a very similar use, to express a future intention or a decision made the moment of speaking. This is in contrast with *going to*, which expresses a pre-planned intention. Students might well perceive this conceptual difference quite easily, but it is another matter to apply the rule thereafter. Selecting appropriate future forms causes many problems for a long time.

Common mistakes

*'Have you booked a holiday yet?' *'Yes. We'll go to Spain.'*
**What will you do tonight?*
**What do you do tonight?*
**What you do tonight?*
*'The phone's ringing.' *'OK. I answer it.'*

Students often use the base form of the verb to express a spontaneous offer or intention, rather than *will.*

**I open the door for you.*

Making offers and expressing intentions are common occurrences in the day-to-day interactions of classrooms, whether students are acting in roles or just being themselves. If (and when!) you hear mistakes with this use of *will*, it is worth reminding learners of the rule. They might learn it all the better for seeing the item in a real context. For example, if a student offers to help you collect in some books and says 'I collect the books for you', take the opportunity to point out to the class how *will* should be used here.

This unit deals with the modal use of *will. Will* as an auxiliary verb to show future time is dealt with in Unit 9.

Vocabulary The *Vocabulary* section introduces the Hot verbs, *have, go,* and *come.* This is the first *Hot verbs* section in the book. These sections aim to focus on the use of common verbs in English, looking at them as vocabulary items, dealing with their range of meanings, confusions as to which one to use, and specific collocations.

Everyday English This section looks at vocabulary and functional language in the context of feelings.

Notes on the unit

STARTER (SB p38)

This starter activity gets students talking about themselves and previews their ability to form and use the verb patterns focused on later in the unit.

Give students a few minutes to prepare some sentences, then either put them in small groups to chat, or nominate a few people and have a brief class discussion. Don't worry about errors made with the verb patterns at this stage, but note how well students can use them.

HOPES AND AMBITIONS (SB p38)

Verb patterns 1

Lead in by asking students about their hopes and ambitions. If they are young, you could ask questions such as *What job do you hope to get? Would you like to go to university/college? What would you like to study? Are you going to travel?*

If they are more mature, you could ask *What do you hope to do in the next ten years? Would you like to travel? Where would you like to go?*

1 **T 5.1** Ask students to look at the pictures and work in pairs to match them with the sentences. Do one as an example. When they are ready, students listen to the recording and check whether their predictions are correct.

Answers and tapescript

1 Justin 2 Sean 3 Alison 4 Martyn 5 Mel 6 Amy

1 **Sean, aged 9**
When I grow up, I want to be a footballer and play for Manchester United, because I want to earn lots of money. After that, I'm going to be an astronaut, and fly in a rocket to Mars and Jupiter. And I'd like all the people in the world and all the animals in the world to be happy.

2 **Mel, aged 19**
I've finished my first year at Bristol University, and now I'm going to have a year off. My boyfriend and I are going round the world. We hope to find work as we go. I really want to meet people from all over the world, and see how different people live their lives.

3 **Justin, aged 29**
What I'd really like to do, because I'm mad about planes and everything to do with flying, is to have my own business connected with planes, something like a flying school. I'm getting married next June, so I can't do anything about it yet, but I'm going to start looking this time next year.

4 **Martyn, aged 39**
My great passion is writing. I write plays. Three have been perfomed already, two in Edinburgh and one in Oxford. But my secret ambition . . . and this would be the best thing in my life . . . I would love to have one of my plays performed on the London stage. That would be fantastic.

5 **Amy, aged 49**
We're thinking of moving, because the kids are leaving home soon. Meg's eighteen, she's doing her A levels this year, so with a bit of luck, she'll be off to university next year. And Kate's fifteen. Jack and I both enjoy walking, and Jack likes fishing, so we're going to move to the country.

6 **Alison, aged 59**
Well, I've just broken my arm, so what I really want to do is to go back to the health club as soon as possible. I really enjoy swimming. At my age, it's important to stay physically fit, and I want to be able to go off travelling without feeling unwell. I'm going to retire next year, and I'm looking forward to having more time to do the things I want to do.

2 Ask students to listen again and complete the chart. You may need to pause after each section to give them time to write.

Answers

	Ambitions/Plans	**Reasons**
Sean	A footballer for Manchester United An astronaut He wants the people and animals in the world to be happy	To earn lots of money
Mel	A year off Going round the world	Wants to meet people from all over the world
Justin	Own business connected with planes, like a flying school Getting married next June	Mad about planes
Martyn	Have a play performed on the London stage	His passion is writing
Amy	Going to move to the country	The kids are leaving home, and she and her husband, Jack, love walking Jack loves fishing too
Alison	Go back to the health club and stay physically fit Wants to be able to travel Going to retire next year	Just broken her arm Enjoys swimming

3 The aim of this activity is to allow students to discover verb patterns and their rules for themselves. Focus students on the example then let them underline the other examples in exercise 1. Ask them which verbs are followed by *to* + infinitive, and which are followed by preposition + *ing*. You may then wish to put students in pairs to find more examples of these patterns in the tapescript on p120.

GRAMMAR SPOT (SB p39)

1 Ask students to work in pairs to complete the sentences using the words *go abroad*. Write the sentences on the board in the feedback and point out the different verb forms.

Answers
I'd like **to go abroad**
I can't **go abroad**
I'm looking forward to **going abroad**
I hope **to go abroad**
I enjoy **going abroad**
I'm thinking of **going abroad**
I'd love **to go abroad**

Point out that the verb *go* is in the infinitive after some verbs and *-ing* after others, and that we use *-ing* after prepositions like *of*. The *to* in *looking forward to* is a preposition.

ADDITIONAL IDEA

So far, students have read the target structures, perhaps written them, and perhaps spoken examples of them, but not to any great extent.

Drill the sentences in the *Grammar Spot* around the class, correcting as necessary. Ask students to practise saying the sentences in pairs.

2 Answer this question as a class. Try to get from students the idea that *like going* is a general, all-time preference. It applies to the past, present, and future. *Would like to go* refers to now or the (near) future. If you feel it would help your class to do so, translate these two sentences.

Refer students to Grammar Reference 5.1 and 5.2 on p134.

Discussing grammar

1 Ask students to work in pairs to do this exercise, or let them do it individually then check with a partner. In the feedback, refer back to the rules if necessary, then get students to work in pairs to make correct sentences with the other verbs.

Answers
1 a,c 2 b,c 3 c 4 a,b 5 b,c 6 a,c

Ask students to make correct sentences with the other verbs.

Answers
1 enjoy living
2 are hoping to go
3 want to go 'd like to go
4 I'm looking forward to seeing
5 want to learn
6 'd love to have

Making questions

2 Ask students to work in pairs to do this exercise.

T 5.2 Play the recording so that students can check their answers then put them in pairs to practise the conversations.

Answers and tapescript
1 **A** I hope to go to university.
B **What do you want to study?**
2 **A** One of my favourite hobbies is cooking.
B **What do you like making?**
3 **A** I get terrible headaches.
B **When did you start getting them?**

4 **A** We're planning our summer holidays at the moment.
B **Where are you thinking of going?**
5 **A** I'm tired.
B **What would you like to do tonight?**

Talking about you

These two exercises provide some personalized free practice for students. Encourage lots of interaction but make sure students are using the verb patterns accurately.

3 Before students work in pairs, make sure they can ask the questions correctly. Drill them around the class. As students ask and answer in pairs, monitor and note any errors regarding the use of verb patterns.

4 Give students some time to prepare the questions in pairs. Change the pairs to ask and answer questions. You could finish the activity by asking one or two pairs to say their questions and answers again while the rest of the class listens. Alternatively, this activity would work well as a mingle activity, where all students stand up and ask one or two questions to as many other students as possible.

Sample questions
Which countries would you like to go to?
When do you want to get married? How many children do you want to have?
What are you going to do/are you thinking of doing after this course? Would you like to go to university?

ADDITIONAL MATERIAL

Workbook Unit 5
These exercises could be done in class to give further practice, for homework, or in a later class as revision.

Exercises 1–3 Verb patterns
Exercises 4–6 *Would like (to do)* and *like (doing)*

Before moving on to the next presentation of *will* and *going to*, you and your class might prefer to do some skills work. You could do the reading activity *Hollywood Kids* on p42 of the Student's Book.

FUTURE INTENTIONS (SB p40)

going to and *will*

If you think your students already have an idea about the difference between *going to* and *will*, do the exercises as they are in the Student's Book. If you think that they would make a lot of mistakes (which is discouraging), do the following introduction first.

Introduction: Write the dialogue below on the board.

Ann *I'm going to buy some sugar. It's on my shopping list.*
Bill *Can you buy some tea?*
Ann *OK. I'll buy some in the supermarket.*

Underline the words as shown, and ask students the following questions.

When did Ann decide to buy some sugar? Before she spoke or while she was speaking?

When did Ann decide to buy the tea? Before she spoke or while she was speaking?

Ask students if they can tell you the difference between the two forms. Explain that *going to* is used to express an intention that is thought about before the moment of speaking, and *will* expresses a spontaneous intention.

At this stage, it is a good idea to remind students that the verbs *go* and *come* are not generally used with *going to* but with the Present Continuous.

Examples
I'm going to go shopping. ✗
I'm going shopping. ✓

I'm going to come to France. ✗
I'm coming to France. ✓

1 Ask a few questions about the pictures to set the situation, get students talking, and perhaps elicit some useful vocabulary such as *backpack, pocket, scarf,* and *parcel.*

Where are they? What are they doing?

Ask students to work in pairs to match a sentence with each picture.

Answers
1d 2f 3b 4a 5c 6e

2 Set this activity up carefully by reading through the sentences with students and checking the vocabulary, then doing one mini-conversation as an example on the board. Ask students to work in pairs to do this exercise.

T 5.3 Students listen to the recording and check their answers, then practise the conversations in pairs. Make sure they try to imitate the pronunciation, stress, and intonation of the sentences on the recording.

Answers and tapescript

1 What are the lads doing this afternoon?
They're going to watch a football match. Arsenal are playing at home.

2 Damn! I've dropped one.
I'll pick it up for you.
Thank you. That's very kind.

3 What's Ali doing next year?
She's going to travel round the world.
Oh, lucky her!

4 The phone's ringing.
It's OK. I'll answer it. I'm expecting a call.

5 I haven't got any money.
Don't worry. I'll lend you some.
Thanks. I'll pay you back tomorrow. I won't forget.

6 What are you and Pete doing tonight?
We're going out to have a meal. It's my birthday.

GRAMMAR SPOT (SB p40)

Answer the questions as a class. Make sure students are concentrating hard at this point.

Answers

1. Point out the pronunciation of *I'll* /aɪl/ and *won't* /wəʊnt/.
2. Spontaneous intentions: *I'll pick it up for you, I'll answer it, I'll lend you some.*
   Before the premeditated intentions, the speaker made some plans: Before going to watch a football match, they put on their scarves, or bought a ticket. Perhaps before travelling, she bought tickets and packed her backpack. Before going for a meal, they talked about which restaurant to go to, and booked a table.
   Going to expresses an intention that is thought about before the moment of speaking. *Will* is used to express a spontaneous intention.

Refer students to Grammar Reference 5.3 on p134.

PRACTICE (SB p41)

Let's have a party!

1 Read the introduction to the exercise as a class. Drill the two sample sentences (*I'll bring the music; I'll buy some crisps*). Make sure that students pronounce the *'ll.*

Do the next part quite briskly, so that suggestions are coming from students all the time. The suggestions must be spontaneous! Try to get an idea from most of the class. If there are any mistakes with *'ll*, correct them.

2 Read the introduction as a class. Model the sample sentences yourself, and exaggerate the stressed *I'm*. If you think it's necessary, ask the class why *going to* is now used, and not *will.*

You need to remember the suggestions your students made. Repeat them, using *will*, and invite the student who made that suggestion to say it again using *going to.* Again, try to do this briskly, otherwise the exercise will pall.

Discussing grammar

3 Students work in pairs to decide which is the correct verb form.

Answers

1. I'll carry
2. I'm going skiing.
3. I'll give
4. We're going to see
5. I won't tell
6. you're going to get
7. I'm going shopping, I'll post
8. are you going

4 **T 5.4** This is a type of prompt drill which aims to help students grasp the idea of the contrasting uses of *going to* and *will* by getting them to make quick decisions as to which one to use. Play each conversation opening and pause the recording for students to respond. Make sure all students are contributing and selecting the correct tense.

Answers and tapescript

1. 'My bag is so heavy.' 'Give it to me. **I'll carry it for you.**'
2. I bought some warm boots because **I'm going skiing.**
3. 'Tony's back from holiday.' 'Is he? **I'll give him a ring.**'
4. 'What are you doing tonight?' '**We're going to see a play at the theatre.**'
5. You can tell me your secret. **I won't tell anyone.**
6. Congratulations! I hear **you're going to get married.**
7. 'I need to post these letters.' '**I'm going shopping soon. I'll post them for you.**'
8. Now, holidays. Where **are you going this year?**

Check it

5 Ask students to work in pairs to correct the sentences.

Answers

1. What do you want to drink?
2. I'll have a Coke, please.
3. I can't help you.
4. It's starting to rain.
5. I'm looking forward to seeing you again soon.
6. I'm thinking of changing my job soon.
7. Phone me tonight. I'll give you my phone number.
8. I'm seeing the doctor tomorrow about my back.

Talking about you

6 Give students some time to prepare a few questions, using either the Present Continuous or *going to.* Before students work in pairs, drill some example questions to focus on the wide tone range required in English.

What are you doing tonight?

What are you going to do next weekend?

Where are you going on holiday?

Students work in pairs to ask and answer questions.

ADDITIONAL MATERIAL

Workbook Unit 5
Exercises 7–9 *will* and *going to*

READING (SB p42)

Hollywood kids

Create interest in the topic by getting your students talking about the problems of teenagers and Hollywood kids in particular. You could elicit *Problems of being a teenager* and write them on the board. (For example, *drugs, arguments with parents, studying for exams.*) Or ask students to look at the title and photos and ask them questions.

What problems do Hollywood kids have?
What is good about their lives?
Would you like to be a Hollywood kid? Why/Why not?

1 Ask students to do this exercise by themselves, then do a brief class feedback to establish that different people have different opinions. Check the vocabulary.

2 Ask students to read the text and tick boxes in the right column according to the information in the text. In the feedback, have a brief discussion as to why Hollywood kids are different (because they are rich, ambitious, grow up really fast and live unreal lives).

Answers
violence in the streets
their parents don't give them enough attention
they worry about how they look
their parents want them to do well in life
they're too old to be children, but too young to be adults

3 Ask students to work in pairs to answer the true/false questions. They will need to read the text again. As you get feedback, encourage discussion and comment.

Answers
1 False. Everyone *wants* to be rich and famous, but that's not the same thing. No doubt there are many people who are rich and famous, but not everyone.
2 True. Their lives are unreal. Their parents are unbelievably rich, they give their kids presents and money which are far too much, they buy the kids anything and everything they want. But all this is more for the parents than for the children themselves.
3 False. They understand the value of nothing because they have everything so easily.
4 True. He has possessions such as a credit card, a driver, and money which a child that age shouldn't have.
5 False. It is true that the parents give their children all that they want, including parties, cars, and clothes. But this is partly to further their own ambitions, and partly because the parents don't have time to give to their children. Giving is a substitute for love.
6 Probably false. The suggestion is that all these people are employed because the mother isn't there herself to do these things.
7 True. The children make all their own decisions, which really they should make in discussion with their parents.
8 False. The children have to do it because the parents aren't at home.
9 True. They want to grow up and be part of the adult world. As Mijanou says 'It's not cool to be a kid.'
10 False. Only Zavier complains, when he says that it is dangerous. The other kids talk about the craziness of living in Hollywood, but it sounds as though they like it.

4 Either put students in groups to do this exercise or do it whole class. Encourage lots of talking from students.

What do you think?

Wind up the lesson by encouraging students to express their own opinions. You could do this with the whole class or in small groups. Small groups maximize students' talking time, allow you to monitor and note errors, and let shyer students speak without having too many people listening to them! A good way to get feedback from groups is to have one student from each group summarize what they talked about.

VOCABULARY (SB p44)

Hot verbs – *have, go, come*

You could introduce this lesson by writing *have, go,* and *come* on the board, putting students in small groups, and giving them a few minutes to think of as many phrases as they can using these very common verbs.

1 Read through the examples with students.

2 Ask students to work in pairs to complete the gaps.

Answers

have an accident	have a cold
come first in a race	go wrong
go out for a meal	have a meeting
come and see me	go abroad
go shopping	

3 Students complete the sentences and check with their partner.

Answers
1 having to come
2 have *or* have got go
3 Come have
4 going Have coming
5 is having go
6 Come to go
7 go have
8 going Do . . . have *or* Have . . . got

ADDITIONAL MATERIAL

Workbook Unit 5
Exercise 10 extends and practises words that go together, and verbs and prepositions.

LISTENING (SB p44)

You've got a friend, by Carole King

This listening exercise is a song, the first of the songs in *New Headway Pre-Intermediate* Student's Book. Songs are fun and motivating, but also very difficult for students at this level to follow. The secret is to create lots of interest at the lead-in, deal with as much vocabulary as you can *before* listening, and guide students to an understanding by means of activities like the gap-fill included here.

A suggested lead-in is to write on the board: *A friend is someone who . . .* . Elicit as many complete sentences as you can from students. For example, *A friend is someone who you can phone at midnight* or *A friend is someone who remembers your birthday.*

1 Make sure students understand the phrases in the box, then ask students to work in pairs to match the phrases with the likely speaker.

Answers
1 Your best friend: *I'll always be there for you.*
2 Your boyfriend/girlfriend: *I'll love you forever, I'll always be there for you, I'll do anything for you, You'll never find anyone who loves you more than I do.*
3 Your ex-boyfriend/girlfriend: *I'll never forget you, I'll always remember the times we had together, You'll never find anyone who loves you more than I do.*

2 Look at the photo and discuss the questions as a class. Encourage as much speculation as you can.

Sample answers
1 No, it seems that they live in different places.
2 Yes. They are best friends.
3 Now they are close friends, but probably in their past they were lovers.

3 **T 5.5** Students listen and complete the song. Play the song through once without writing, give students time to complete the gaps, then play it again, pausing if necessary to give students time to write. If your students like singing, then play it again and sing along. Students may query the use of *will* here. If they do, tell them that here, it is not used for *spontaneous decisions*, but rather for *promises/truths.*

Answers and tapescript
When you're down and troubled
And you need a **helping hand**
And nothing, but **nothing is going right**
Close your eyes and think of me
And soon I **will be there**
To brighten up even your darkest nights.

(Chorus)

You just call out my name,
and you know wherever I am
I'll come running to see you again.
Winter, spring, **summer, or fall**
All you have to do is call
And I'll be there, yeah, yeah, yeah,
You'**ve got a friend**.

If the sky above you
Turns dark and full of clouds
And that old north **wind begins to blow**
Keep your head together
And **call my name out loud**
And soon I'll be knocking on your door.
Hey, **ain't it good to know** that you've got a friend?
People can be so cold.
They'll hurt you and desert you.
Well they'll take your soul if you let them
Oh, yeah, but **don't you let them**.

(Chorus)

EVERYDAY ENGLISH (SB p45)

How do you feel?

1 Set the scene by asking students to look at the photos and say how they think the people in the photos feel. At this stage, you could try to elicit some expressions by asking students what they think the people are saying.

2 Ask students to work in pairs to match the phrases.

Answers

I feel nervous.	I've got an exam today.
I don't feel very well.	I think I'm getting the 'flu.
I'm feeling a lot better, thanks.	I've got a lot more energy.
I'm really excited.	I'm going on holiday to Australia tomorrow.
I'm fed up with this weather.	It's so wet and miserable.

I'm really tired.	I couldn't get to sleep last night.
I'm a bit worried.	My grandfather's going into hospital for tests.
I feel really depressed at the moment.	Nothing's going right in my life.

3 Now ask them to choose a reply from a–h.

T 5.6 Students listen to the mini-dialogues and check their answers. You may choose to pause the recording after each phrase so that students can repeat for pronunciation, or ask them to work in pairs to practise after each dialogue. Alternatively, drill some of the phrases with particularly interesting or unusual intonation patterns. For example:

Why don't you go home to bed?

That's great!

Poor you!

Answers and tapescript

1 A I feel nervous. I've got an exam today.
B **Good luck! Do your best.**
2 A I don't feel very well. I think I'm getting the 'flu.
B **Why don't you go home to bed?**
3 A I'm feeling a lot better, thanks. I've got a lot more energy.
B **That's good. I'm pleased to hear it.**
4 A I'm really excited. I'm going on holiday to Australia tomorrow.
B **That's great. Have a good time.**
5 A I'm fed up with this weather. It's so wet and miserable.
B **I know. We really need some sunshine, don't we?**
6 A I'm really tired. I couldn't get to sleep last night.
B **Poor you! That happens to me sometimes. I just read in bed.**
7 A I'm a bit worried. My grandfather's going into hospital for tests.
B **I'm sorry to hear that, but I'm sure he'll be all right.**
8 A I feel really depressed at the moment. Nothing's going right in my life.
B **Cheer up! Things can't be that bad!**

4 Students work in pairs to prepare and practise conversations using some or all of the situations. Monitor and help with preparation. Let some pairs act out their dialogues to the class. Ask other students to comment on the pronunciation.

Don't forget!

Workbook Unit 5

Exercise 11 revises adjectives and asks students to write a postcard.

Pronunciation book Unit 5

Word list

Photocopy the Word list for Unit 5 (TB p155) for your students, and ask them to write in the translations, learn them at home, and/or write some of the words into their vocabulary notebook.

Progress test

There is a Progress test for Units 1–5 on p138 of the Teacher's Book.

What ... like? • Comparatives and superlatives
Synonyms and antonyms
Directions

Tell me! What's it like?

Introduction to the unit

The theme of the unit is describing people and places. This provides a useful context to practise the grammar for this unit, *What ... like?* and comparatives and superlatives. The *Listening and speaking* section describes life in Sweden and compares it to Britain. The *Reading* section contains texts about the meanest and most generous millionaires in the world.

Language aims

Grammar – *What ... like?* This question, which asks for a description, causes difficulties for students.

POSSIBLE PROBLEMS

- *Like* is used as a preposition in *What ... like?*, but students only have experience of it as a verb, as in *I like dancing.*
- The answer to the question *What ... like?* does not contain *like* with the adjective.
  Common mistake
  What's John like? **He's like nice.*
- Students may find *What ... like?* a strange construction to ask for a description. In many languages the question word *how* is used to do this. In English, however, *How is John?* is an inquiry about his health, *not* about his character and/or looks, and the answer is *He's very well.*

What ... like? is introduced first in the unit to provide a staged approach to the practice of comparatives and superlatives in the second presentation. It is a useful question in the practising of these.

Comparatives and superlatives It is assumed that students will have a certain familiarity with these, although of course mistakes will still be made. The exercises bring together all aspects of comparatives and superlatives:

- the use of *-er/-est* with short adjectives, *-ier/-iest* with adjectives that end in *-y*, and *more/most* with longer adjectives.
- irregular adjectives such as *good/better/best* and *bad/worse/worst.*
- *as ... as* to describe similarity.

Students experience little difficulty with the concept of these structures but experience more difficulty in producing and pronouncing the forms because of all the different 'bits' involved. One of the most common problems is that they give equal stress to every word and syllable, so that utterances sound very unnatural.

Common mistakes
**She's more big than me.*
**He's the most rich man in the world.*
**She's tallest in the class.*
**It's more expensive that I thought.*
**He is as rich than the Queen.*

There are a lot of controlled activities which aim to practise the form, and a pronunciation drill to practise natural connected speech.

Vocabulary Adjectives are practised in the *Vocabulary* section, where students are asked to explore the use of synonyms and antonyms.

Everyday English This section practises getting and giving directions with prepositions of place, e.g. *behind*, *in front of*, and prepositions of movement e.g. *along*, *across*. A map is used to do this. The final activity is personalized, and students give each other directions to get to their homes from school.

Notes on the unit

STARTER (SB p46)

The aim of this activity is to personalize the theme by getting students to describe the capital cities of their countries. Hopefully, they will use some of the adjectives and other vocabulary used in the unit. Pay careful attention to how well they can use descriptive language.

WORLD TRAVEL (SB p46)

What's it like?

1 Read through the introduction to Todd Bridges with your students.

2 Check that your students know where Melbourne, Dubai, and Paris are. You may need to refer to a map to do this. Elicit as many facts about these places as you can and write the words and phrases on the board.

3 **T 6.1** Play the recording. You could ask students to listen to see if their predictions are the same as what Todd says.

Tapescript
T = Todd E = Ellen

E You're so lucky, Todd. You travel all over the world. I never leave Chicago!
T Yeah – but it's hard work. I just practise, practise, practise and play tennis all the time. I don't get time to see much.
E What about last year? Where did you go? Tell me about it.
T Well – in January I was in Melbourne, for the Australian Open. It's a beautiful city, sort of big and very cosmopolitan, like Chicago. There's a nice mixture of old and new buildings. January's their summer so it was hot when I was there.
E And what's Dubai like? When were you there?
T In February. We went from Australia to Dubai for the Dubai Tennis Open. Boy is Dubai hot! Hot, very dry, very modern. Lots of really modern buildings, white buildings. Interesting place, I enjoyed it.
E And Paris! That's where I want to go! What's Paris like?
T Everything that you imagine! Very beautiful, wonderful old buildings but lots of interesting modern ones too. And of course very, very romantic, especially in May. Maybe I can take you there sometime.
E Yeah?

After listening for the first time, students write down as many adjectives as they can remember. You may need to replay the recording once or twice, but they should be familiar with most of the adjectives, although possibly *crowded*, *polluted*, and *noisy* will need some explanation, and they will certainly need some pronunciation practice: *crowded* /ˈkraʊdɪd/, *polluted* /pəˈluːtɪd/, *noisy* /ˈnɔɪzi/.

In the feedback, write the adjectives on the board.

Answers
Melbourne beautiful, sort of big, very cosmopolitan, old and new (buildings), hot (in summer)
Dubai very hot, very dry, very modern, interesting
Paris very beautiful, wonderful, old (buildings), interesting, modern (buildings), very romantic

NOTE
The first stage of the lesson focuses only on the adjectives and giving descriptions before moving to the introduction of the question *What … like?* This is so that when the question is introduced students will understand from the start that the answer to this question is a description and does not contain *like*.

GRAMMAR SPOT (SB p46)

Before you ask students to match the questions and answers, give them the opportunity to tell you if they heard the question *What … like?* Ask *Did anyone hear the question the friend asked about all the cities?*

Now do the matching activity as a class. The aim is to make clear the difference between the verb *to like* and the preposition *like*.

Answers

1	Do you like Paris?	Yes, I do./No, I don't.
	What's Paris like?	It's beautiful./It's got lots of old buildings.
2	The second question, *What's Paris like?*	

You could ask students to read the tapescript on p121 to see the questions in context. You could ask them to underline the questions in the text.

Refer students to Grammar Reference 6.1 on p135.

4 The aim of the exercise is very controlled oral practice. You could chorus drill the question to practise the contraction *What's*, and the intonation.

Ask students to work in pairs. Go round, helping and correcting.

Ask your students to do this exercise without looking at the tapescript if possible.

Sample answers
What's Melbourne like? It's a beautiful city, sort of big and very cosmopolitan. There are old and new buildings, and it's hot in summer.
What's Dubai like? It's very hot, very dry and very modern, but it's very interesting too.
What's Paris like? It's got very beautiful, wonderful, old buildings, and interesting, modern buildings too. It's very romantic.

PRACTICE (SB p47)

What's Chicago like?

1 Ask students to do this on their own and compare their answers with a partner when they finish. They should be able to do it quite quickly.

Answers and tapescript
T = Todd F = Friend
1 **F** What's **the weather** like?
T Well, Chicago's called 'the windy city' and it really can be windy!
2 **F** What **are the people** like?
T They're very interesting. You meet people from all over the world.
3 **F** What **are the buildings** like?
T A lot of them are very, very tall. The Sears Tower is 110 storeys high.
4 **F** What **are the restaurants** like?
T They're very good. You can find food from every country in the world.
5 **F** What's **the night-life** like?
T Oh, it's wonderful. There's lots to do in Chicago.

2 **T 6.2** Students listen and check their answers. Drill the questions around the class, or play and pause the recording for students to repeat.

3 This activity allows students to practise the new structure, *What's … like?*, in a fairly controlled yet personalized way. Ask students to work in pairs, model what you want them to say, then monitor and correct errors thoroughly.

ADDITIONAL MATERIAL

Workbook Unit 6
These exercises could be done in class to give further practice, for homework, or in a later class as revision.
Exercises 1–2 *What … like?*

BIG, BIGGER, BIGGEST! (SB p47)

Comparatives and superlatives

It is assumed that your students will already have some familiarity with comparatives and superlatives, and so different aspects of them are brought together in this text, including the uses of *as … as*, *much* as an intensifier, and *different **from***. The aim is to find out how much they know.

1 **T 6.3** Ask students to work in pairs to complete as many sentences as they can. Find out how much they know. Then play the recording to check their answers.

In the feedback, point out that *as* is pronounced /əz/, that *different* is followed by *from* not *than*, and that *much* is strongly stressed and used to show a big difference when comparing. A clear way of showing this is to write *Melbourne 30°*, *Madrid 32°*, and *Dubai 45°* on the board: *Madrid is hotter* but *Dubai is **much** hotter.*

Answers and tapescript
Melbourne was interesting, but, for me, Paris was **more** interesting **than** Melbourne, and in some ways Dubai was the **most** interesting of all because it was so different **from** any other place I know. It was also the **hottest**, driest, and **most** modern. It was hot in Melbourne but not **as** hot **as** in Dubai. Dubai was **much** hotter! Melbourne is **much** older **than** Dubai but not **as** old **as** Paris. Paris was **the** oldest city I visited, but it has some great modern buildings, too. It was the **most** romantic place. I loved it.

GRAMMAR SPOT (SB p48)

1 As a class, ask students to tell you the comparative and superlative of each adjective. Make sure students pronounce the comparatives accurately, particularly the weak stress /ə/ on *-er*. You may wish to do this as a repetition drill.

Answers

	Adjective	Comparative	Superlative
a	small	smaller	smallest
	cold	colder	coldest
	near	nearer	nearest
b	big	bigger	biggest
	hot	hotter	hottest
	wet	wetter	wettest
c	busy	busier	busiest
	noisy	noisier	noisiest
	dry	drier	driest
d	beautiful	more beautiful	most beautiful
	interesting	more interesting	most interesting
	exciting	more exciting	most exciting

Ask your students to work in pairs to find out what the rules are.

Answers
One-syllable adjectives: add *-er* or *-est*.
Two-syllable adjectives ending with *-y*: drop the *-y* then add *-ier* or *-iest*.
Adjectives with two syllables or more: use *more* or *most*.

NOTE
At this point, explain the rule about the doubling of the consonant: where there is *one* vowel then *one* consonant at the end of the word, the consonant doubles.

2 Check that students know the comparative and superlative forms of these irregular adjectives.

Answers

far	farther	farthest
good	better	best
bad	worse	worst

Refer students to Grammar Reference 6.2 on p135.

2 **T 6.4** This is a short pronunciation exercise. The aim is to practise the links between words in connected speech and weak forms, which students often find difficult because they are trying to remember all the different 'bits' of these structures.

Play the first sentence on the recording (or model it yourself) and highlight the weak forms, *hotter* /hɔtə/ and *than* /ðən/ and the word links:

This summer's hotter than last.

/ðɪs sʌməz hɔtə ðən lɑ:st/

Do the same with the second sentence, pointing out the weak stresses on *as* … *as* and the word links:

It wasn't as hot as this last year.

/ɪt wɔznt əz hɔt əz ðɪs lɑ:st jɪə/

Check that students understand the use of *(not) as* … *as* in the example. Point out that *so* can only be used with the negative. See if students can find or remember other examples from Todd's conversation in exercise 1.

3 Ask students to work in pairs on the next set of sentences. They could mark in the word links and say them to each other. If your students know the phonemic script you could transcribe the sentences (see below) and give them out to help them practise.

It isn't as cold today as it was yesterday.

/ɪt ɪznt əz kəʊld tədeɪ əz ɪt wɔz jestədeɪ/

But it's colder than it was last week.

/bʌt ɪts kəʊldə dən ɪt wɔz lɑ:st wi:k/

I'm not as tall as you, but I'm taller than Anna.

/aɪm nɔt əz tɔ:l əz ju: bʌt aɪm tɔ:lə ðən ænə/

This car's more expensive than John's.

/ðɪs kɑ:z mɔ:(r) ɪkspensɪv ðən dʒɔnz/

But it isn't as expensive as Anna's.

/bʌt ɪt ɪznt əz ɪkspensɪv əz ænəz/

T 6.5 Play the sentences on the recording one by one (or model them yourself) and get the whole class to chorus them, then ask individual students to repeat them or practise them with a partner.

4 Poems and rhymes are good ways of remembering irregulars and exceptions. Your students may like to learn this by heart. They could invent their own poem for *bad, worse, worst*.

PRACTICE (SB p48)

Comparing four capital cities

These exercises bring together the grammar from both the presentations – *What … like?* and comparatives and superlatives.

1 Ask students to match the cities with the photographs. Ask them about the buildings, the weather, the size of theatres, etc.

Answers

Picture 1	Stockholm (Sweden)
Picture 2	Paris (France)
Picture 3	Brasilia (Brazil)
Picture 4	Beijing (China)

2 This is an information gap activity which needs to be set up carefully. Photocopy enough copies of the information about Paris and Beijing, and Stockholm and Brasilia, for students in your class. You can find the information on p121 of the Teacher's Book. Put students into two groups, A and B. Give the students in each group information about the *same* cities. Give students time to read. Monitor and help with vocabulary.

When students are ready, focus them on the questions and drill them for pronunciation.

Now put students in pairs with one from Group A and one from Group B, each with different information. Model the activity by asking a confident student some of the questions, then let students work in their pairs to ask and answer. Monitor and note errors.

3 Ask students to do this in their pairs. Tell them to write sentences using all of the structures and remind them to use the adjectives in the *Grammar Spot* on p48. Tell them that they do not have to make sentences just using the

facts about the cities – if they know the cities they can give their own opinions.

Sample answers
Facts
Paris is older than Stockholm.
The population is bigger.
It's bigger than Stockholm.
It's not as cold as Stockholm.
It's wetter than Stockholm.
It's farther from the sea.
Opinions
Paris is more romantic/cosmopolitan/crowded than Stockholm.

4 Students work individually to choose two cities in their own country that they know something about, and to think of ideas to compare. You could give them an example with two cities from your own country if you think this will help. Ask students to work in pairs to tell each other about their two cities. When students have finished, you could get them to feed back what their partner told them to the rest of the class.

Conversations

5 Allocate different conversations to different pairs, or let the pairs choose one for themselves, but make sure that there is variety in the class.

Some sample answers are given here so that you can give additional prompts to reluctant students. Make it clear to students that not every line of the conversation needs to contain examples of the structures – the idea is to broaden the context of use.

Sample answers
1 *New flat*: It's more expensive – it has a much more beautiful garden. It has more bedrooms. It's nearer to the town centre, but further from the countryside. I am very happy there.
2 *New boyfriend*: He's taller, more attractive and very funny, much funnier than Al. He's got a good job.
3 *New teacher*: She's the best/friendliest/funniest/most caring/most intelligent.
4 *New car*: It's bigger, more comfortable, and it has more space for luggage. It was more expensive than my old car, but it's much better. I love driving it.

Go round and help with ideas and ask them to go back through their dialogues to get them right and aim for good pronunciation. At the end, ask one or two pairs to act out their conversation to the rest of the class.

T 6.6 Play the recording. Students repeat the last lines.

Tapescript
1 **A** I moved to a new flat last week.
B Oh, really? What's it like?
A Well, it's bigger than my old one but it isn't as modern, and it's further from the shops.
2 **A** I hear Sandy and Al broke up.
B Yeah. Sandy's got a new boyfriend.
B Oh, really? What's he like?
A Well, he's much nicer than Al, and much more handsome. Sandy's happier now than she's been for a long time.
3 **A** We have a new teacher.
B Oh, really? What's she like?
A Well, I think she's the best teacher we've ever had. Our last teacher was good but she's even better and she works us much harder.
4 **A** Is that your new car?
B Well, it's second-hand, but it's new to me.
A What's it like?
B Well, it's faster than my old car and more comfortable, but it's more expensive to run. I love it!

Check it

6 Go round and monitor the pairs as they correct the sentences.

Answers
1 He's **older** than he looks.
2 Jessica's **as tall as** her mother.
3 'What **is** New York like?' 'It's really exciting!'
4 Trains in London are more crowded **than** in Paris.
5 Oxford is one of **the** oldest universities in Europe.
6 He isn't as intelligent **as** his sister/He isn't **more** intelligent than his sister.
7 This is **harder** than I expected.
8 Who is the **richest** man in the world?
9 Everything is **cheaper** in my country.
10 Rome was hotter **than** I expected.

Conduct feedback with the whole class.

ADDITIONAL MATERIAL

Workbook Unit 6
Exercises 3–8 Comparatives and superlatives

LISTENING AND SPEAKING (SB p49)

Living in another country

The aim of the lead-in is to create awareness of and interest in Sweden. You could bring in a map or pictures if you have any.

1 Ask students the questions in the Student's Book and brainstorm as many suggestions as you can. Put them on

the board without comment. They will find out whether they are true or not later.

Go through the statements with students. Check that they understand words that are key to the understanding of the listening: *insulated, the sun sets/rises, luxurious, sauna.* Put students in pairs or or groups of three to tick whether they think they are true or false.

2 **T 6.7** Read through the information about Jane Bland with students. Play the recording. Students listen and check their answers. They may need to listen twice.

Answers (to questions in exercise 1) and tapescript

1 True
2 False (they look forward to spring)
3 False (they are well-insulated)
4 True
5 True
6 True
7 False (only in summer)
8 False (they are primitive – with no running water or toilets)
9 False (every house *she has been to* has a sauna)
10 True

J = Jane F = Fran, a friend

J When I say that I live in Sweden, everyone always wants to know about the seasons . . .

F The seasons?

J Yeah . . . you know, how cold it is in winter – what it's like when the days are so short.

F So what *is* it like?

J Well, it *is* cold, very cold in winter, sometimes as cold as –26° and of course when you go out you wrap up warm, but inside, in the houses, it's always very warm, much warmer than at home. Swedish people always complain that when they visit England the houses are cold even in a good winter. In Sweden the houses are much better insulated than in Britain and they always have the heating on very high.

F And what about the darkness?

J Well, yeah, around Christmas time, in December, there's only *one* hour of daylight – so you really look forward to the spring. It is sometimes a bit depressing but you see the summers are amazing – from May to July, in the north of Sweden, the sun never sets, it's still light at midnight, you can walk in the mountains and read a newspaper.

F Oh, yeah – the land of the midnight sun.

J That's right. But it's wonderful, you want to stay up all night and the Swedes make the most of it. Often they start work earlier in summer and then leave at about two or three in the afternoon, so they can really enjoy the long summer evenings. They like to work hard but play hard too. I think Londoners work longer hours, but I'm not sure this is a good thing.

F So what about free time? Weekends? Holidays? What do Swedish people like doing?

J Well, every house in Sweden has a sauna . . .

F *Every* house!?

J Well, every house I've been to. And most people have a country cottage, so people like to leave the town and get back to nature at weekends. These cottages are sometimes quite primitive, – no running water or not even toilets and . . .

F No *toilet*?

J Well, *some* don't have toilets but they *all* have a sauna and all the family sit in it together, then run and jump into the lake to get cool.

F What!? Even in winter?

J Yeah – Swedish people are very healthy.

F Brrr! Or mad!

3 In a monolingual class, students can do this in pairs. In a multilingual class, they will have to work alone. Give students time to prepare a few sentences. You may wish to give them some headings to think about: *the seasons, the weather, houses, work,* and *free time.*

Put students in small groups to discuss. Monitor and note errors, particularly those involving comparatives.

ADDITIONAL MATERIAL

Workbook Unit 6

Exercises 10 and 11 do some work on relative clauses and provide a model text, which leads to students writing a description of their home town.

READING AND SPEAKING (SB p50)

A tale of two millionaires

1 Have a general discussion about the richest people in students' countries. If students have little to say, you could mention some well-known millionaires, such as Bill Gates, (the owner of *Microsoft*, and probably the richest man in the world today), or Queen Elizabeth II, (popularly believed to be the richest woman in Britain, if not the world. It is estimated that she owns lands, property, and other assets worth £6.7 billion.)

2 Ask students to work in pairs to match the verbs and nouns. They will probably need to use dictionaries, but try to get them to make guesses first. Do the first as an example: *buy – stocks and shares.*

Answers

buy	stocks and shares
spoil	a child
wear	ragged clothes
open	a bank account
live in	poverty
inherit	a lot of money from someone

make	a will
arrest	a thief
invest	a lot of money in something
amputate	a leg

3 Focus students on the headline and ask them to read quickly about Milton Petrie and find examples of his kindness.

Answers

He paid the hospital bill and funeral costs of the man he bought his newspaper from.

Whenever he read about personal disasters in the newspaper, he sent generous cheques to the families, including the families of injured policemen and firemen, a mother who lost her children, and a model whose face was cut.

4 Ask students to read about Hetty Green and find examples of her meanness.

Answers

She ate in the cheapest restaurants.

She argued about prices in shops.

She bought broken cookies and got free bones for her dog from the local grocery store.

She lost a two-cent stamp and spent the night looking for it.

She never bought clothes.

She always wore the same skirt.

She refused to pay for a doctor and her son's leg was amputated.

5 Read through the questions with students, and check understanding, then ask half the class to read about Milton and half to read about Hetty. Put students in pairs, one who read about Milton with one who read about Hetty, and ask them to discuss their answers.

Answers

1 Milton was born in 1902, Hetty in 1835.
2 Milton's family were poor but kind-hearted. His father was a Russian immigrant and a policeman who was too kind to arrest anyone.
Hetty's mother was often ill. Her father was a millionaire businessman.
3 Milton was 'lucky in business'.
Hetty inherited $7.5 million, invested on Wall Street and saved every penny.
4 Hetty.
5 She refused to pay for a doctor when her son injured his leg. His leg was amputated.
6 Because he could help more people.
7 Milton married four times. His last wife's name was Carroll.
Hetty married Edward Green, a multi-millionaire.
8 Milton died in 1994, aged 92. Hetty died in 1916, aged 81.
9 Milton left most. Hetty left her money to her children.
Milton left his money to 383 people.

What do you think?

Students work in small groups to discuss the questions. Monitor and encourage as much speaking as you can. It is a good idea to make one student in each group the *discussion leader*, responsible for asking the questions and making sure everybody has a chance to speak.

Sample answers

- Milton's family were poor and kind-hearted. Hetty was rich and spoilt.
- It made Milton kind and generous and Hetty mean.
- Perhaps because his father was a policeman.
- Perhaps because her brother's leg was amputated because her mother refused to pay for a doctor.
- A matter of opinion.
- A matter of opinion, but most students will probably say Milton. He says he was lucky. Hetty was the most hated woman in the world.

VOCABULARY AND PRONUNCIATION (SB p52)

Synonyms

Check that your students know what synonyms are: *words that are the same or similar in meaning.* You could make the point by asking them to give you some examples in their own language, and also by reading through the introduction to the exercise with them.

1 Ask students to work in pairs to complete the conversations. They may need to use dictionaries to check the meaning of some of the words, but encourage them to try to guess first.

2 **T 6.8** Students listen to the recording to check their answers.

Now play the dialogues through one at a time and after each one ask the pairs of students to repeat the dialogues, and to try to imitate the stress and intonation. Let them practise the conversations in pairs.

Answers and tapescript

1 'Mary's family is very rich.'
'Well, I knew her uncle was very **wealthy**.'
2 'Look at all these new buildings!'
'Yes. Paris is much more **modern** than I expected.'
3 'Wasn't that film wonderful!'
'Yes, it was **brilliant**.'
4 'George doesn't earn much money, but he's so kind.'
'He is, isn't he? He's one of the most **generous** people I know.'
5 'Ann's bedroom's really untidy again!'
'Is it? I told her it was **messy** yesterday, and she promised to clean it.'
6 'I'm bored with this lesson!'
'I know, I'm really **fed up** with it, too!'

Antonyms

3 Remind students what antonyms are: *words that are opposite in meaning*. You could do this in the same way suggested for synonyms above.

Let your students stay in the same pairs. You need to focus them again on the adjectives in the previous exercise to do this exercise. Look at the examples.

Answers

interested	bored, fed up
horrible	wonderful, brilliant
mean	kind, generous
old	new, modern
poor	rich, wealthy
tidy	untidy, messy

4 Read through the introduction with your students. Draw particular attention to the response containing *not very* + the antonym. Then ask them to work together in their pairs to construct more polite answers.

Sample answers and tapescript

1 'London's such an expensive city.'
'Well, it's not very cheap.'
2 'Paul and Sue are so mean.'
'They're certainly not very generous.'
3 'Their house is always so messy.'
'Mmm . . . it's not very tidy.'
4 'Their children are so noisy.'
'Yes, they're certainly not very quiet.'
5 'John looks so miserable.'
'Hmm, he's not very happy.'
6 'His sister's so stupid.'
'Well, she's certainly not very clever.'

5 **T 6.9** Students listen to the recording to check their answers.

Allocate pairs of students across the class to be A or B and get them to act out the little dialogues. Encourage good stress and intonation. The main stress in both sentences is on the adjective.
Example

● ● ● ●
Paul and Sue are so mean.

● ● ●
They're certainly not very generous.

ADDITIONAL MATERIAL

Workbook Unit 6
Exercise 9 looks at the use of suffixes in adjective formation.

EVERYDAY ENGLISH (SB p53)

Directions

The aim is to direct students in stages towards being able to understand and give directions. Students could work in pairs from the start of the lesson.

1 Ask them to look at the map and find the different things. Go round the pairs to check and then go through with the whole class together.

2 Tell them to read the descriptions of the places not yet on the map and to insert them in the correct place. The aim of this is to teach/revise prepositions of place.

Answers

1 hotel	6 greengrocer's
2 bank	7 flower shop
3 baker's	8 The Red Lion
4 supermarket	9 The Old Shepherd
5 chemist's	

3 This activity is very controlled. Before you ask students to do it in pairs, go through the introductory example with the whole class, and then do one or two further examples yourself with individual students across the class, to check their understanding of the prepositions.

Go round helping and correcting.

4 This is designed to teach/revise prepositions of movement. Ask students to do it on their own and then compare with a partner.

T 6.10 Students listen and check their answers. The route is marked on the map in **2** above.

Answers and tapescript
You go **down** the path, **past** the pond, **over** the bridge, and **out of** the gate. Then you go **across** the road and take the path **through** the wood. When you come **out of** the wood you walk **up** the path and **into** the church. It takes five minutes.

5 Finally, personalize the activity by asking students to give directions from the school to their houses, or other places not too far from the school.

Don't forget!

Pronunciation book Unit 6

Word list
Photocopy the Word list for Unit 6 (TB p156) for your students, and ask them to write in the translations, learn them at home, and/or write some of the words into their vocabulary notebook.

Video
Report (Section 4) ***Purple Violin*** This video section supplements Units 5 and 6 of the Student's Book. It is a short documentary about a musician in Oxford who busks with an electric violin.

7

Present Perfect • *for, since*
Adverbs, word pairs
Short answers

Famous couples

Introduction to the unit

This unit uses the theme of fame to introduce the Present Perfect. The theme naturally lends itself to talking about people's experiences, which is one of the main uses of the Present Perfect. The new structure is introduced by means of texts about two famous writers, the *Reading* section has an interview with an imaginary famous couple, and the *Listening and speaking* section has an interview with an imaginary rock band. There are opportunities to roleplay interviews with celebrities.

Language aims

Grammar – Present Perfect This is the first unit in *New Headway Pre-Intermediate* where the Present Perfect is dealt with. The simple aspect is introduced and practised. In Unit 13, the simple aspect is revised, and the continuous aspect is introduced.

The Present Perfect means 'completed some time before now, but with some present relevance', and so joins past and present in a way that many other languages do not. In English, we say *I have seen the Queen* (at some indefinite time in my life), but not **I have seen the Queen yesterday.* Other languages express the same ideas, but by using *either* a past tense *or* a present tense. In many other European languages, the same form of *have* + the past participle can be used to express both indefinite (Present Perfect) and definite (Past Simple) time.

Common mistakes
**I have watched TV last night.*
**When have you been to Russia?*
**Did you ever try Chinese food?*

Many languages use a present tense to express unfinished past. However, English 'sees' not only the present situation, but the situation going back into the past, and uses the Present Perfect.

Common mistakes
**I live here for five years.*
**She is a teacher for ten years.*
**How long do you know Paul?*

Students are usually introduced to the Present Perfect very gently in their first year course, so they will not be unfamiliar with the form. This unit aims to introduce students to some uses/meanings of this tense, but your class will not have mastered it by the end of the unit. It takes a long time to be assimilated.

Vocabulary The first vocabulary exercise practises adverbs of different kinds: adverbs of manner (*slowly*), adverbs of frequency (*usually*), focusing adverbs (*only, too, especially*), comment adverbs (*of course, fortunately*) and adverbs of degree (*nearly*).

The second exercise looks at word pairs, idiomatic expressions consisting of two words joined by *and*, such as *salt and pepper*, and *now and then.*

Everyday English This section practises short answers. There are exercises on short answers throughout the Workbook whenever a new tense or verb form is introduced, and this section aims to bring the area together, and to give some oral practice.

Notes on the unit

STARTER (SB p54)

This is a quick check that students know the Past Simple and past participle forms of these common irregular verbs. Ask students to work in pairs to help each other with the answers. They can check their answers in the irregular verbs list on p143 of the Student's Book.

FAMOUS WRITERS (SB p54)

Present Perfect and Past Simple

NOTE

We usually suggest that students look at the *Grammar Reference* at the back of the Student's Book for homework *after* the presentation in class. However, with certain difficult items, it is worth asking students to spend five or ten minutes looking at the information in the *Grammar Reference before* you introduce the structure in class, so that they can begin to understand and think about the area. The Present Perfect is a case in point, so set this for homework (see Student's Book p136).

ADDITIONAL IDEA

If you feel you would like to remind your students of the form and basic use of the Present Perfect (to express experience) before you begin the 'Famous Writers' section, you could do the following mini-revision lesson.

Ask a student (who you know has travelled) *Which countries have you been to?* If the student is puzzled by the verb form, prompt with *in your life.*

Write the names of the countries on the board. Say to the class *Claudia has been to France, Germany, Italy, and Portugal. Do we know when Claudia went to France?* Ask her a question with *When ... ?* to elicit the question in the Past Simple *When did Claudia go to France?*

The class now asks Claudia the questions, and she replies with the dates.

Put two sentences on the board.

Claudia ***has been*** *to France, Germany, Italy, and Portugal.*

Claudia ***went*** *to France in (1998).*

Ask the class if they know the names of these two tenses. The Past Simple should be known, but probably not the Present Perfect. Explain (in L1, if possible, or through the use of timelines) that the Past Simple is used to talk about definite time, and the Present Perfect is used to talk about indefinite time, to talk about an action which happened some time before now.

Suggested timelines and check questions

past ——x?——x?——x?—— **present**

Claudia **has been** to France.
Is Claudia in A now? (No.)
Do we know when? (No.)
Is when important? (No.)

past ——x—————— **present**
1998

Claudia **went** to France in 1998.
Is Claudia in France now? (No.)
Do we know and say when? (Yes.)

Ask some other students *Which countries have you been to?* Encourage the class to ask *When did you go there?*

Lead in to the topic by asking students about writers and novels. Personalize and create interest by asking questions.

Who are your favourite novelists? What sort of books do you like?
When did you last read a novel? Do you know any British writers?

1 Ask students to look at the photographs in their book and ask them a few questions.

When were they born? How do you think they are related? What do you think their novels are about?

NOTE

- The Victorian novelist Anthony Trollope wrote novels about clerical life in a provincial English town. His most famous novel is *Barchester Towers* (1857).
- The romantic novelist Joanna Trollope writes historical and contemporary novels – some of which also describe clerical life in rural England. Her best known novels are *A Village Affair*, *The Rector's Wife*, and *The Choir*. Although related, Joanna is not a direct descendant of Anthony Trollope.

Ask students to complete the sentences with *He* or *She*. Do the first as an example. Check that students understand why the answer is *He:* because Anthony Trollope is dead, and therefore what he did is finished and has no connection to now, or *She:* because Joanna is still alive and writing now.

Answers and tapescript

1 **He** wrote novels about Victorian life. **She** writes novels about modern people and their relationships.
2 **He** wrote 47 novels, travel books, biographies, and short stories. **She** has written over twenty novels. She started writing in her thirties.

3 **She** has lived in the west of England for forty years. **He** lived in Ireland for eighteen years.
4 **She** has been married twice, and has two daughters. **She** married for the first time in 1966. **He** was married and had two sons.

T 7.1 Play the recording so students can check their answers. At this stage you may wish to play and pause the recording to drill the sentences containing the Present Perfect around the room, paying particular attention to the contracted *has.*

GRAMMAR SPOT (SB p54)

1 Ask students to work in pairs to underline the examples of the Past Simple. The aim is to consolidate what is known (i.e. the Past Simple) before moving on to the new (i.e. the Present Perfect), and to reinforce the idea that the Past Simple is used to refer to definite past time.

Answers
1 wrote
2 wrote/started
3 lived
4 married/was married

Ask students why the Past Simple is used. Then ask them to underline examples of the other tense, the Present Perfect.

Answers
1 –
2 has written
3 has lived
4 has been married

2 Complete the rule as a class.

We make the Present Perfect with the auxiliary verb *have* + the past participle.

3 Students work in twos or threes to answer the third Grammar question. They might be able to infer the answers, or they might have no idea. If students can manage something such as *Anthony Trollope is dead,* they are doing well.

Answers
Anthony Trollope wrote forty-seven novels – Past Simple, because he is dead and can write no more.
Joanna Trollope has written twenty novels – Present Perfect, because she is still alive, and can write more in the future.

Refer students to Grammar Reference 7.1 and 7.2 on p136.

2 Ask students to work in pairs or small groups to put the verbs in the correct tense. Encourage them to look back at the sentences in exercise 1 to help them.

Answers and tapescript
1 Anthony Trollope **travelled** to South Africa, Australia, Egypt, and the West Indies. Joanna Trollope **has travelled** to many parts of the world.
2 She **has won** many awards, and several of her stories **have appeared** on TV.
3 Her first book **came** out in 1980. Since then, she **has sold** more than 5 million copies.
4 She **went** to school in the south of England, and **studied** English at Oxford University, but she **has lived** in the country for most of her life.
5 She writes her books by hand. She **has had** the same pen since 1995.

T 7.2 Play the recording so that students can check their answers.

3 Do 1 and 2 as a class to establish the two question forms, one in the Present Perfect and one in the Past Simple, and drill them to establish a model.

Answers and tapescript
1 **'How long has she lived in the west of England?'**
'For forty years.'
2 **'What did she study at university?'**
'English.'
3 **'How many novels has she written?'**
'More than twenty.'
4 **'How many books has she sold?'**
'Over five million.'
5 **'When did her first novel come out?'**
'In 1980.'
6 **'How many times has she been married?'**
'Twice.'
7 **'Has she got any children?'**
'Yes, two daughters.'
8 **'How long has she had her pen?'**
'Since 1995.'

T 7.3 Play the recording so that students can check their answers. Drill the questions around the room, making sure students start with the voice high.

At this stage you could ask students to ask and answer the questions about Joanna in pairs. Monitor and correct.

PRACTICE (SB p55)

Discussing grammar

1 The aim of this exercise is to check that students have grasped the form and use of the Present Perfect. It tests some of the typical errors and confusions made by

students learning this tense. Students work in pairs to choose the correct verb form.

Answers

1 Have you ever been	4 was
2 saw	5 have bought
3 have liked	6 have been

Find someone who . . .

2 This is a mingle activity, where students ask the same question to everyone in the class. Photocopy p122 of the Teacher's Book, and cut it up into sentences. (If you paste them onto card, you can use them again.)

Every student must have a sentence. Read the example in the Student's Book, showing that they have to turn their sentences into a question beginning *Have you ever … ?* Make sure students don't go round the class saying 'Find someone who has been to China.'

Before you ask the class to stand up, check that everyone's question is correct. Model the activity with a strong student, asking a *Have you ever … ?* question and three or four follow-up questions to show that you want students to find out as much as they can.

Students stand up and ask everyone, making a note of the answers.

3 When they have finished and have sat down, allow them a minute to decide what they are going to say when they report back to the class. Ask all students to report back.

for and *since*

4 Students work in pairs to complete the sentences with *for* and *since*. Before they start, tell students that *for* is used with a *period of time*, and *since* is used with a *point in time*. Compare:
. . . for ten minutes.
. . . since January 2000.

Answers

1 for	5 since
2 for	6 for
3 since	7 for
4 since	8 since

5 Ask students to work in pairs to match the lines to make sentences. Do the first as an example to give them the idea then monitor and help.

T 7.4 Play the recording so that students can check their answers. You could play and pause and drill the sentences around the class. Get students to make similar sentences about themselves then read them out to the class.

Answers and tapescript

1 I've known my best friend for years. We met when we were 10.
2 I last went to the cinema two weeks ago. The film was rubbish.
3 I've had this watch for three years. My Dad gave it to me for my birthday.
4 We've used this book since the beginning of term. It's not bad. I quite like it.
5 We lived in our old flat from 1988 to 1996. We moved because we needed somewhere bigger.
6 We haven't had a break for an hour. I really need a cup of coffee.
7 I last had a holiday in 1999. I went camping with some friends.
8 This building has been a school since 1985. Before that it was an office.

Asking questions

6 **T 7.5** Ask students to work in pairs to complete the conversation then play the recording so they can check their answers. Ask students to tell you why the different tenses are used.

Answers and tapescript

A	Where **do you** live, Olga?	Present Simple, because it is true now.
B	In a flat near the park.	
A	How long **have you lived** there?	Present Perfect, because it is unfinished past – starting in the past and continuing until now.
B	For three years.	
A	And why **did you** move?	Past Simple, because it asks about a finished past event.
B	We wanted to live in a nicer area.	

Drill the three questions round the class, paying particular attention to the intonation pattern of *Wh-* questions, then ask students to work in pairs to practise the conversation.

7 This activity gives students lots of controlled speaking practice in manipulating the question forms of three different tenses. Be prepared to have to do a lot of prompting and correcting.

Model the first conversation with a confident student then ask students to work in pairs to practise. Ideally, they should be able to do this without having to write, just using the prompts, although it may be a good idea to let them write out the first conversation for confidence. Ask two or three pairs to model one of their conversations for the class at the end.

Sample answers

1 **A** What **do you** do?
B I work (**for a bank**).
A How long **have you worked there**?
B For **a year**.
A What **did you** do before that?
B I worked **for** (**an insurance company**).

2 **A** **Have you** got a car?
B Yes, I **have**.
A How long **have you had it**?
B Since **1998**.
A How much **did you** pay for it?
B It was **about two thousand pounds**.

3 **A** **Do you** know Pete Brown?
B Yes, I **do**.
A How long **have you known him**?
B For **ten years**.
A Where **did you** meet him?
B We **met at college**.

8 Extend the previous two activities by doing some personalized speaking practice, using the prompts suggested in the Student's Book. This could be done in pairs or as a mingle activity.

ADDITIONAL MATERIAL

Workbook Unit 7
These exercises could be done in class to give further practice, for homework, or in a later class as revision.
Exercises 1–5 practise the form of the Present Perfect.
Exercise 6 practises *for* and *since*.
Exercises 7 and 8 Students are asked to discriminate between the Present Perfect, the Present Simple, and the Past Simple in the Tense revision.

LISTENING AND SPEAKING (SB p57)

The band *Style*

1 Talk to students about the kind of music they like. Ask the questions in Student's Book. Focus on the last question, *If you could meet your favourite band or singer, what would you ask them?* You could prompt with questions such as: *How long have you been together? What are you doing at the moment? When are you going to make another record?*

2 **T 7.6** Read the introduction and look at the picture. Check that students understand the names of the instruments in the chart. Play the recording. Students listen and complete the chart.

Ask students to work in pairs to compare their answers before feedback.

Answers and tapescript

1 What do they do in the band?	2 Bands they have played with	3 Places they have visited
G guitar	G UB40	✔ Holland
S keyboards	S Lionel Ritchie	✘ Hungary
G drums	S Phil Collins	✘ America
G harmonica	G Genesis	✔ Sweden
S vocalist	G Happy Mondays	✔ Japan
	S Bon Jovi	✔ Italy
	S Ace	✔ Australia

T 7.6
I = Interviewer S = Suzie G = Guy

I . . . and that was the latest record from *Style* called *Give it to me*. And guess who I've got sitting right next to me in the studio? I've got Suzie Tyler and Guy Holmes, who are the two members of *Style*. Welcome to the programme!
S Thanks a lot.
I Now you two have been very busy this year, haven't you? You've had a new album out, and you've been on tour. How are you feeling?
S Pretty tired. We've just got back from Holland, and in April we went to Japan and Australia, so yeah . . . we've travelled a lot this year.
G But we've made a lot of friends, and we've had some fun.
I Tell us something about your background. What did you do before forming *Style*?
G Well, we both played with a lot of other bands before teaming up with each other.
I Who have you played with, Suzie?
S Well, over the years I've sung with Lionel Richie and Phil Collins, and a band called *Ace*.
I And what about you, Guy?
G I've recorded with *Genesis* and *UB40* , and of course, *Happy Mondays*.
I Why is *Happy Mondays* so important to you?
G Because I had my first hit record with them. The song was called *Mean Street*, and it was a hit all over the world . . . that was in 1995.
I So how long have you two been together as *Style*?
S Since 1997. We met at a recording studio while I was doing some work with *Bon Jovi*. We started chatting and Guy asked me if I'd like to work with him, and it all started from there.
I Suzie, you're obviously the vocalist, but do you play any music yourself?
S Yes, I play keyboards.
I And what about you, Guy?
G I play guitar and harmonica. I can play the drums, but when we're doing a concert we have a backing group.
I So where have you two travelled to?
S Well, I . . . er . . . I sometimes think that we've been everywhere, but we haven't really. We've toured in Europe, Italy, Holland, and we've done Japan and Australia, but we've never been to America. That's the next place we'd

like to go. And then Eastern Europe. I'd love to play in these places.
G You forgot Sweden. We went there two years ago.
S Oh yeah.
I Over the years you've made a lot of records. Do you know exactly how many?
G That's a difficult question, erm . . .
I Well, about how many?
S Oh, I don't know. Perhaps about twenty-five.
G Yeah, something like that.
I And how long have you been in the music business?
G I guess about fifteen years. I've never had another job. I've only ever been a musician, since I was seventeen.
S I've had all sorts of jobs. When I left college, I worked as a waitress, a shop assistant, a painter, a gardener . . . I could go on and on . . .
I Well, stop there, because now you're a member of a band. Suzie and Guy, it was great to talk to you. Good luck with the new record.
S/G Thanks.
I And now for something different. We're . . .

Ask individual students to tell you the bands Suzie and Guy have played with, and the countries they have been to. This is to give further controlled practice of the Present Perfect. You could also ask about the bands they *haven't* played with, and the countries they *haven't* been to, to get practice of the negative.

3 Play the recording again. Ask students to work in pairs to answer the comprehension questions.

Answers
1 Because they have been busy and have travelled a lot this year.
2 They've had a new album out, been on tour, travelled a lot, and been to Holland, Japan, and Australia.
3 Yes. They have made a lot of friends and had some fun.
4 It was Guy's first hit record, a hit all over the world in 1995.
5 Since 1997.
6 America and then Eastern Europe.
7 Guy has never had another job.
She's worked as a waitress, a shop assistant, a painter, a gardener . . .

Language work

The aim of these two exercises is to give further practice of the Present Perfect.

4 Ask students to work in pairs to make sentences. Give them one or two examples to get them started.

In the feedback, point out that the verb forms in the sentences from **A** are in the Past Simple, because they refer to definite time. The verb forms in the sentences from **B** are in the Present Perfect, because they refer to the past up to the present, and probably into the future.

Sample answers
A
They went to Japan and Australia in April.
Guy had his first hit record in 1995.
They went to Sweden two years ago.
Suzie worked as a waitress when she left college.
B
They have been together as *Style* since 1997.
They have made about twenty-five records.
Guy has been in the music business (for) fifteen years.
He has been a musician since he was 17.

5 Ask students to work in pairs and give them a little time to prepare the questions. When they are ready, let them ask and answer in pairs, using the information from the *Listening*. Monitor and make sure they are using both tenses correctly.

Answers
What did they do before forming *Style*?
Have they ever been to America?
How did they meet each other?
How many records have they made?

Roleplay

6 This activity could last a short while or nearly an hour, depending on how you organize it (and whether you and your class are interested). If you allow the musicians and journalists about fifteen minutes to prepare, then have the interviews and record them, then listen to the recorded interviews for feedback, you should easily fill an hour, depending on the size of your class. You could ask students to prepare their roles for homework. You could save some of the recorded interviews for the next class. The success of a roleplay often depends on the effort put in during preparation.

Here are some ideas to help students prepare their roles.
Musicians
Students should talk together to decide the following:
– the kind of music they play
– the name of their band / orchestra
– who plays what instrument
– what has influenced their music
– how long they have been together
– the records they have made
– the countries they have toured
Journalists
Students should work together to think of questions to ask the musicians. They could use the ideas for musicians to help them, although they should also try to think of follow-up questions to get further information.

When students are preparing, the journalists will probably be ready before the groups of musicians. If this happens, tell the journalists that they too are a group of musicians and should prepare information.

Decide whether you want all the interviews to go on at the same time or one by one. The advantage of the latter is that students are often interested in each other, and want to hear what the 'groups' have to say. Expect some funny answers!

Recording students from time to time can also be useful. You need a good microphone and a long lead! Ideally, you need a tape recorder with batteries to be able to get round the groups easily.

READING (SB p58)

Celebrity interview

1 The aim of the lead-in is to get students talking about the topic of celebrities. It is a good idea to bring in covers of magazines like *Hello!* or *OK!* as well as photos of celebrities in the news in students' countries. Ask students the questions in the Student's Book and encourage a whole-class discussion. You may wish to pre-teach vocabulary around the topic: *celebrity, pop star, film star, well-known, world famous, glamorous lifestyle, luxurious home.*

2 Ask students to look at the headline and photographs from *Hi! Magazine.* Ask the questions in the Student's Book. You could ask students what they think Donna and Terry are like, or what their relationship and lifestyle will be like.

NOTE

Hello! and *OK!* are two popular glossy magazines which feature friendly articles and glamorous photographs of the rich and famous, usually at home or at celebrity parties.

3 Read through the questions with students to check their understanding, then ask them to read the article quickly to match the questions with the paragraphs. They don't have to read every word – just enough of each paragraph to match it with a question. It is a good idea to set a strict time limit of about five minutes.

Answers

3, 5, 4, 1, 2

4 Read through the comprehension questions with students. Give them longer this time to find and write answers from the text. Let them check fully with a partner before feedback.

Answers

1 Because Donna is a pop star. Terry is a footballer with England and Manchester United.
2 Donna has had six number one records, and Terry has scored fifty goals for Manchester United and played for England thirty times. They earn £20m a year.
3 **Normal**: Their perfect Saturday night is sitting in front of the TV with a take-away (*meal*). They don't go to pubs and clubs with famous people. They are shy and in love.
Not normal: They have flown all over the world to spend a few hours together. Newspapers write about them. They are very rich and famous.
4 Possible answers include: They will fly all over the world to be together. They are prepared to give and take. There is a trust between them. They have been together for two years and live together. They spend a lot of time together. They want to get married and spend the rest of their lives together. They mean the world to each other.
5 Yes.
6 They don't like them because they tell terrible stories and tell lies.
7 Probably because they are jealous of their fame, wealth, and perfect relationship.
8 Possible answers may include: He has good taste! He's shy. He doesn't like going to pubs and clubs with famous people. Of course, students may disagree and think he is a typical footballer.

5 Students work in groups of three to read the text aloud.

Language work

6 Ask students to choose the correct tense.

Answers

1 Donna and Terry **have been** together for two years.
2 They **like** watching TV on Saturday night.
3 They **met** after a football match.
4 They **have lived** in their new home since April.
5 Terry **has been** in love just once.

Project

7 If students are particularly interested in this topic encourage them to research an article about a famous couple from a magazine like *Hello!* or *OK!* and present their findings in the next lesson. You could give the project a framework by asking them to find the answers to certain questions, for example:

Why are they famous? What have they done?
How did they meet? How long have they been together?
How do they find being famous? What are their lives like?

VOCABULARY (SB p60)

Adverbs

1 Ask students to find adverbs that end in *-ly* in the interview on p58–9.

Answers
really, obviously, fortunately, naturally, totally

2 Ask students to find the example adverbs in the text.

3 Ask students to work in pairs to complete the sentences with words from the box.

Answers

1 Of course	4 only
2 still	5 nearly
3 together	

4 Students work in pairs to complete the sentences.

Answers

1 especially	4 just
2 too	5 At last
3 Exactly	

Word pairs

The aim of this activity is to introduce students to some common expressions consisting of two words joined by *and.*

1 Read through exercise 1 as a class.

2 Ask students to work in pairs to match the words. Do the first as an example.

Answers
ladies and gentlemen
fish and chips
now and then
yes and no
do's and don'ts
up and down
peace and quiet
safe and sound
salt and pepper

3 **T 7.7** Ask students to complete the sentences with the expressions. Play and pause the recording. Students must try to remember the correct expression to complete each conversation.

Answers and tapescript
1 'Do you still play tennis?'
'Not regularly. Just **now and then**, when I have time.'
2 This is a pretty relaxed place to work. There aren't many **do's and don'ts**.
3 Here you are at last! I've been so worried! Thank goodness you've arrived **safe and sound**.
4 'Do you like your new job?'
'**Yes and no**. The money's OK, but I don't like the people.'
5 Sometimes there are too many people in the house. I go into the garden for a bit of **peace and quiet**.
6 Good evening, **ladies and gentlemen**. It gives me great pleasure to talk to you all tonight.
7 'How's your Gran?'
'**Up and down**. There are good days, and then not such good days.'
8 'Here's supper. Careful! Its hot.'
'**Fish and chips**! Yummy!'

ADDITIONAL MATERIAL

Workbook Unit 7
Exercise 9 looks at nouns that refer to men and women, such as *waiter* and *waitress.*

EVERYDAY ENGLISH (SB p61)

Short answers

Short answers have been practised throughout the Workbook. The aim here is to bring them all together and practise them orally.

1 **T 7.8** Read the instruction as a class. Play the recording. Pause after each pair of conversations and ask the questions. Students should be able to tell you that in the second of each pair of conversations the speaker uses short answers and a more animated intonation to be more polite.

Tapescript
1 'Do you like learning English, Elsa?'
'Yes.'
'Do you like learning English, Elsa?'
'Yes, I do. I love it. It's the language of Shakespeare.'
2 'Are those new jeans you're wearing?'
'No.'
'Are those new jeans you're wearing?'
'No, they aren't. I've had them for ages.'
3 'Have you got the time, please?'
'No.'
'Have you got the time, please?'
'No, I haven't. I'm so sorry.'

4 'Can you play any musical instruments?'
'Yes.'
'Can you play any musical instruments?'
'Yes, I can, actually. I can play the violin.'

Read through the Caution Box as a class then ask students to work in pairs to complete the short answers.

Answers

Do you like cooking?	Yes, I **do**.
Is it raining?	No, it **isn't**.
Have you been to France?	Yes, I **have**.
Are you good at chess?	No, **I'm not**.
Can you speak Spanish?	Yes, I **can**.

Remind students that we cannot use *I've, they've, he's,* etc. in short answers.

Drill the short answers by asking the class or individuals the prompt questions above and eliciting short answers with a good intonation pattern in response.

Yes, I do.

Ask students if they can remember any other phrases used on the recording to add more information.

2 Ask students to work in pairs to complete the short answers. Do the first as an example.

Answers
1 No, **I don't. I prefer rock'n'roll.**
2 Yes, **I did. It was a great game.**
3 No, **I haven't. I'm sorry. I haven't got a penny on me.**
4 Yes, **I have.** I **went there last weekend with Frank.**
5 Yes, I suppose **they are. But they give me a lot of freedom, too.**
6 No, **I'm not. Why? What are you doing?**

Students work in pairs or groups of three to continue the conversations.

At this stage, you could drill the conversations to practise the pronunciation. Let students practise one or two conversations in pairs.

3 Students work alone or in pairs to think of questions, using the prompts.

4 Ask students to stand up and mingle, asking their questions to as many different students as possible. Learners often find short answers difficult. Although it is a purely mechanical process to know which auxiliary to use, and whether it should be positive or negative, these decisions have to be made so quickly in the natural course of conversation that learners complain they don't have time to think.

Try to be aware of short answers in your teaching generally, and remind students of them whenever appropriate. The use of short answers, reply questions, and question tags is often quoted as the sign of a successful speaker of English, as they are employed to 'lubricate' conversation.

Don't forget!

Workbook Unit 7
Exercise 10 is a writing activity on relative clauses.
Exercise 11 asks students to write a biography.

Pronunciation book Unit 7

Word list
Photocopy the Word list for Unit 7 (TB p156) for your students, and ask them to write in the translations, learn them at home, and/or write some of the words into their vocabulary notebook.

Video
Situation (Section 5) ***The Hotel*** This is a short situation in which Paola has to make a complaint at the hotel where she is staying in Cornwall. Students practise making complaints and ordering from the room service menu.

8

have (got) to • *should/must*
Words that go together
At the doctor's

Do's and don'ts

Introduction to the unit

This unit, 'Do's and don'ts', introduces the functional language of obligation and advice. In the two presentation sections, 'Work, work', and 'Problems, problems', students talk about the duties and disadvantages of different professions and what they have to do at home, and offer advice to friends and to visitors to their country. In the *Listening* section, students listen to three people from different parts of the world giving advice about holidays in their countries, and the *Reading* section contains extracts from a newspaper problem page.

Language aims

Grammar – *have (got) to* This might be the first time that your class has been introduced to *have to* or *have got to* to express obligation. *Must* is often taught in first-year courses to express the obligation of the speaker. This can cause students problems, as they don't realize that *must* with second and third persons sounds too authoritarian. *Should* would be more appropriate. They also use *must* to refer to a general obligation, when *have to* sounds more natural. In British English, particularly informal English, *have got to* is normally used when talking about *one thing* we are obliged to do, (e.g. *I've got to do my homework this evening*), whereas *have to* is used when the obligation is habitual, (e.g. *I usually have to visit my family at the weekend*). In American English only *have to* is used.

Common mistakes
**You've got hiccups. You must have a glass of water.*
**My parents must work six days a week.*

In *New Headway Pre-Intermediate*, we do not introduce *must* to express obligation. This is because the difference between *must* to express the obligation of the speaker, and *have (got) to* to express obligation in general, is too subtle for the level. However, *must* is used to express strong advice or recommendation, for example, *You must see that new film – it's marvellous!*

Students often find the verb *have* a problem, because it has so many guises. In Unit 2, it was seen as a full verb with two forms, one with *got* and one with *do/does*. In Unit 7, it was seen as an auxiliary verb in the Present Perfect. In this unit, it is seen operating with another verb in the infinitive.

should/must There is an introduction to modal auxiliary verbs on p137 of the *Grammar Reference*. Ask students to read this before you begin the presentation of *should* and *must* to make suggestions and give advice.

Both *must* and *should* present few problems of meaning, but learners often want to put an infinitive with *to*.

Common mistakes
**You should to do your homework.*
**You must to see the doctor.*

Vocabulary Two areas of collocation are dealt with, verbs and nouns that go together, and compound nouns.

Everyday English The functional situation, *At the doctor's*, is practised. It introduces the vocabulary of illnesses and revises the language of advice.

Notes on the unit

STARTER (SB p62)

The aim of this Starter is to find out how well students can use *have (got) to*. Ask students as a class some questions to get them started, for example:

What's good about your life? What's bad about your life?

Put students in pairs to make sentences using the prompts in the box.

WORK, WORK (SB p62)

have (got) to

1 **T 8.1** Look at the photograph and read the introduction as a class. Students listen to Steven talking about his job, and answer the questions. Ask students to discuss the questions with a partner before you get feedback.

Answer and tapescript
Steven is a chef.
I = Interviewer S = Steven

I What sort of hours do you work, Steven?
S Well, I have to work very long hours, about eleven hours a day.
I What time do you start?
S I work nine till three, then I start again at five thirty and work until eleven. Six days a week. So I have to work very unsocial hours.
I And do you have to work at the weekend?
S Oh, yes. That's our busiest time. I get Wednesdays off.
I What are some of the things you have to do, and some of the things you don't have to do?
S Er . . . I don't have to do the washing-up, so that's good! I have to wear white, and I have to be very careful about hygiene. Everything in the kitchen has to be totally clean.
I What's hard about the job?
S You're standing up all the time. When we're busy, people get angry and shout, but that's normal.
I How did you learn the profession?
S Well, I did a two-year course at college. In the first year we had to learn the basics, and then we had to take exams.
I Was it easy to find a job?
S I wrote to about six hotels, and one of them gave me my first job, so I didn't have to wait too long.
I And what are the secrets of being good at your job?
S Attention to detail. You have to love it. You have to be passionate about it.
I And what are your plans for the future?
S I want to have my own place. When the time's right.

2 The aim of this exercise is to focus students on the positive, negative, and past forms of *have to*. Put students in pairs to complete the sentences. They may need to listen to the recording again.

Answers
I **have to** work very long hours.
Do you have to work at the weekend?
I **don't have to** do the washing-up.
We **had to** learn the basics.
I **didn't have to** wait too long to get a job.

3 Ask students to work in pairs to change the sentences. Do the first as an example.

Answers
He has to work very long hours.
Does he have to work at the weekend?
He doesn't have to do the washing-up.
He had to learn the basics.
He didn't have to wait too long to get a job.

GRAMMAR SPOT (SB p62)

Read through the *Grammar Spot* as a class.

Answers

3 What time **do** you **have to get** up?
I **don't have to get** up early.
Yesterday, I **had to get** up early.

Refer students to Grammar Reference 8.1 on p137.

4 Ask students to give you sentences about what other things Steven said he has to do. Insist on good pronunciation.

Answers
He has to work about eleven hours a day.
He has to work six days a week.
He has to work unsocial hours.
He has to wear white.
He has to be very careful about hygiene.

PRACTICE (SB p63)

Pronunciation

1 **T 8.2** If your students don't know phonemic script very well, focus on the six different pronunciations and drill them round the class. Ask students to listen to the sentences and write the correct number next to the sentences according to the pronunciations.

Answers and tapescripts

1 [b]	I have a good job.	[d]	I have to work hard.
2 [a]	He has a nice car.	[e]	She has to get up early.
3 [c]	I had a good time.	[f]	I had to take exams.

Play the recording again. There are pauses to allow your class to repeat. Drill the sentences around the class.

Jobs

2 Check that students know all the jobs in the box, and drill the longer words for pronunciation. Model the activity by choosing a job and getting students to ask you questions. Refuse to answer unless they ask a grammatically correct question, and make sure they are trying to use *have to* in some of the questions. When they have guessed your job, put them in pairs to ask and answer. Monitor and correct errors.

3 Ask students to discuss as a class the jobs they would like to do, and those they wouldn't like to do. This second question, *Why?*, should prompt examples of *have to*. Notice that students are expected to use the third person plural here, not second person singular.

Talking about you

4 Introduce the discussion by asking one or two students some of the questions or by telling students about what you had to do when you lived at home with your parents. Put students in small groups of three or four to discuss the questions. In the feedback, ask one student from each group to summarize some of the more interesting comments made.

ADDITIONAL MATERIAL

Workbook Unit 8
These exercises could be done in class to give further practice, for homework, or in a later class as revision.
Exercises 1–5 practise *have to/had to, don't have to/didn't have to.*

PROBLEMS, PROBLEMS (SB p64)

should, must

1 Match the problems and suggestions as a class. Read out the problems, using intonation and mime to get over the meaning, and ask students to give you the correct suggestion. Then ask students what advice they would give. If any students use *should* or *must* correctly then encourage them, but the aim at this stage is to set the context and find out what they know.

2 **T 8.3** Students listen and complete the sentences, using the phrases in the box.

Play the recording, allowing time for students to complete the conversations.

Answers and tapescript

1 'I'm working 16 hours a day.'
'I think you **should** talk to your boss.'
2 'I can't sleep.'
'You **shouldn't** drink coffee at night.'
3 'My ex-boyfriend's getting married.'
'I **don't think you should** go to the wedding.'
4 'I've had terrible toothache for weeks.'
'You **must** go to the dentist.'

Drill the sentences round the class, paying particular attention to the strong stresses and wide intonation range used when giving advice.

You should talk to your boss.

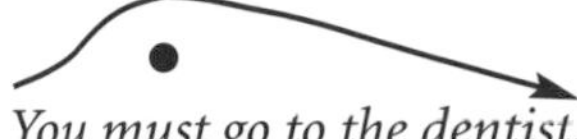

You must go to the dentist.

Students practise the conversations in pairs.

3 Check students understand the vocabulary used in each situation, and give them a few minutes to think of advice for each. Model the first situation by reading out the sentence and getting advice from students. Put them in groups of three to do the exercise.

GRAMMAR SPOT (SB p64)

Answer the questions as a class.

Answers

1 *You should go on a diet.* expresses a suggestion.
You must go to the doctor's. expresses strong obligation.

2 We do not add *-s* in the third person, or use *do* or *does* in the question and negative. Questions are formed by inverting subject and the modal verb. Negatives are formed by adding *not* or, more commonly, *n't*.

3 Using *I don't think . . .* makes the suggestion more tentative.

Refer students to Grammar Reference 8.2–8.4 on p137–8.

PRACTICE (SB p64)

Grammar

1 Students work in pairs or small groups to make sentences. You may wish them to write a few sentences for consolidation.

Sample answers

If you want to learn English,	you have to work hard. you have to learn the grammar. you don't have to go to university. you should buy a dictionary. you shouldn't speak your language in class.
If you want to do well in life,	you should go to university. you have to believe in yourself.
If you want to keep fit,	you should do some sport. you shouldn't smoke.

A trip to your country

2 Students work in groups to think of advice to give someone coming to their country for six months. You could set this task for homework, so that when they start to talk about it, students have some ideas prepared.

ADDITIONAL MATERIAL

Workbook Unit 8
Exercises 6–9 practise *should*, *have to*, and *must*.

LISTENING AND SPEAKING (SB p65)

Holidays in January

1 Students discuss the questions in groups. Let this go on for as long as they are interested. Ask students to complete the sentence and read it out loud to the class.

NOTE
Many British people go abroad in summer, especially to Europe. Spain is the most popular destination. People also take holidays in Britain, either in the countryside or on the coast, especially the south coast. Skiing holidays in the winter, especially in the Alps, are increasingly popular.

2 **T 8.4** Read the instructions as a class and look at the chart. Check that students understand key words: *chilly*, *temple*, *pottery*, *spicy*, *cool*, *mosque*, *cruise*, *mint*, *melt*.

Students listen and take notes. Stop the recording after each section for students to compare notes with a partner.

Tapescript and answers

Holidays in January

1 Silvia
In January the weather is wonderful. It's the most perfect time of year, not too hot, not too cold, but the temperature can change a lot in just one day. It can go from quite chilly to very warm, so you should perhaps bring a jacket but you don't need any thick winter clothes. The capital city is the most populated city in the world and there are lots of things to see and do there. We have lots of very old, historic buildings. We are very proud of our history, with Mayan and Aztec temples. But you should also go to the coast. We have beautiful beaches. Perhaps you've heard of Acapulco.
You don't need a lot of money to enjoy your holiday. There are lots of good cheap hotels and restaurants, and of course you must visit the markets. You can buy all kinds of pottery and things quite cheaply, and don't forget our wonderful fruit and vegetables. We have one hundred different kinds of pepper. You should try tacos, which are a kind of bread filled with meat, beans, and salad. And our beer is very good, especially if you add lemon and salt. Or, of course, you can always drink *tequila*.

2 Fatima
It's usually quite mild in January, and it doesn't often rain, so you don't have to bring warm clothes. But you'll need a light coat or a jumper because it can get cool in the evenings. There is so much to see and do. We have some wonderful museums, especially the museum of Islamic Art and the mosques are beautiful, but of course what everyone wants to see is the Pyramids. You must visit the pyramids. Go either early in the morning or late in the afternoon, the light is much better then. And if you have time you should take a cruise down the Nile, that's really interesting, you can visit all sorts of places that are difficult to get to by land.
The best place to try local food is in the city centre. You should try *koftas* and *kebabs*, which are made of meat, usually lamb. You should also try *falafel*, which is a kind of ball made of beans mixed with herbs, it's fried until it's crispy. It's delicious. One of the nicest things to drink is tea, mint tea. It's especially good if the weather is very hot, it's really refreshing.

3 Karl
Well, of course in January in my country it can be very cold, with lots of snow everywhere, so you must bring lots of warm clothes, coats and woolly hats, and, if you can, snow boots. Many people go skiing in the mountains at the weekends and when you are up so high and the sky is blue, the sun can feel really quite hot – warm enough to have lunch outside. You can even sunbathe, so you should bring sun cream! But you don't have to go skiing, there are lots of other things to do and see. A lot of our towns are very pretty. They look exactly the same today as they did four hundred years ago. And we have beautiful lakes. If the weather's fine you can go for a boat trip and you can get really wonderful views of the

mountains all around, from Lake Geneva you can sometimes see as far as Mont Blanc.
The food you must try is *fondue*, which is cheese melted in a pot. You put pieces of bread on long forks to get it out. Also you could try *rösti* made with potatoes and cream – mmm! They're both delicious.

Answers

	Weather and clothes	**Things to do, etc.**	**Food and drink**
Silvia	It's not too hot and it's not too cold. Bring a jacket but you don't need any thick winter clothes.	Visit historic buildings, Mayan and Aztec temples. Go to beautiful beaches.	Good, cheap restaurants. Tacos, local beer, and Tequila.
Fatima	It's mild, and doesn't often rain. Take a light coat or a jumper.	Go round museums and mosques. Visit the Pyramids. Go on a Nile cruise.	The local food is koftas, kebabs, and falafel. Mint tea is refreshing.
Karl	Very cold, lots of snow, but in the mountains it can be warm. Bring warm clothes and waterproof shoes.	Go skiing and walking. Visit the towns. Go for a boat trip on the lake.	Fondue is cheese melted in a pot, and you eat it with bread.

3 Answer question 1 as a class, then ask students to discuss questions 2–6 in pairs. Question 6 might lead to a class discussion.

Answers
1 The first speaker, Silvia, is talking about Mexico. Her capital city is the most densely populated in the world, and that is Mexico City. She talks about Aztecs and Acapulco. The second speaker, Fatima, talks about Egypt. She suggests visiting the Pyramids and going on a Nile cruise.
The third speaker, Karl, is talking about Switzerland, where there are mountains and lakes. It is famous for its winter sports.
2 a, b, c – Switzerland
d, e, f – Mexico
g, h, i – Egypt
3 The third speaker, Karl talked about skiing.
4 The first speaker, Silvia, said that you don't need a lot of money to enjoy your holiday. There are good cheap hotels and restaurants, and markets.
5 The second and third speakers suggested a boat trip. Fatima talked about a cruise down the Nile, and Karl talked about a boat trip on the lakes.
6 Students' own answers.

Speaking

4 Students work in pairs to form the questions.

Answers
1 What is the weather like in January?
2 What clothes should I take?
3 What sort of things can I do?
4 Are there any special places that I should visit?
5 What food do you recommend?

5 Students work in pairs to practise asking the questions.
If you have a monolingual class, you could ask one student to talk about a place he/she has visited that the others don't know. It needn't have been in January. Alternatively, *you* could talk about a place you know, or you could invite in a guest speaker. Inviting someone into your class can be very motivating and interesting.

READING AND SPEAKING (SB p66)

Problem page

Lead in by introducing students to the topic. It is a good idea to bring in a problem page to show students. Ask students about problem pages.

What sort of problems do people write in with? Do you think problem pages are a good idea? Why? Why not?
Would you write to a problem page? Do you ever read them?

1 Read the introduction as a class. Ask students to read the three problems and summarize them in the feedback. What advice would they give? Focus on and explain some of the expressions used in the texts.
*She **longs** to change her life = wants very much*
*She should **act her age** = do things like a woman of 47 usually would*
*He **dropped out** of school = left before he should, probably because of bad behaviour*
*His father wants to **throw him out** = make him leave home*

2 Ask students to read the problems more carefully and match them to the letters. Let them check in pairs before feedback.

Answers
a 2,5 b 4,6 c 1,3

3 **T 8.5** Ask students to work in pairs to put the lines into the correct letter. Then play the recording for them to check.

Answers and tapescript

1 Children always need the support of their parents, whether they're four or 24. I think you should pay for him to get some qualifications, and when he's ready, **you should help him** to find somewhere to live. Meanwhile, **you've got to give** him all the love that he needs.
Jenny Torr
Brighton

2 I decided to give it all up and change my life dramatically three years ago. Since then, **I have had** the most exciting three years of my life. It can be scary, but if you don't do it, you won't know what you've missed. I don't think **she should worry**. Go for it.
Mike Garfield
Manchester

3 He's using you. I think **you should tell him to leave home**. It's time for him to go. Twenty-four is too old to be living with his parents. He's got to take responsibility for himself. And **you must tell the police** about his drug-taking. Sometimes you have to be cruel to be kind.
Tony Palmer
Harrow

4 Why **should he accept** it? He isn't their slave, they don't own him. And I too can't stand the way people use their mobiles in restaurants, on trains and buses. They think that the people around them are invisible and can't hear. **It is so rude**.
Jane Sands
London

5 I think **she should be very careful** before she gives up her job and goes to live abroad. Does she think that the sun will always shine? If there is something in her life that makes her unhappy now, this will follow her. She should take her time **before making a decision**.
Nigella Lawnes
Bristol

6 **He must keep it**! He should have a word with his company and come to an arrangement with them. Why can't he turn it off sometimes? Mobile phones are great, and if he's got one for free, **he's very lucky**. They are one of the best inventions ever.
Pete Hardcastle
Birmingham

4 Students work in pairs to answer the questions. Let them refer back to the text. The aim here is to make sure students have a good detailed understanding of the letters and to get them to express their own opinions.

Answers
Nigella Lawnes suggests waiting (letter 5)
Jenny Torr thinks love is the answer (letter 1)
Mike Garfield has been adventurous (letter 2)
Jane Sands thinks that employers shouldn't exploit their employees (letter 4)
Pete Hardcastle loves mobile phones (letter 6)
Tony Palmer suggests being tough (letter 3)

Ask students which advice they agree with.

What do you think?

Put students in small groups to discuss the questions which arise from the text. Ask one student from each group to summarize what was said.

Roleplay

Put students in pairs to choose and roleplay one of the situations. Give them time to prepare and encourage them to use *should* and *must* and the ideas from the letters in exercise. When they are ready let some of the pairs perform their roleplays for the class.

Group work

Elicit a few typical 'problem page' situations from students, for example: *My boyfriend/girlfriend has left me*, *I have lost my job*, *My best friend hates me*, or less personal ideas such as *I can't do my homework* or *My teacher never listens to me*. Put students in small groups of three or four to write a short letter to a problem page. Encourage them to use the ideas on the board and their own ideas. When the groups have written their letters, exchange them with another group. Students must write a reply using *should* or *must*. Return the letters and replies to the group that wrote them and get feedback.

VOCABULARY (SB p68)

Words that go together

1 Read the introduction as a class. See if students can give you any other common verb + complement. Put students in pairs to match the verbs and complements in the two boxes. They can refer to the letters from the *Problem page* to check their answers. You could save time by asking half the class to match the words in one box, and half to match the words in the other box. Check all the answers as a class in the feedback.

Answers
live abroad
write poetry
stop being silly
act your age
take responsibility
take your time
stay in bed
don't know what you've missed
have to be cruel to be kind
give up your job
have a word with someone

2 Ask students to close their books and, in twos or threes, to see how many sentences they can remember involving the phrases in the boxes. Prompt students with a verb if necessary.

3 Read the introduction as a class. Drill the compounds *post office*, *headache*, and *horse-race* to make the point about the stress being on the first word. You will probably need to exaggerate the stress pattern yourself as students' natural inclination is to give both words equal stress.

Students work in pairs to match the nouns to make new words. Tell students that English people have to check whether compounds are spelt as one word, two words, or hyphenated, and dictionaries often disagree.

T 8.6 Play the recording so that students can listen and check. Ask students to repeat the list, making sure that the stress is on the first word.

Answers and tapescript

alarm clock	hair-drier (can also be spelt *hair-dryer*)
car park	sunset
traffic lights	earring (or ear-ring)
credit card	signpost
ice-cream	bookcase
sunglasses	rush hour
timetable	cigarette lighter
raincoat	earthquake

4 On their own or in pairs, students think of sentences to define the compound nouns. Give some more examples if necessary.

It wakes you up in the morning.
It's where you leave your car.
They have red, orange, and green lights.

ADDITIONAL MATERIAL

Workbook Unit 8
Exercise 10 is a vocabulary activity which practises verb + noun collocations associated with job descriptions.

EVERYDAY ENGLISH (SB p69)

At the doctor's

This section deals with the vocabulary and functional language of going to the doctor's. Lead in to the situation by asking students about their own experiences, without getting too personal.

When did you last go to the doctor? What's your doctor like?

Alternatively, you could introduce the situation by writing a few of the symptoms of a cold or 'flu on the board; *a sore throat, a runny nose, a high temperature, a terrible headache*, and telling students that they are all doctors. Say, for example, *I've got a terrible headache, what should I do?* and elicit advice from different students. This introduces vocabulary, revises advice, and previews the speaking activity at the end of the section.

1 Read out the phrases in the box and drill any that are difficult. Note that *diarrhoea* is pronounced /ˌdaɪəˈrɪə/. Check students understand the words. You could mime some of the difficult words, *swallow, sneeze, runny nose*.

Ask students to work in pairs to complete the table and answer the check question.

Answers

Illnesses	Symptoms
I've got a cold.	**I can't stop sneezing, and my nose is runny.**
I've got **'flu**.	I've got a temperature, my whole body aches, and I feel awful.
I've twisted my ankle.	**It hurts when I walk on it.**
I've got **diarrhoea**.	I keep going to the toilet.
I've got a sore throat.	**My glands are swollen, and it hurts when I swallow.**
I've got **food poisoning**.	I keep being sick, and I've got diarrhoea.

I feel sick means *I feel ill*. It can also mean *I want to vomit*.
I was sick last night means *I vomited last night*.

2 Read through the sentences with students and check any unknown words, or alternatively students could try to guess the words from the context as they do the exercise. Put students in pairs to put the sentences in order.

Answers
1 I didn't feel very well.
2 I phoned the doctor's surgery and made an appointment.
3 I went to the surgery and saw the doctor.
4 I explained what was wrong.
5 She took my temperature and examined me.
6 She told me I had an infection.
7 She gave me a prescription.
8 I went to the chemist's, paid for the prescription, and got some antibiotics.
9 After a few days, I started to feel better.

3 Focus students on the photo of Manuel and set the scene with a few questions.

Where is he?
What do you think is the matter?
What is the doctor saying?

You could pre-teach difficult words from the listening, such as *pale*.

T 8.7 Read through the questions with students then play the recording. Let them check in pairs before getting feedback. They may need to listen twice.

Answers and tapescript

1 He's got a bit of a temperature, feels terrible, and has a stomach ache. He's been sick and he's had diarrhoea.
2 What seems to be the matter? Have you felt sick? Have you had diarrhoea at all? Have you had anything to eat recently which might have disagreed with you?
3 She thinks he has food poisoning.
4 She prescribes something for a stomach ache and diarrhoea.
5 She tells him to drink a lot, spend a day or two in bed, and take things easy.
6 Only the prescription, which is £6.

T 8.7

D = Doctor M = Manuel

D Hello. Come and sit down. What seems to be the matter?
M Well, I haven't felt very well for a few days. I've got a bit of a temperature, and I just feel terrible. I've got stomach ache as well.
D Have you felt sick?
M I've been sick a few times.
D Mm. Let me have a look at you. Your glands aren't swollen. Have you got a sore throat?
M No, I haven't.
D Have you had diarrhoea at all?
M Yes, I have, actually.
D Have you had anything to eat recently which might have disagreed with you?
M No, I don't think . . . Oh! I went to a barbecue a few days ago and the chicken wasn't properly cooked.
D It could be that, or just something that was left out of the fridge for too long.
M Yes, I started being ill that night.
D Well, you should have a day or two in bed, and I'll give you something that will look after the stomach ache and diarrhoea. Drink plenty of liquids, and just take things easy for a while. I'll write you a prescription.
M Thank you. Do I have to pay you?
D No, no. Seeing me is free, but you'll have to pay for the prescription. It's £6.
M Right. Thanks very much. Goodbye.
D Bye-bye.

4 Students look at the tapescript on p124 and practise the dialogue in pairs. You could point out and drill the doctor's questions first, noting that they are mostly in the Present Perfect.

5 Ask students to imagine they feel a bit ill and write down a list of symptoms. Put them in pairs, and nominate one student to be the doctor, the other to be a patient. Students roleplay the situation. You could change pairs to give them more practice.

Don't forget!

Workbook Unit 8
Exercise 11 is an exercise on writing formal letters.

Pronunciation book Unit 8

Word list
Photocopy the Word list for Unit 8 (TB p157) for your students and ask them to write in the translations, learn them at home, and/or write some of the words into their vocabulary notebook.

Video
Report (Section 6) ***Wales*** This is a short documentary about the Welsh-speaking areas of Wales and the threats to the survival of the Welsh language.

EXTRA IDEAS UNITS 5–8

1 On p123 of the Teacher's Book there is a questionnaire about ambition, 'How ambitious are you?', and suggested activities to exploit it.
2 On p124 of the Teacher's Book there is a song, *Killing me softly with his song*, and suggested activities to exploit it. You will find the song after Unit 8 on the Class Cassette/CD.

If you have time and feel that your students would benefit from one or both of these activities, photocopy them and use them in class.

The answers to the activities are on p147 of the Teacher's Book.

Stop and check 2 (TB p132)
A suggestion for approaching the *Stop and check* tests is in the introduction on p5 of the Teacher's Book.

Time clauses • *if*
Hot verbs
In a hotel

Going places

Introduction to the unit

The title of this unit is 'Going places'. The future form *will* and its use in time and conditional clauses is introduced and practised in the context of two friends talking about their plans for a gap year. There is a *Reading* text about the building of the biggest city in the world, and the *Listening* is an interview with Michio Kaku, a professor of theoretical physics who explains how science will revolutionize the 21st century.

Language aims

Grammar – *will* The use of *will* to express an offer was presented in the *Everyday English* section of Unit 4, and the use of *will* to express a future intention or decision made at the moment of speaking was presented in Unit 5. In this unit we see *will* as an auxiliary of the future, where it merely signals future time. This use is also called 'the neutral future'. The distinction is very fine, and not always discernible.

The house will cost fifty thousand pounds is an example of the neutral future.
I'll phone you when I arrive is an example of a decision.
I'll see you tomorrow can have elements of both meanings.
We don't suggest you explore this area with your students.

First conditional Tense usage in any sentence containing the word *if* causes learners of English a lot of problems. In this unit, the first conditional is presented, and in Unit 12 the second conditional is introduced. The problems seem to be that there are two clauses to get right, and whereas *will* is used in the result clause, it is *not* used in the condition clause, even though it might refer to future time. In many languages, a future form is used in both clauses.

Common mistakes
**If it will rain, we'll stay at home.*
**If it rains, we stay at home.*

Time clauses This unit looks at clauses introduced by the time phrases *while*, *when*, *before*, *until*, *as soon as*, and *after*. These phrases are often used to refer to the future but generally they include a present tense. Speakers of Germanic languages confuse *when* and *if*, as they are translated by the same word. Tense usage in time clauses presents the same problems as in the first conditional, i.e. a future verb form is not used in the time clause, even though it might refer to future time.

Common mistakes
**When it rains, we'll stay at home.*
**When I will arrive, I'll phone you.*
**As soon as I arrive, I phone you.*

Vocabulary This is the second *Hot verbs* section in *New Headway Pre-Intermediate.* It looks at common collocations of the verbs *take*, *get*, *do*, and *make*.

Everyday English Students practise the vocabulary and functional language involved in staying at a hotel.

Notes on the unit

STARTER (SB p70)

The aim of this activity is to preview the use of *will* in time clauses by getting students to talk about the future in a personalized activity. Ask students to work in pairs to ask the questions. Note how well students use the structures in the feedback.

THE GAP YEAR (SB p70)

Time and conditional clauses

1 Look at the photo of Clare and Ally with students. Set the scene by asking questions about the picture.

What are they doing? Where are they going? What are their plans?

Read the introduction as a class and explain *gap year*, (a year out taken by students, often between school and college or college and work, in which they often travel).

T 9.1 Ask students to work in pairs to complete the sentences with phrases from the box. Play the recording so that they can check their answers.

Answers and tapescript

1c 2f 3e 4b 5h 6a 7g 8d

T 9.1

1 We're travelling round the world before we go to university.
2 We're going to leave as soon as we have enough money.
3 When we're in Australia, we're going to learn to scuba dive on the Great Barrier Reef.
4 If we get ill, we'll look after each other.
5 After we leave Australia, we're going to the USA.
6 We can stay with my American cousins while we're in Los Angeles.
7 Our parents will be worried if we don't keep in touch.
8 We'll stay in the States until our visa runs out.

2 Either play and pause the recording for students to repeat or drill some of the sentences open class. Ask students to work in pairs then ask them to cover the box and see if they can remember how to complete the sentences.

GRAMMAR SPOT (SB p70)

There is quite a lot to do and to understand in this *Grammar Spot*. It is a good idea to ask students to work in pairs to do each task, discussing each as a class before moving on to the next task.

Answers

1 *while, if, before, until, when, as soon as, after*

2 They are in the present tense but they refer to the future. This is because in time and conditional clauses the verb after *if, when*, etc. stays in the present form.

3 Sentences 1 and 5 use the Present Continuous to talk about a future arrangement, something planned before speaking. Sentences 2 and 3 use *going to* + infinitive to talk about a future intention, a plan already decided before speaking. Sentences 4, 7, and 8 use *will* to refer to future time.

4 Both sentences express future facts. The first sentence with *when* expresses something that is sure to happen. The second sentence with *if* expresses a possibility.
You could also ask students the following questions:
*What's the difference between **when** and **as soon as**?*
Explain that ***when*** refers to a point in time whereas ***as soon as*** has the idea of *immediately*.
*What's the difference between **when** and **while**?*
Explain that ***when*** refers to a *point in time* whereas ***while*** refers to a *period of time*.

Refer students to Grammar Reference 9.1–9.3 on p138.

PRACTICE (SB p71)

when, as soon as

1 Look at the first picture as a class. Elicit completed sentences from students. Ask students to work in pairs to complete the other sentences suggested by the pictures. Tell them to think about whether to use *will*, the Present Continuous, or *going to* + infinitive.

T 9.2 When they are ready, play the recording for them to compare their answers, but accept any variations from students if they are accurate.

Sample answers and tapescript

1 When I get home, **I'm going to have a bath**.
2 As soon as this lesson finishes, **I'm going home.**
3 If I win, **I'll buy a new car**.
4 After I leave school, **I want to go to college**.
5 While I'm in New York, **I'll do some shopping**.
6 **I'm going to travel the world** before I get too old.

You could play and pause the recording at this stage for students to repeat for pronunciation.

What if . . . ?

2 Do the sentences on the left about hopes for the future all together as a class, and drill the sentences around the class. Pay careful attention to contractions and sentence stress.

If I don't go out so much, I'll do more work.

Answers
If I do more work, I'll pass my exams.
If I pass my exams, I'll go to university.
If I go to university, I'll study medicine.
If I study medicine, I'll become a doctor.
If I become a doctor, I'll earn a good salary.

Ask students for suggestions to continue the sentences.

Students work in pairs to do the same with the sentences on the right.

If I stop smoking, I'll have more money.
If I have more money, I'll save some every week.
If I save some every week, I'll be rich when I'm thirty.
If I'm rich when I'm thirty, I'll have my own business.
If I have my own business, I'll make a lot of money.
If I make a lot of money, I'll retire when I'm forty.

What will you do?

3 Read the introduction and the examples as a class. You could ask your students who can ski and who can't then pair a novice skier with a good skier to do the exercise. Do the first three or four questions and answers as a class, so students see what they have to do, then put them in pairs.

Questions and sample answers
A What will you do if you don't like the food?
B I'll buy some from a shop.
A What will you do if it rains?
B I'll wait for it to stop./I'll go to a movie.
A What will you do if you don't learn to ski?
B I'll go for walks in the snow.
A What will you do if you hurt yourself?
B I'll go to the doctor.
A What will you do if there's nothing to do in the evening?
B I'll watch the TV./ I'll go to bed early.
A What will you do if you don't make any friends?
B I'll read a book.
A What will you do if you lose your money?
B I'll phone you and ask for some.
A What will you do if you get lost in a snowstorm?
B I'll shout for help.

Extend the practice by getting students to make a conversation in pairs about going on safari. Elicit a few ideas to get them started. Have one or two pairs act out their conversation for the class at the end.

Discussing grammar

4 Do the first two sentences as a class, then ask students to do the rest in pairs.

Answers

1 before	5 If
2 when	6 before
3 If	7 until
4 until	8 before

When I get to New York . . .

5 Read the introduction as a class. Ask students to work in pairs or small groups to complete the dialogue. Do the first couple to give students the idea.

T 9.3 Play the recording so that students can check their answers.

Answers and tapescript
P = Paul M = Mary
P Bye, darling. Have a good trip to New York.
M Thanks. **I'll ring** you **as soon as** I arrive at the hotel.
P Fine. Remember **I'm going** out with Henry tonight.
M Well, **if** you**'re** out **when** I **ring**, **I'll leave** a message on the answerphone so you'll know I've arrived safely.
P Great. What time do you expect you'll be there?
M **If** the plane **arrives** on time, **I'll be** at the hotel at about 10.00.
P All right. Give me a ring **as soon as** you **know** the time of your flight back, and **I'll pick** you up at the airport.
M Thanks, darling. Don't forget to water the plants **while I'm** away.
P Don't worry. I won't. Bye!

Refer students to Grammar Reference 9.1 on p138.

ADDITIONAL MATERIAL

Workbook Unit 9
These exercises could be done in class to give further practice, for homework, or in a later class as revision.
Exercises 1–4 practise *will*, *will* versus the Present Simple, and the first conditional.
Exercises 5–9 practise the first conditional further and time clauses.

Pronunciation book Unit 9

LISTENING AND SPEAKING (SB p73)

Life in 2050

One way of introducing this activity and exploiting it subsequently is to incorporate current issues regarding new technology, both local to you and global, particularly computer technology and how that will change our lives. Have a discussion about what is happening in the world, both the good news and the bad, and what life will be like in 2050.

1 Focus students on the description of the airline of the future. What do they think the story says about life in the future?

Answer
It suggests that we will lose control of our future, that computers will take over.

2 Read the introduction as a class. Put students in small groups to discuss the questions. If there is a lot of interest, you could develop this into a full class discussion.

3 **T 9.4** Play the recording. Students listen and make notes in response to the questions in exercise 2. They may wish to listen twice. In the feedback, discuss whether their ideas differed from Michio Kaku's.

Answers and tapescript
- He is generally optimistic. He sees no reason why improvements can't continue.
- Some people think they are too old. He thinks we must learn to use new technology now.
- Yes and no. As we get richer, the population will stop increasing.
- Everyone will have a computer.
- Probably. We will have to manage the world and its resources on a global level.
- We will begin to control the weather and the environment. There will be no illness.
- People will still be the same, intelligent but stupid and cruel. They will want to fight wars, they won't look after forests, oceans and the atmosphere, and they will think money is everything.

T 9.4
I = Interviewer MK = Michio Kaku
I Are you optimistic about the future?
MK Generally, yeah. If we go back to 1900, most Americans didn't live after the age of 50. Since then we've had improvements in healthcare and technology. There's no reason why these won't continue far into the 21st century.
I Are we ready for the changes that will come?
MK Changes are already happening. The future is here now. We have DNA, microchips, the Internet. Some people's reaction is to say 'We're too old, we don't understand new technology.' My reaction is to say 'We must educate people to use new technology now.'
I Is world population going to be a big problem?
MK Yes and no. I think that world population will stop increasing as we all get richer. If you are part of the middle class, you don't want or need twelve children.
I What will happen to people who don't have computers?
MK Everyone will have computers. The Internet will be free and available to everyone.
I Will there be a world government?
MK Very probably. We will have to manage the world and its resources on a global level, because countries alone are too small. We already have a world language called English, and there is the beginning of a world telephone system, and that's called the Internet.
I Will we have control of everything?
MK I think we'll learn to control the weather, volcanoes and earthquakes. Illness won't exist. We will grow new livers, kidneys, hearts, and lungs like spare parts for a car. People will live till about 130 or 150. For two thousand years we have tried to understand our environment. Now we will begin to control it.
I What are your reasons for pessimism?
MK People will still fundamentally be the same, with all their intelligence and stupidity. There will still be cruel people, people who want to fight wars against other races and religions, people who don't see that we have to look after our forests, our oceans, our atmosphere, people who think that money is everything. We will have the technology. The question is, will we have the wisdom to use the technology to our advantage?

4 Ask students to work in pairs to answer the questions. They may need to listen again.

Answers
1 Improvements in healthcare and technology.
2 They say they are too old to understand. He says they must be educated.
3 Because we will all get richer.
4 To manage the world's resources on a global scale. Countries are too small.
5 The weather, volcanoes and earthquakes, illness and our environment.
6 They will want to fight wars, neglect the environment, and think that money is everything.

What do you think?

Encourage a class discussion.

Michio Kaku isn't so sure about people – they will continue to be stupid, cruel and wasteful. He doubts whether we will have the wisdom to use the technology to our advantage.

ADDITIONAL MATERIAL

Workbook Unit 9

Exercise 11 is a writing exercise on linking words to express advantages and disadvantages on the theme of travel.

READING AND SPEAKING (SB p74)

The world's first megalopolis

The aim of the lead-in is to create interest in the topic, China. It also aims to find out how much students know about the subject. It is a good idea to bring in lots of pictures of China if you can find any, or if you have a student who comes from or has been to China, get the other students to think up and ask him/her questions. Alternatively, before doing the first exercise in the Student's Book, put students in small groups to quickly think of five things they know are true and five things they think are true about China, then discuss them as a class.

1 Put students in small groups of three or four to discuss the statements. Arguably, all the statements are true, but students may well disagree that Chinese people love tradition or prefer bicycles. The text contradicts both these assumptions, and suggests that China is more capitalist than communist.

2 Look at the pictures and the headline, and read the introductory paragraph with students. Ask them what they would like to find out about the world's biggest city. Ask students to read the text and say which subjects in exercise 1 are discussed. What else did they find out about the new city?

Answers

It talks about all the subjects, except that Chinese families can have only one child.
It says the new city will be the **biggest** city on earth, with a population of 40 million people. (line 16)
It says the old China of **bicycles** and little red books is disappearing, and the new China will be a world of mobile phones and **capitalism**. (line 26)
It says the Chinese don't worry about losing **traditional** ways of life. (line 33)
It says people don't want **bicycles**. If you have a car, it means you have money. (line 68)

3 Ask students to label the map.

Answers

1 Guangzhou
2 Pearl River Estuary
3 the Hopewell Highway
4 Shenzhen

4 Ask students to work in pairs to discuss the questions. They will probably need to read the text again.

Answers

1 No. It hasn't got a name yet.
2 It is ugly because it has no boundaries or centre, just concrete office blocks, factories and housing blocks. It is exciting because it is so big and growing so fast, and it will be powerful and wealthy.
3 Remarkable statistics:
It has a population now of 3 million, and will have a population of 40 million in ten years.
It takes only six months to build a 60-storey skyscraper.
It takes two hours to travel 123 kilometres on the new superhighway.
4 It is no longer a world of state control and bicycles, but a world of developers, mobile phones, cars, and capitalism. Deng Xiaoping's words are significant because, perhaps, they signify that China is embracing change, wealth creation and some sort of capitalism.
5 They welcome change and want cars and wealth. Owning a car means you are rich.
6 It looks like a big, ugly, shocking building site.
7 Because its power, energy and wealth will be felt all over the world.
8 **1982**: when Shenzhen was a fishing village.
3 million: the population now.
less than ten years: the time it will take for the population to reach 40 million.
40 million: the population in less than ten years' time.
thousands: the number of buildings being built.
six months: the time it takes to design, build and finish a 60-storey skyscraper.
two hours: the time it takes to travel the superhighway from Shenzhen to Guangzhou.
four hours: the time people spend commuting.

What do you think?

Put students in groups to write what they think are the ten largest cities in the world. This will probably cause a lot of disagreement, particularly in a multilingual classroom.

Answers

1	Tokyo–Yokohama	29,971,000
2	Mexico City	27,872,000
3	São Paulo	25,354,000
4	Seoul	21,976,000
5	Mumbai	15,357,000
6	New York	14,648,000
7	Osaka–Kobe–Kyoto	14,287,000
8	Tehran	14,251,000
9	Rio de Janeiro	14,169,000
10	Calcutta	14,088,000

(Source: US Bureau of Census estimate for the year 2000)

Ask the groups to make a list of problems the cities face. Give students two or three suggestions to get them started, for example *overcrowding, shortage of accommodation, crime, poverty, poor health and sanitation.*

VOCABULARY (SB p76)

Hot verbs – *take, get, do,* and *make*

Lead in by writing *take, get, do,* and *make* on the board and putting students in small groups to think of as many phrases they can using these words. Give them a time limit of three or four minutes. You could give each group a different word.

1 Read the introduction as a class and get students to find the examples in the text.

Answers

'To get rich is glorious.'	(line 25)
. . . as it gets bigger and bigger . . .	(line 71)
. . . it takes just two hours . . .	(line 67)
. . . it means you have made money.	(line 79)

2 Read through the examples and check understanding, then students work in pairs to ask and answer.

3 Ask students to work in pairs to put the phrases in the correct column.

Answers

TAKE	two tablets a day, a photo, somebody out for a meal, care
GET	back home, a cold, angry, on well with someone
DO	some shopping, me a favour
MAKE	sure, friends, up your mind, a reservation, a complaint

4 **T 9.5** Check students can use the phrases by getting them to complete the sentences then listen to the recording and check.

Answers and tapescript

1 I did some shopping while I was in town. I bought myself a new jumper.
2 'I don't know if I love Tom or Henry.'
'Make up your mind. You can't marry both of them.'
3 Bye-bye! See you soon. Take care of yourself.
4 Aachoo! Oh dear. I think I'm getting a cold.
5 'Are the doors locked?'
'I think so, but I'll just make sure.'

5 Finish with some personalized practice in which students work in pairs or small groups to ask and answer the questions.

EVERYDAY ENGLISH (SB p76)

In a hotel

1 Lead in and personalize the topic by asking students the questions in the Student's Book. If they all come from the same town, you could put them in small groups to discuss their answers first. Alternatively, you could ask them *What's the best hotel you've ever been to?*, or you could bring in hotel brochures and start the lesson with a skimming task. Ask students to look at the brochure(s) quickly and answer the following questions:

How much is a double room? What facilities does the hotel have?
Would you like to stay there? Why/Why not?

2 Read through the information about the Grand Hotel with students. Model and drill the example question and answer, paying particular attention to the intonation of the question form.

Where's the conference centre?

Point out that we say *on* the second floor but *in* the basement, then ask students to work in pairs to practise.

NOTE
In British English, the ground floor is the floor at street level, and the first floor is the one above it. In American English, the floor at street level is called the first floor.

3 **T 9.6** Ask students to work in pairs to re-order the conversation. Do the first as a class to get them started. When they have finished, play the recording so that they can check their answers.

Answers and tapescript
R = Receptions C = Client

R Hello, the Grand Hotel. Cathy speaking. How can I help you?
C **I'd like to make a reservation, please.**
R Certainly. When is it for?
C It's for two nights, the thirteenth and the fourteenth of this month.
R **And do you want a single or a double room?**
C A single, please.
R OK. Yes, that's fine. I have a room for you. And your name is?
C Robert Palmer. **Can you tell me how much it is**?
R Yes. That's £95 a night. Can I have a credit card number, please?
C Yes, sure. It's a Visa. 4929 7983 0621 8849.
R Thank you. **And could I have a phone number**?
C Uh huh. 01727 489962.
R That's fine. **We look forward to seeing you on the thirteenth**. Bye-bye.
C Thanks a lot. Goodbye.

At this stage you could drill the sentences around the class for pronunciation, and/or ask students to work in pairs to practise reading the conversation.

4 Students work in pairs to prepare the conversation between Robert Palmer and the receptionist. It is a good idea to brainstorm what you have to do when you check into a hotel to give students some ideas for their dialogue: *fill in a form, get the key, order meals.* Monitor and help them prepare. Make sure they are using the language of polite requests correctly: *I'd like …* , *Could I …* , *Could you …* , *please?* Write these phrases on the board as prompts to help them. When students are ready, let them perform their dialogues for the class.

5 This activity gives students further practice in making requests in a hotel. Give them time to think how to make the initial request, (e.g. *Could you bring me an extra pillow, please?*), then put them in pairs to improvise conversations.

Don't forget!

Workbook Unit 9
Exercise 10 is a vocabulary exercise on preposition + noun.

Pronunciation book Unit 9

Word list
Photocopy the Word list for Unit 9 (TB p157) for your students, and ask them to write in the translations, learn them at home, and/or write some of the words into their vocabulary notebook.

10

Verb patterns 2
manage to, used to
-ed/-ing adjectives • Exclamations

Scared to death

Introduction to the unit

The title of this unit is 'Scared to death', and the texts all reflect this theme. The opening presentation text is an article about a frightening adventure in the mountains of southern Spain, the *Reading* text is about a young man lost in Alaska, and the *Listening* is about how a group of friends scare a boy by kidnapping him as a practical joke on his birthday. The opening text provides a context for the grammar of the unit, verb patterns and infinitives. The introduction of *used to* has the subsidiary aim of allowing revision of the Past Simple and comparing and contrasting similarities and differences in their uses.

Language aims

Grammar – verb patterns and infinitives This is the second presentation section that deals with verb patterns. They were also dealt with in Unit 5, where the emphasis was on patterns that referred to the future. This unit focuses on *go* + *-ing* for an activity, *used to* + infinitive to talk about past states and habits, and then several verbs followed by either the infinitive or *-ing*. It also focuses on the use of the infinitive in English.

These verb patterns do not present students with many problems of concept. However, students often make mistakes of form, as they inevitably confuse those verbs that are followed by an infinitive with *to* and those that are followed by an infinitive without *to*, and once *-ing* forms have been looked at, students begin to put *-ing* where it doesn't belong!

Common mistakes
**He enjoyed dance.*
**He enjoyed to dance.*
**Let's go to shop.*

Start is one of the few verbs that can be followed by either the infinitive or the *-ing* form with no change of meaning. However, English doesn't like two *-ing* forms together, so in a continuous tense form, we use the infinitive.

It's starting to rain. (NOT **It's starting raining.*)

We also deal with adjectives followed by the infinitive (*It's easy to learn English.*) and the infinitive to express purpose (*I went to the shops to buy a paper.*) Students often translate this second item from their own language and insert *for*, which is wrong in English.

Common mistakes
**I went to the shops for to buy a paper.*
**I went to the shops for buy a paper.*

used to *Used to* may well be a new structure for your students. The aim of the practice here is to compare life now with life as a child, thus putting *used to* in a very clear context and contrasting it with a common confusion: the use of *usually* and the Present Simple.

Used to + infinitive exists only in the past, and expresses past habits or states that do not happen now. The Past Simple can express the same idea but needs a clear context and/or an adverbial expression of frequency to convey the idea of habit. Compare the following sentences:

When I was a child, we went to Scotland for our holidays.
When I was a child, we used to go to Scotland for our holidays.

The first sentence needs the addition of *often* or *every year* to convey habit, otherwise it could mean once only, because the Past Simple is also used to talk about an event that happened only once in the past. *Used to* cannot do this.

Students may find it strange that this structure only exists to express past habit, not present habit and sometimes they try to use it in the present.

Common mistake
**He uses to get up at seven o'clock.*

The pronunciation of *used to* /ju:stʊ/ or /ju:stə/ compared with the verb *to use* /ju:z/ can also cause students problems, and needs to be highlighted.

Another problem is that the pronunciation of *used to* is the same in positive and negative sentences. This means that students forget to drop the 'd' in the negative when writing the structure *I used to* /ju:stʊ/ *smoke. I didn't use to* /ju:stʊ/ *smoke.*

Common mistake
**I didn't used to smoke.*

Vocabulary Participle adjectives such as *bored/boring, surprised/surprising* are practised. These pairs of words are often confused.

Common mistakes
**I am very interesting in art.*
**It was an embarrassed situation.*

Everyday English Exclamations with *so* + adjective/adverb and *such* + noun are introduced, as are *so many/so much* + count and uncount nouns. *So* is used to make the meaning of the adjective much stronger.

Common mistake
**He is so handsome man.*

Notes on the unit

STARTER (SB p78)

This starter is a lead-in to the theme of the unit. It gets students talking about fears and dangers. You could introduce vocabulary around the subject of fear here: *afraid, scared (to death), frightened, terrified, scary, dangerous.* Put students in small groups to discuss the questions then feed back to the class. Allow time to hear what students are afraid of.

Answers

Cartoon 1	She's afraid of spiders.
Cartoon 2	She's afraid of confined spaces.
Cartoon 3	He's afraid of heights.
Cartoon 4	He's afraid of the dark.

A WALK WITH DEATH (SB p78)

Verb patterns and infinitives

1 Focus students on the photograph of *El Camino del Rey.* Ask them questions.

Does the path look safe? How would you feel if you had to walk across it?

Ask students to read the story and answer the question in the Student's Book.

Answers
Before the adventure began, he was very excited.
On the footpath he was very frightened and thought he was going to die.
At the end, he was shaking, covered in sweat from heat and fear, and exhausted.

2 **T 10.1** Ask students to complete the text with the phrases in the box, then play the recording so that they can check their answers.

Answers and tapescript
I have always enjoyed walking. When I was a boy, I used to go walking at weekends with my father. We (1) **went camping** and climbing together.
I try to visit a new place every year. Last year I decided to walk a path in Spain called *El Camino del Rey*, which means the King's Way. It is one of the highest and most dangerous footpaths in Europe. It used to be very safe, but now it is falling down.
I took a train to the village of El Chorro and started to walk towards the mountains. I was very excited.
Then the adventure began. The path was about three feet wide and there were holes in it. It (2) **used to have** a handrail, but not any more. I didn't know what to do – should I go on my hands and knees, or stand up? I (3) **decided to stand up** and walk very slowly. At times the path was only as wide as my two boots. I stopped to have a rest, but there was nowhere to sit.
I (4) **began to feel** very frightened. It was impossible to look down or look up. I was concentrating so hard that my body (5) **started aching**. There was no thrill of danger, no enjoyment of the view. I thought I was going to die.
I finally managed to get to the end. I was shaking, and I was covered in sweat from heat and fear. I fell to the ground, exhausted.

3 Ask students to work in pairs to answer the comprehension questions.

Answers
1 walking
2 He used to go walking, camping and climbing with him.
3 No. He goes to a new place every year.
4 No. It is falling down.
5 Because there was nowhere to sit.
6 Because he was too frightened. There was no thrill of danger, no enjoyment of the view. He thought he was going to die.

GRAMMAR SPOT (SB p79)

There are two ways of approaching this. You could work through all the tasks in the *Grammar Spot* with students, letting them do each discovery or gap fill task in pairs before discussing as a class. Alternatively, you could do one activity then follow it with the relevant activities in the *Practice* section before moving on to the next.

1 **Answers**

enjoy + *-ing*	try + **infinitive**	decide + **infinitive**
start + *-ing*	begin + **infinitive**	manage + **infinitive**

Exercises 1 and 2 of the *Practice* section practise these uses.

2 Read through the rules of form, use, and pronunciation with students.

Answers

I used to go walking	(line 7)
It used to be very safe	(line 17)
It used to have a handrail.	(line 27)

You could briefly drill *used to* /ju:stʊ/ with the whole class and then get individuals to repeat it. You could highlight at this point the difference between /s/ in /ju:stʊ/ and the /z/ in the verb *to use* /ju:z/. Ask students to repeat the sentences above and make sure they pronounce the weak form of *to* /tʊ/, or /tə/. Alternatively, you could simply model the sentences yourself.

Exercise 3 in the *Practice* section practises *used to* + infinitive.

3 **Answers**

I used to go **walking** at weekends.
I didn't know what **to do**.
I stopped **to have** a rest.
It was impossible **to look down**.
There was nowhere **to sit**.

Exercises 4 and 5 in the *Practice* section practise infinitives.

Refer students to Grammar Reference 10.1–10.4 on p139.

PRACTICE (SB p79)

Discussing grammar

1 Students work in pairs to complete the sentences.

Answers

1 skiing	4 ski
2 to ski	5 skiing
3 to ski	6 to ski

2 Students work in pairs to choose the correct form.

Answers

1 to stop	4 go
2 to find	5 to eat
3 shopping	6 to make

When I was young, I used to . . .

3 **T 10.2** The aim of this activity is to compare *used to* for past habit and the Present Simple for present habit in controlled written and oral practice.

Read through the introduction and the prompt questions in the chart. Tell students to listen to the man talking about his childhood and his life now and make notes. Put students in pairs to compare their notes. They may need to listen more than once. When they have complete notes, ask them to work in pairs to write one sentence for each question using *used to*. They could refer to the tapescript on p125 to check their answers. Conduct a feedback session, making sure students are pronouncing *used to* correctly.

Answers and tapescript
Life as a child

1 He used to go to school on Saturday morning. The family used to get together for Sunday lunch.
2 He used to watch TV and do his homework.
3 He used to go camping in Europe.
4 He used to play rugby, tennis, swimming, hockey.
5 He used to watch cartoons, comedies, and action films like James Bond.
6 He used to love beans, pizza, fizzy drinks, and chips.

T 10.2

1 Now I usually go shopping on Saturday, and on Sunday morning I play tennis. When I was a child, I used to go to school on Saturday morning. On Sunday all the family used to get together for Sunday lunch.
2 In the evening I used to watch TV and do my homework. Now I read, or go out with friends.
3 We go to a hotel somewhere hot and just do nothing. When I was young, we used to go camping in Europe. We went everywhere – France, Italy, Austria, Germany.
4 I was very sporty. I used to play everything. Rugby, tennis, swimming, hockey. Now I just play tennis. Oh, and walk the dog!
5 I like documentaries and sport. When I was a kid, I used to like cartoons, comedies, action films, you know, like James Bond.
6 I liked all the things that kids like. Beans, pizza, fizzy drinks. I used to love chips. Still do. Now I eat everything. Except peppers. Really don't like peppers.

NOTE
Point out to your students that it is more common to ask questions about past habit in the Past Simple and answer with *used to*, rather than to ask the questions using *used to*. 'What did you use to do?' is not very common.

Read through and drill the example questions and answers with your students and then put them in pairs to ask and answer questions from the chart.

Formation of questions
What do/did you do at the weekend?
What do/did you do in the evening?
Where do/did you go on holiday?
What sports do/did you play?
What TV programmes do/did you like?
What kind of food do/did you like?

Conduct a feedback session with the whole class. Ask different pairs to give you examples of their questions and answers.

Infinitives

4 Check that students understand that we use the infinitive here to express purpose, to say *why* we do something, *why* we go to these places. It is a good idea to ask students how they express this idea in their language. Many languages use *for* to express purpose.

Do the example, then do a prompt drill with the class, asking *Why do you go to the post office/bookshop, etc. … ?* and prompting a response from the class. Put students in pairs to ask and answer questions about other places.

Sample answers

post office	to buy stamps, to send a parcel, to pay a bill, to post a letter
petrol station	to buy/get petrol
bookshop	to buy a book
newsagent's	to buy a newspaper/magazine/lottery ticket
library	to borrow a book, to return a book
market	to do your shopping, to buy fruit/vegetables/ meat/cheese/clothes

5 **T 10.3** Ask students to work in pairs to match the parts of the sentences.

Answers and tapescript
1 'I'm hungry. I need something to eat.'
'Have a sandwich.'
2 'I'm going to a posh party, but I don't know what to wear.'
'I think you should wear your black dress.'
3 'My CD player's broken. Can you show me how to repair it?'
'I'm sorry. I haven't a clue.'
4 'Don't talk to me. I have nothing to say to you.'
'Oh, dear! What have I done wrong?'
5 'Do I turn left or right? I don't know where to go.'
'Go straight on.'
6 'I'm bored. I haven't got anything to do.'
'Why don't you read the dictionary?'
7 'Can you get some meat?'
'Sure. Tell me how much to buy.'
'A kilo.'
8 'I feel lonely. I need somebody to talk to.'
'Come and talk to me. I'm not doing anything.'

Ask students to think of replies in pairs then play the recording so that they can check. Let students practise the dialogues in pairs, using their replies or those on the recording.

Check it

6 Students work individually to choose the correct form. This could be done for homework.

Answers

1 to buy	4 to say
2 dancing	5 swimming
3 to go	

Ask students to read Grammar Reference 10.1–10.4 on p139, perhaps before they do some of the Workbook exercises for homework (see below).

ADDITIONAL MATERIAL

Workbook Unit 10
These exercises could be done in class to give further practice, for homework, or in a later class, as revision.
Exercises 1–4 practise verb patterns.
Exercises 5–6 practise *used to*.

VOCABULARY (SB p81)

-ed/-ing adjectives

You could lead in to this activity, get students talking, and link the lesson with the theme of the unit by asking students *What's the most frightening experience you have ever had?*

1 Read through the words in the box, drilling them for pronunciation. Put students in pairs to match the adjectives with an experience. Do the first as an example.

Sample answers
1 frightening, terrifying
2 exhausting
3 frightening, exciting, terrifying
4 frightening, terrifying
5 boring
6 surprising

Ask students how people feel when they get stuck in a lift. Elicit *They're frightened/terrified.*

2 Ask students how the people in the photos feel.

Answers
He's frightened/terrified.
He's exhausted.
She's surprised.
They're excited.
She's bored.

T 10.4 Play the recording. Students listen and repeat to practise the pronunciation of the words. Ask students to work in pairs to say how people feel in the other situations. Conduct a feedback session.

Tapescript
frightened excited surprised terrified bored exhausted

Read through the rules in the Caution Box for using *-ed/-ing* adjectives with students.

3 Ask students to work in pairs to complete the sentences using the adjectives in the box.

Sample answers
1 'I met a famous film star today.' 'Really? How **exciting**!'
2 'I spent four hours going round a museum.' 'Was it **interesting**?' 'No, it was **boring**.'
3 'I haven't heard from my parents for two months.' 'You must be **worried**.'
4 'Wow, Maria! What are you doing here?' 'Why are you so **surprised** to see me?'
5 I failed my exam. I worked really hard for it. I'm so **disappointed**.
6 'A man started to follow me home last night.' 'Weren't you **worried/frightened**?'
7 My computer's broken, and I don't understand the manual. It's so **confusing**.

T 10.5 Students listen to the beginnings of the lines and have to remember how to complete them. Pause the recording after each line and ask individuals to complete. Make sure they say the adjectives with appropriate feeling.

Really? How exciting!

4 Give students a little time to prepare, then put them in pairs or small groups to discuss TV programmes, films, and books. Monitor and make sure they are using the adjectives correctly.

READING AND SPEAKING (SB p82)

Into the wild

1 Lead in by discussing the picture on the page with your students. Put them in pairs or small groups to discuss the questions.

Sample answers
The country is Alaska.
Conditions are extreme. There are a lot of mountains and rivers. It is often cold, with little daylight.

2 Read the introductory paragraph and the words in **bold** as a class. Put them into pairs and give them a few minutes to decide whether the statements are true or false. Then get feedback on their ideas. Ask them what else they want to know about Chris.

Answers
- True.
- False. He was found by hunters.
- False. He had a good life.
- True.
- False. He says, 'It's great to be alive.'
- True.

3 Focus students on the questions then ask them to read to line ending "… *Thank you!' his diary reads.*" and answer them. Put students in pairs to check before feedback.

Answers
1 No. They last heard from him in June 1990.
2 He needed no possessions because he wanted to survive with nature.
3 He needed nothing. He didn't need possessions or money.
4 He had total freedom to live how he wanted and work when he wanted. He felt it was great to be alive.

4 Focus students on the choices then ask them to read to line ending "… *I didn't know where he was.*" and choose the best answers. Put students in pairs to check before feedback.

Answers
1 Chris didn't get on with his father because his father **tried to tell Chris what to do**.
2 When the parents didn't hear from Chris, **they got in touch with the police**.
3 In July 1992 **his mother is sure that she heard Chris calling her**.

5 Read through the summary with students. They must read the rest of the text then correct the mistakes in pairs.

Answers
Chris **hitchhiked** to Alaska, and arrived in **April** 1992. He lived in a bus, and there was a bed and a **stove** in it. He was very happy. There was **very little** to eat – small animals, fruit and vegetables, which he **found in the wild**.

After **three** months of living alone, he started to feel ill. He had no strength because he was eating poisonous plants, and **he knew this was the reason**. He **couldn't eat any more**. He died of **starvation**.
He knew he was dying. He wrote a **note** to his parents, and took a photo of himself. He seemed **at peace** to die in these circumstances.

What do you think?

Ask students to discuss these questions in pairs. Try to encourage a class discussion if your students are interested in the issues raised.

Sample answers
- Total freedom, living with nature, and being at peace were important. Money, possessions and, arguably, his family were not important.
- He was trying to live his life on his own terms, to escape from the rat race, to live with nature, to be totally free.
- Because they want freedom and independence.

LISTENING AND SPEAKING (SB p84)

It was just a joke

Lead in by explaining 'practical joke' to students: a trick that is played on somebody to make them look stupid and to make other people laugh (*OALD*). Ask some questions.

Have you ever played a practical joke on someone? What did you do?
Have your friends ever played a practical joke on you? What did they do?

1 Have a brief class discussion about which birthdays are special in students' country or countries.

NOTE
In Britain, people often have a big party on their eighteenth birthday. Friends and family often mark the occasion by buying large plastic, silver-coloured keys to signify being adult enough to possess a key to the door. The 21st birthday is also significant for the same reason.

2 Read the introduction with students. Look at the cartoon pictures as a class and ask them to tell you what they can see. Use the pictures to explain the vocabulary in the box in the Student's Book, (picture 2 shows a man in a *balaclava*, picture 5 shows Tom *tied up* and *blindfolded*). Put students in pairs or threes to invent a story based on the pictures. Tell them they can put the pictures in any order. Listen to one or two stories from the pairs or groups in the feedback.

3 **T 10.6** Play the recording. Students listen to find out whether the pictures are in the same order as events are described. Conduct a feedback session. Is the story similar to their stories?

Answers and tapescript
Yes, he does.
T 10.6
I = Interviewer J = Jamie

I So you decided to kidnap this boy, Tom, for his eighteenth birthday?
J Yeah, just for a joke. We wanted to give him a real scare.
I So how did you organize it?
J About eight of us planned it. Tom thought he was going round to Richard's house, and Dave was driving him there. They came to a place which is quite dark, and there in the middle of the road was this body, this . . . dead body.
I And this was one of you?
J Yeah, it was Andrew. Dave stopped the car and got out, and then said to Tom, 'Hey, Tom, come and help. This looks really serious.' So Tom got out. I was hiding behind a tree, and I jumped on him. There were about six of us, all dressed in black with balaclavas on our heads. And I had this gun, well, a toy gun, and I put it in his face and started screaming at him to lie on the ground. Then we tied him up, put a blindfold on him, and threw him in the back of the car.
I Did anyone see you doing this?
J Well, yeah, but I'll tell you about that later.
I And how was Tom? Wasn't he terrified?
J Yeah, it was all so real. Tom started to say things like 'Please, I haven't seen your faces. Please let me go.' We were all so worried . . . you know, that it was getting too real, but we couldn't stop. 'Please,' he said, 'don't kill me!' Anyway, we got him to Richard's house and put him in a room with just a chair in the middle and all these lights pointing at him, so we could see him but he couldn't see us, and then we all started singing Happy Birthday.
I That's amazing!
J Tom tried to say that he knew it was us from the start, but that's just not true. He was so terrified.
I So what about these people who saw the kidnap?
J Well, someone saw what was happening from a bedroom window and called the police, and soon there were police cars and armed police everywhere, dogs, and a police helicopter all looking for terrorists. And that was us!
I And they found you?
J We were driving past later that evening, and the police were stopping everyone and asking if they knew anything about a kidnap, and we had to confess that it was just a joke.
I Weren't they angry with you for wasting so much police time?
J Yeah, well. We're still waiting to hear if we're going to be taken to court.

I And has Tom forgiven you?
J Oh, yeah. He'll never forget his eighteenth birthday, though.

4 Students work in pairs to answer the questions. Play the recording again for them to check.

Answers

1 **Tom**: picture 1, passenger in the car; picture 2, standing in the road; pictures 3 and 4, lying on the ground; picture 5, tied up and blindfolded; picture 6, sitting on the chair
Jamie: pictures 2 and 3, kidnapper with toy gun
Dave: picture 1, driving the car
Andrew: picture 1, lying in the road
The witness: picture 4, looking out of the window

2
I've had a . . .	Jamie
Lie on the . . .	Jamie
Please let me . . .	Tom
Send the police . . .	The witness
Come and help . . .	Dave
Happy birthday . . .	Jamie, Dave, and Andrew
You *****s!	Tom
I knew it . . .	Tom
Excuse me, . . .	The police
I think we . . .	Jamie, Dave, and Andrew

Roleplay

Ask students to work with a partner to choose one of the situations and prepare a conversation. Let them perform their roleplays for the class.

EVERYDAY ENGLISH (SB p85)

Exclamations with *so* and *such*

1 **T 10.7** Ask students to read and listen to the sentences on the recording. Drill students, making sure they attempt the stress and intonation pattern of the sentence with *so*.

He was so scared!

Discuss the questions as a class.

Answers
This use of *so* is more spoken.
It has the effect of making the adjective stronger, more emphatic. The whole sentence is more dramatic.

2 Put students in pairs or groups of three to look at the sentences and work out the rules of use.

Answers
so + adjective
such an + singular, count noun beginning with a vowel
such a + singular, count noun beginning with a consonant
such + plural noun
such + uncount noun
so many + plural noun
so much + uncount noun
We use *so many/so much* to make expressions of quantity more emphatic.
Compare:
I have a lot of money.
I have so much money!

Drill the sentences round the class.

3 **T 10.8** Ask students to work in pairs to complete the sentences. Play the recording so that they can check their answers.

Answers and tapescript
1 Their house is **such a** mess! I don't know how they live in it.
2 There were **so many** people at the party! There was nowhere to dance.
3 I'm **so** hungry! I could eat a horse.
4 Jane and Pete are **such** nice people! But I can't stand their kids.
5 I've spent **so much** money this week! I don't know where it's all gone.
6 A present! For me? You're **so** kind! You really didn't have to.
7 We've had **such a** nice time! Thank you so much for inviting us.
8 Molly's **such a** clever dog! She understands every word I say.

Students practise in pairs. Monitor and make sure they are putting a lot of emphasis on *so* and *such*.

4 Put students in small groups to think of ideas using *so* and *such*. Get class feedback to check their ideas and correct any mistakes.

Don't forget!

Workbook Unit 10
Exercises 7–9 practise infinitives.
Exercises 10 and 11 are vocabulary exercises on *-ed/-ing* adjectives, and words which rhyme.

Pronunciation book Unit 10

Word list
Photocopy the Word list for Unit 10 (TB p158) for your students, and ask them to write in the translations, learn them at home, and/or write some of the words into their vocabulary notebook.

Video
Report (Section 7) ***BBC World Service*** This is a short documentary about the development of BBC World Service radio.

Progress test
There is a Progress test for Units 6–10 on p141 of the Teacher's Book.

Passives
Verbs and nouns that go together
Notices

Things that changed the world

Introduction to the unit

The title of the unit is 'Things that changed the world' and the theme is the history of some internationally well-known products: Coca-Cola, hamburgers, tobacco, sugar, cotton, and chewing gum. Texts about these products in the presentation and skills sections contextualize the grammatical area of the unit, passive forms, and provide many opportunities for practice.

Language aims

Grammar – passives The unit introduces four passives: Present Simple passive, Past Simple passive, Present Perfect passive, and Future Simple passive. In the opening presentation section, 'Sold worldwide', they are introduced together rather than dealt with one at a time. There is a lot of emphasis on how to form the passive and when and why to use it. With this approach, students at this level can cope with studying and practising four passive tenses at one time, especially as the tense use is the same as for the active, and your students should already be familiar with this.

It is worth reminding yourself that English generally makes more use of the passive voice than many other languages where the equivalent of *one* is used to avoid it – for example *on* in French and *man* in German. In English, *one* is rarely used and it can sound very formal and distant.

They is sometimes used to replace the passive in English. It is less formal.

They make good cars in Sweden./Good cars are made in Sweden.

Vocabulary This activity is on words that go together (collocation). In the first exercise in this unit students have to say which nouns go with which verbs. In the second exercise they have to say which prepositions go with which verbs. It is important to introduce students to the idea of collocation quite early in the learning of English. It is a language with many synonyms or near synonyms, and so it is important for students to develop an awareness of which words go together.

Everyday English This is an exercise on recognizing notices in common locations around Britain.

Notes on the unit

STARTER (SB p86)

This Starter introduces students to the form of the Present Simple passive in a context and use that they have probably come across before. As such, it is a good way of gently easing students into the grammatical area of the unit.

1 Ask students in pairs to make sentences from the chart in open class.

Answers
Champagne is made in France.
Whisky is made in Scotland.
Rice is grown in Japan and China.
Rolls Royce cars are made in England.
Nikon cameras are made in Japan.
Coffee is grown in Brazil.
Pineapples are grown in Hawaii.

2 Ask them to work in pairs to write some sentences about what is made or grown in their own country.

SOLD WORLDWIDE (SB p86)

Passives

1 To introduce the topic ask your students a few general questions about Coca-Cola:

How many of you like to drink Coca-Cola? Do you know where it comes from?
Can you tell the difference between Coca-Cola and Pepsi?
Do you know any advertisements for Coca-Cola?

Ask them to look at the facts about Coca-Cola and decide whether they are true or false. Check with a partner, then read the article. They should have no difficulty with the vocabulary.

Answers
1 False. 1.6 billion gallons are sold every year.
2 False. But it is drunk in over 160 countries.
3 True.
4 False. It is over 100 years old.

NOTE
1 gallon = 4.5 litres
1.6 billion gallons = 7.2 billion litres

GRAMMAR SPOT (SB p87)

After the reading, go through the *Grammar Spot* with the whole class. The aim here is to check the form and establish that the passive is used when the main interest and focus is on the object of the sentence not the subject.

Answers

2

Present Simple	**Past Simple**
is enjoyed	was invented
are sold	was given
is (still) made	was (originally) made
is (still) kept	were sold
	was bought
	was opened
Present Perfect	***will* Future**
have been produced	will be drunk
has been made	
have been used	

3 Coca-Cola is the main interest of the text. Therefore it is the subject of many of the sentences in the text. Dr John Pemberton and Frank Robinson are only interesting because of their relation to the central theme of Coca-Cola. We use the passive because we are more interested in Coca-Cola, the object of the active sentence.

Refer students to Grammar Reference 11.1 on p140.

2 Use the verb forms in the table in exercise 2 of the *Grammar Spot* as prompts to get students producing passive sentences.

PRACTICE (SB p88)

Active and passive

1 Ask your students to do this on their own then check with a partner before feedback. Do the first as an example.

Answers

Active	**Passive**
They make Rolls Royce cars in England.	Rolls Royce cars **are made** in England.
They **grow** rice in China.	Rice is grown in China.
Bell invented the telephone in 1876.	The telephone **was invented** by Bell in 1876.
Thieves **stole** two pictures from the museum last night.	Two pictures were stolen from the museum last night.
They have built three new factories this year.	Three new factories **have been built** this year.
They **have sold** the picture for £3,000.	The picture has been sold for £3,000.
The factory will produce 10,000 cars next year.	10,000 cars **will be produced** next year.
Did they **make** many cars last year?	Were many cars made last year?
Bell didn't invent the television.	The television **wasn't invented** by Bell.

2 This is an exercise in recognizing when to use an active or a passive verb form, and putting it into the appropriate tense. The text is about the history of the hamburger. To introduce the topic, ask students to look at the pictures and ask some questions.

Do you know when hamburgers were invented? When did McDonald's start?
How many McDonald's are there in the world? Have a guess.

Ask students to read the text quickly and find the answers to the questions. Then put them in pairs to put the verbs in the correct tense, active or passive.

Answers

1	were made	6	were bought
2	called	7	preferred
3	was given	8	opened
4	became	9	have opened/have been opened
5	grew	10	are eaten

Go through the answers as a class.

Questions and answers

3 Ask students to match question words and answers.

Answers

When?	In 1895./In 1948.
Where?	In Connecticut.
Who?	Louis Lassen.
Why?	Because the recipe came from Hamburg.
How many?	25,000/35 million.

4 **T 11.1** Ask students to work in pairs to write questions using the prompts in exercise 3. They must use the passive form. Monitor and help with question forming, then play the recording for students to check. You could drill these questions for pronunciation at this stage. Write the question words on the board as prompts, model each question with a clear, slightly exaggerated pronunciation, and get the class, then individuals to repeat.

Ask students to ask and answer in pairs.

Answers and tapescript

1 When was the first hamburger made?
In 1895.
2 When was the first McDonald's opened?
In 1948.
3 Where were the first hamburgers made?
In Connecticut.
4 Who were they made by?
Louis Lassen.
5 Why were they called hamburgers?
Because the recipe came from Hamburg.
6 How many McDonald's restaurants have been opened since 1948?
25,000.
7 How many hamburgers are eaten every day?
35 million.

5 This is further controlled practice of forming the passive. It also revises short forms.

T 11.2 Read through the example with students then let them work in pairs to complete the mini-conversations. Play the recording so that they can check. Before letting students practise the dialogues in pairs, play the recording again, pausing after each conversation for students to repeat.

Answers and tapescript

1 A Are Coca-Cola and hamburgers sold *only* in America?
B No, they aren't. They**'re sold all over the world.**
2 A Was Coca-Cola invented by Louis Lassen?
B No, it **wasn't. It was invented by John Pemberton.**
3 A Were the first hamburgers made in 1948?
B No, they **weren't. They were made in 1895.**
4 A Was the first McDonald's restaurant opened in New York?
B No, it **wasn't. It was opened in San Bernadino, in California.**
5 A Have 2,500 restaurants now been opened worldwide?
B No, not 2,500. **25,000 have been opened worldwide.**

Check it

6 This exercise checks the rules of form and use of passives. It could be done in class or for homework with some other exercises from the Workbook.

Answers

1 were	5 don't carry
2 by	6 drunk
3 has stolen	7 been eaten
4 sells	

Refer students to Grammar Reference 11.1 on p140.

ADDITIONAL MATERIAL

Workbook Unit 11
These exercises could be done in class as further practice, for homework, or in a later class as revision.
Exercises 1–5 practise the passive.

VOCABULARY (SB p89)

Verbs and nouns that go together

The aim of this exercise is to develop students' awareness of the collocations of some common verbs. The verbs in this exercise have been chosen because they should all be familiar to students, but they are often incorrectly used in relation to some nouns. You may wish to do it as a dictionary exercise, developing students' ability to use dictionaries to extend their vocabulary.

1 Ask your students to work in pairs to find the noun that does not go with the verb. They could do this by guessing, or by having a guess then checking in a dictionary. Tell your students to check the *nouns* in the dictionary first. This is more likely to tell them which verbs go with them than vice versa.

Answers

You *can't* say:

grow £3,000	**give** a complaint
carry a watch	**lose** the bus
tell hello	**keep** an idea

2 Now ask the same pairs of students to write two more examples for each verb. Go round and check as they do this. Then ask several students to read aloud their sentences for the others to comment on.

3 Students think of verbs to go with the nouns that didn't fit in exercise 1.

Answers

earn £3,000	**make** a complaint
wear a watch	**miss** the bus
say hello	**have** an idea

Ask students to complete the sentences. Again, they could use dictionaries.

Answers

1 Say	4 have . . . had
2 missed	5 earned
3 wore	6 made

READING AND SPEAKING (SB p90)

Three plants that changed the world

This is a jigsaw reading. Think of a way of leading in and creating interest. One suggestion is to ask students *Which plants are important to humans?* and write some on the board. Ask them to tell you which one is the most important in their opinion and why, or ask them if they can think of ways that plants have changed history.

1 Ask students to read the introduction to the book review. The book is about how plants have changed history.

Answers

2 The plants are: 1 cotton 2 tobacco 3 sugar cane.

3 Ask students to work in pairs to match the words with each plant. They will probably need to use a dictionary to check the words.

Sample answers
A cotton plant: soil, fabric, silk, plantation, slaves, luxury, harvest
A tobacco plant: addict, soil, plantation, lung cancer, luxury, chain-smoke, inhale, ban, refine, chew, harvest.
A sugar cane plant: addict, soil, plantation, slaves, luxury, sweeten, refine

4 Divide students into three groups at this stage, Group A, Group B, and Group C. If you have a large class, have two sets of each group. You don't want more than four or five students in each group. Make sure they know which text to read.

5 Ask students to read their text and answer the questions. When they have finished reading, ask them to discuss their answers with their group. Then divide the class into new groups with one student from Group A, one from B, and one from C, in each group. Students must compare their answers to each question.

Answers
Tobacco
The words used are soil, chewed, slave plantations, refined, chain-smoking, addicts, lung cancer, banned.
Bad effects: addictive, lung cancer
Good effects: The US tobacco industry makes over $4.2 billion a year (though it is debatable that this is a good effect)
Sugar
The words used are luxury, plantations, slaves, sweeten, addictive.
Bad effects: addictive, you can lose your teeth
Good effects: used to make sweets and chocolate
Cotton
The words used are luxury, silk, slaves, fabric, plantations, banned.
Bad effects: none
Good effects: cheap fabric

Students may suggest that the slave trade was a bad effect of all three plants.

6 Ask students to return to their original groups. Ask them to answer the questions in their group.

Answers
All the plants have been grown for thousands of years.
Sugar was known as white gold because the plantation owners made so much money out of it.
Both sugar and cotton were luxuries.
Cotton caused the American Civil War. It was fought because the Southern States wanted to keep slaves on their plantations.
Tobacco was the main American export until 1820.
Cotton became the main American export after 1820.
All the plants were harvested by slaves.
Tobacco has, because of lung cancer, but all the plants have caused the death of many people because of the slave trade.

What do you think?

The aim here is to round off the lesson with a personalized discussion. You could do it open class, or in groups. You could turn it into a debate by asking each group, A, B, and C, to prepare and present reasons why their plant has changed history most.

LISTENING AND SPEAKING (SB p92)

The world's most common habit: chewing gum

1 Lead in to the listening by asking one or two students the following questions.
Do you ever chew gum? When do you chew gum? Where do you chew gum?
How often do you chew gum? What sort of gum do you chew?

Set up the mini-survey. Focus students on the questions in the Student's Book and the chart. They may need to copy it so that they can write down other students' names as they walk round the classroom.

Ask students to walk round asking questions and completing their charts. However, don't let it go on too long, especially if you have a large class.

2 Discuss the questions as a class. It will probably be quite light-hearted.

3 Ask students to check the words in their dictionary. To *freshen (the breath)*, to *wrap*, and *packet* have the most obvious connections, as mint-flavoured gum does freshen your breath, and gum usually comes wrapped in a packet. Students may speculate that it is made from tree sap and often advertised on billboards.

4 **T 11.3** Ask students to work in pairs to read the statements and decide whether they are true or false. Have a quick feedback. There will probably be a lot of disagreement, but don't tell them the answers yet. Play the recording. Students must check their ideas.

Answers and tapescript

1 False. 100,000 tons is chewed.
2 True.
3 True.
4 False. It was made of tree sap and honey.
5 False. They are born wanting just to chew.
6 True.
7 True. However, the gum was wrapped in leaves, so it wasn't a packet in the modern sense.
8 False. The North American Indians gave it to the English.

T 11.3

P = Presenter I = Interviewer
LW = Leanne Ward, chewing gum expert
A B = Interviewees
Part one

P Today in Worldly Wise, the world's most common habit ... Yes, chewing gum. We chew 100,000 tons of it every year but how many of us actually know what it's made of?
I Excuse me, I see you're chewing gum ...
A Yeah.
I Have you got any idea what it's made of?
A Nah – no idea. Never thought about it.
I Have *you* any idea what chewing gum is made of?
B Er ... no, not a clue. Rubber maybe?
I And do you have any idea who invented it?
A The Americans?
B Yeah – sure – I reckon it was invented in America, yeah.

P Well no. It wasn't the Americans who invented chewing gum. It was the Swedes. The Swedes, I hear you say? But listen to Leanne Ward, a chewing gum expert.
LW The history of chewing goes back thousands of years. In Sweden in 1993, the skeleton of a teenager was found, he was nine thousand years old. And in his mouth was a gum made of tree sap and sweetened with honey – the first known chewing gum.
P It seems we've always chewed things of no real food value. Babies are born wanting to chew. Everything goes straight into their mouths. So why do we chew? Here's Leanne again.
LW We chew to clean our teeth and freshen our breath but also because we just like chewing. The ancient Greeks chewed a gum called *mastica*, which is a type of tree sap. They thought it was good for their health and women really enjoyed chewing it as a way to sweeten their breath. Then in the first century AD we know that the Mayan Indians in South America liked to chew a tree sap, called *chiclay*. They wrapped it in leaves and put it in their mouths so this was, if you like, the first packet of chewing gum. The American Indians also chewed tree sap – they gave it to the English when they arrived, but it wasn't until a few hundred years after, that it became really popular in America.

After the feedback, ask students to correct the false sentences in pairs.

5 **T 11.4** Ask students if they know anything about William Wrigley. They may recognize his name from chewing gum packets. Read through the questions then play part two.

Answers and tapescript

1 He was a salesman, a business and advertising genius who popularized chewing gum.
2 He hired 'the Wrigley girls' to walk up and down in the street handing out gum, and had huge electric signs and billboards.
3 After the Second World War.
4 'Got any gum, chum?'
5 It's a secret recipe.

T 11.4

P = Presenter
LW = Leanne Ward, chewing gum expert
Part two

P The history of modern chewing gum begins in 19th century America. In 1892 a clever young salesman called William Wrigley decided that chewing gum was the thing of the future. Wrigley was a business genius. He was the first to use advertising to sell in a big way. Here's Leanne.
LW William Wrigley was really an advertising genius. He hired hundreds of pretty girls, who he called 'the Wrigley girls'. They walked up and down the streets of Chicago and New York City handing out free gum. Millions of pieces were given away. He also had huge electric signs and billboards – one billboard was a mile long, it ran along the side of the train track. So with all this, chewing gum became very popular all over the USA.
P So how did the world get to know and love chewing gum? Leanne again.

LW Well, during the Second World War American soldiers were given Wrigley gum to help them relax. In 1944 *all* gum production went to the US Army and they took their gum overseas and gave it to children. Soon they were followed everywhere by the cry: 'Got any gum, chum?'.

P And so the popularity of gum spread to other countries. After the war sales of gum exploded worldwide. Chewing gum was even taken into space by the first astronauts. So what exactly *is* it made of?

LW Well, the strangest thing about gum today is that nobody knows what it's made of. Nobody will tell you. The chewing gum industry keeps the recipe top secret.

Let students check their answers in pairs before feedback. They may wish to listen to the recording a second time.

What do you think?

End with a short personalized discussion in groups or open class.

Possible homework
Ask the class to underline all the examples of passive forms in the tapescript on p126.

EVERYDAY ENGLISH (SB p93)

Notices

Introduce the topic by asking your students for examples of any typical notices in their country. Ask which ones might be difficult for foreigners visiting there to understand.

1 Put students into pairs or small groups to do this. Check through the answers with the whole class.

Answers
2c 3b 4k 5f 6d 7i 8j 9e 10g 11a 12h 13m

NOTE

d People under the age of 18 are not allowed to buy alcohol in Britain.

h The opposite of *vacant* is *engaged* on a toilet door.

a Banbury is near Oxford in the centre of England. Trains from London to Banbury often stop in Slough, Reading and Oxford.

i The Northern Line is just one of the lines on the London Underground. Some of the other lines are: the Jubilee Line, the Bakerloo Line, the Piccadilly Line, the Victoria Line.

2 **T 11.5** These five dialogues take place in one of the places in exercise 1. Play the dialogues one at a time and after each ask your students:

Where are the people? Who are the people?
How can you tell where they are? What are they talking about?

Answers and tapescript

1 **A** Are we nearly there yet, Dad?
B No. It's miles to go, but we'll stop soon and have something to eat.
A All right. I need the toilet, anyway.

Father and child in a car, probably on a motorway.

2 **A** How much is it to send this letter to Australia?
B Give it to me and I'll weigh it. That's . . . £1.20.
A OK. That's fine. And a book of ten first-class stamps, please.
B All right.

Customer and clerk in a post office. You can buy stamps in some shops, but you can't have letters weighed to find out how much it costs to send them.

3 **A** Hi. Can I pay for my petrol, please.
B Which pump?
A Er . . . pump number . . . five.
B Forty-one pounds 78p, please.

Customer and shop assistant at a petrol station. Most petrol stations in Britain are self-service, so you fill up your own tank and pay in the shop.

4 The 7.56 from Bristol is now arriving at platform 4. Virgin Rail would like to apologize for the late arrival of this service. This was due to circumstances beyond our control.

At a railway station. The station announcer is apologizing because the train is late. (Note: British Rail is the name of the British railway system. It is a common joke that the trains are always late whenever the weather isn't perfect, which is quite often in Britain!)

5 **A** A vodka and orange, please.
B How old are you?
A Eighteen.
B Hmm. Have you got any identification on you?
A No.

In a pub. A barman and a young girl. The barman is asking for means of identification because the girl does not look old enough (18) to buy alcohol.
(Note: British people do not have identity cards, so to prove your age you would need, for example, a driving licence, a passport, or a student card. However, it is not very common to be asked your age, although there are notices about under-age drinking in most pubs.)

3 Students work in pairs and ask them to choose two other places from the list and write very short dialogues typical for those places.

Ask the pairs to read their dialogues aloud, taking different parts. Tell the rest of the class to listen and try to guess where they are taking place.

ADDITIONAL MATERIAL

Workbook Unit 11
Exercise 6 contains more notices and could be used after the *Everyday English* section.

Don't forget!

Workbook Unit 11
Exercise 7 is a contrast between the active and passive.
Exercise 8 is a vocabulary exercise which practises homonyms (words with more than one meaning).
Exercise 9 Students are guided towards writing a short review of a book they have seen.

Pronunciation book Unit 11

Word list
Photocopy the Word list for Unit 11 (TB p158) for your students, and ask them to write in the translations, learn them at home, and/or write some of the words into their vocabulary notebook.

Video
Situation (Section 8) ***Lost Property*** Paola loses her bag and goes to the police station to report it.

Report (Section 9) ***The Mini*** This is a short documentary about the history and development of the Mini – Britain's most successful car.

12

Second conditional • *might*
Phrasal verbs
Social expressions 2

Dreams and reality

Introduction to the unit

The title of this unit is 'Dreams and reality'. There are two presentation sections. In the first, 'Sweet dreams', the dreams of a young girl, set against the reality of her day-to-day life, provides the context to introduce and highlight the unreality and improbability in the use of the second conditional. In the second, 'Who knows?', two students, one decisive, one unsure, talk about what they are going to do after university, and this is the context used to introduce *might*.

The combined *Reading and listening* section contains texts about ghosts and a listening where a woman talks about hearing voices in her head.

Language aims

Grammar – second conditional The first conditional was introduced in Unit 9.

The concept of the conditionals does not seem to cause students as much difficulty as the formation. There are two common problems with this area:

1 The tenses used in the main clause and *if* clause do not seem logical.
2 The complicated structural patterns are difficult for students to manipulate and get their tongues around.

Where the second conditional is concerned, the use of a past tense in the *if* clause to express an unreal present or improbable future often strikes students as strange and illogical, especially as in many languages unreality is expressed by separate subjunctive verb forms.

Common mistake
**If I would live in the country, I would have a dog.*

The subjunctive has largely disappeared from English, but one last remnant is the use of *were* in all persons of the verb *to be* in the second conditional, for example:

If I ***were*** *rich, I'd buy a new car.*
If I ***were*** *you, I'd go to the doctor.*
If he ***were*** *here, he'd know what to do.*

However, nowadays this too seems to be disappearing, and it is equally acceptable to say:

If I ***was*** *rich, …* etc.

The contraction of *would* to *'d* can also be a problem, not only in terms of pronunciation but also because *'d* can also be a contraction for the auxiliary *had* (there is an exercise on this later, in Unit 14, Student's Book p112, after the Past Perfect has been introduced).

might The use of *might* is very common in English but much avoided by learners of English, who often prefer to use *maybe/perhaps* + *will* to express lack of certainty about the future, for example:

Maybe she will come.
Perhaps I will play tennis this afternoon.

These are not incorrect, but it sounds much more natural to say:

She might come.
I might play tennis this afternoon.

We are not suggesting that your students will immediately start using *might* after studying this unit, but we hope their awareness of it will be raised and *might* could eventually become part of their repertoire.

Vocabulary Students will already be familiar with some phrasal verbs. There are so many in English that it is impossible to study the language for even a short time and not come across some of the more common ones, for example: *put on, take off* (a coat, etc.), *get on, get off* (a bus, etc.).

In the vocabulary section there is a gently-staged introduction to the different types of phrasal verbs. There are four exercises which move from literal use of these verbs to non-literal use and finally to problems of word order.

Everyday English Some very common social expressions are practised. They are the sort of expressions that occur very frequently in any day-to-day English conversation.

Notes on the unit

STARTER (SB p94)

The aim of this starter is to get students using the second conditional in a personalized speaking activity. Note that two of the questions contain the structure *would like*, which is a second conditional form that students have already met. Discuss the questions as a class or let students discuss them in small groups first. Note how competently students manipulate *would*.

SWEET DREAMS (SB p94)

Second conditional

1 Tell your students to look at the picture of Nicola, and to read the two short texts about her life as it really is and her dreams. Check that your students understand *flat*, *budgie*, and *uniform*. Make sure students know that the first text describes her life, and the second text her dreams. Ask them *What tense is used in the first text? Why?* The answer is the Present Simple because it talks about her everyday life.

Now ask your students to read the 'dream' text again and complete the text with the words in the box.

Answers and tapescript

If I were a princess, I'd live in a **palace**. I'd have **servants** to look after me. My Mum would be Queen, and she wouldn't work. I wouldn't go to school. I'd have a private **teacher**. I'd ride a white **horse**, and I'd wear a long **dress**. I could have all the **sweets** I wanted.

At this stage you could check that students understand the use of the second conditional in this context. Ask:

What would Nicola like to be? Is she a princess? Is it probable that she will be a princess?

Use the questions to establish that she is dreaming about being a princess, it is not real and not probable, unlike the first text.

Now ask your class to read the 'dream' text more carefully and then ask them to work with a partner and compare the verb forms in the two texts.

2 **T 12.1** Students listen and check their answers. Use the recording to drill the structure. Play and pause after each sentence and ask individuals to repeat. Make sure students are pronouncing *I'd* /aɪd/ and *wouldn't* /wʊ(d)nt/ correctly. The grouping of the consonants with *wouldn't* can be difficult for many students, and the /d/ sound almost disappears.

GRAMMAR SPOT (SB p95)

Go through the questions with the whole class to establish the form and use of the second conditional.

Answers

1 The Present Simple.

2 No, she doesn't live in a palace, she lives in a block of flats.
lived is Past Simple.
The palace and the servants are a dream.

3 The unreal conditional clause is formed with *if* + the **Past Simple** tense. In the result clause, we use the auxiliary verb ***would*** + the infinitive without *to*.
Would is often reduced to *'d*.

4 It is acceptable to use either *was* or *were* here, although *were* is considered more correct.

Refer students to Grammar Reference 12.1 on p141.

3 This exercise is very controlled to give students practice at manipulating the question forms. First model the example questions and short answers yourself. You could do it as a chorus drill.

Students work in pairs to take turns asking and answering questions using the prompts.

Sample answers

What **would** her mother do?	**She would be Queen.**
Would she work?	**No, she wouldn't.**
Would Nicola go to school?	**No, she wouldn't. She'd have a private teacher.**
What pet **would she** have?	**She'd have a white horse.**
What **would she** wear?	**She'd wear a long dress.**
Would she have a lot of sweets?	**Yes, she would.**

NOTE

Short positive answers cannot be contracted.
**Yes, she'd.* is wrong. *Yes, she would.* is correct.

This should not really be a problem to students, as they will already be familiar with the short answer in *Would you like a coffee? Yes, I would./No, I wouldn't.*

PRACTICE (SB p95)

Discussing grammar

These are very controlled exercises to give further practice. It is a good idea to vary doing them as written and spoken.

1 Ask students to do this orally in pairs. Ask them to make the most natural sounding sentences.

Sample answers
If I found some money in the street, I wouldn't keep it.
If I were president, I'd build more hospitals.
If I were taller, I'd get a job in the police.
If I knew the answer, I'd tell you.
If I had a lot of money, I wouldn't buy a big house.
If I had a car, I'd give you a lift.
If I didn't eat cakes and ice-cream, I'd lose weight.
If I didn't smoke so much, I'd feel better.

NOTE

It is important to point out to students that the sentence parts can be reversed and the main clause can equally well come before the *if* clause, for example:

I'd lose weight if I didn't eat so much.
I'd give you a lift if I had a car.

Notice that there is no comma when this happens.

2 Ask students to do this on their own and then compare with a partner before you check through the exercise with the whole class.

Answers
1 If I **were** rich, **I'd travel** round the world. First **I'd** go to Canada, then **I'd** go to New York.
2 If he **worked** harder, he**'d have** more money.
3 **I'd go** to work if I **felt** better, but I feel terrible.
4 If I **could** speak perfect English, I **wouldn't be** in this classroom.
5 'What **would** you **do** if a stranger **gave** you £1 million?'

What would you do?

3 The aim here is for some less controlled speaking practice. Students might warm to some topics more than others. Put students into pairs or small groups to discuss the situations. The aim is to practise the result clause only, and ideally there will be a rapid exchange of ideas. Encourage students to give their real opinions.

Sample ideas
- I'd scream and shout and call the police.
- I'd say thank you very much then put it in a drawer and forget about it.
- I don't know what I would do. If the thief were old or poor, perhaps I wouldn't do anything.
- I'd take it to the police or, if there was an address inside I'd return it to the owners and hope for a reward.
- I'd try and find a policeman. I wouldn't interfere.

Bring the class together to share some of the ideas.

If I were you . . .

4 **T 12.2** Explain to students that we often use the second conditional structure *If I were you, I'd . . .* to give advice. Play the recording. Students listen and repeat the examples. Put students in pairs to take turns giving and receiving advice about the problems.

T 12.3 Students listen and check. Let some pairs perform one of their conversations for the class.

Answers and tapescript
1 'I have no money. What am I going to do?'
'If I were you, I'd try to spend less.'
'What do you mean?'
'Well, you buy a lot of clothes, designer clothes. Stop buying such expensive clothes.'
'But I like them!'
2 'My hair's awful. I can't do anything with it.'
'It's not that bad.'
'It is, really. Just look at it.'
'Well, if I were you, I'd try that new hairdresser, Antonio. He's supposed to be very good, and not that expensive.'
'Mmm. OK, I'll try it. Thanks.'
3 'I've got toothache.'
'Have you seen a dentist?'
'No.'
'Well, if I were you, I'd make an appointment right now.'
4 'I've had a row with my boyfriend.'
'What about?'
'Oh, the usual thing. He gets jealous if I just look at another boy.'
'And did you?'
'No, of course not!'
'Well, if I were you, I'd love him and leave him. He won't ever change, you know.'
'Oh, I couldn't do that.'
5 'My car won't start in the morning.'
'If I were you, I'd buy a new one. Yours is so old.'
'I know it's old, but I can't afford a new one.'
'Well, take it to a garage. Let them have a look at it.'
'All right.'

6 'My neighbours make a lot of noise.'
'Do they? That's awful.'
'Mmm. We can't get to sleep at night.'
'Have you spoken to them about this?'
'No, we're too frightened.'
'If I were you, I'd invite them round to your flat for coffee and say that you're having problems.'
'That's probably a good idea. I'm not sure they'll come, but I'll try it.'

ADDITIONAL MATERIAL

Workbook Unit 12
These exercises could be done in class as further practice, for homework, or in a later as class revision.
Exercises 1–5 practise the second conditional.

> **NOTE**
> At this point you might like to take a break from grammar and move forward to the *Reading and listening* on p98, before doing the grammar presentation of *might* on p96.

WHO KNOWS? (SB p96)

might

This introduction to *might* provides a good opportunity to revise the Present Continuous and *going to* for future plans and arrangements.

1 Ask your students to look at the pictures of the two students. Ask some questions to set the situation.

What do you think Ruth is going to do when she leaves university? What about Henry?

T 12.4 Read the introduction and play the recording. Ask questions.

Did they predict students' plans correctly? Which student is more sure of his or her plans? (Ruth)

Put students in pairs to complete the texts. They will probably need to listen again. You may need to play and pause for them to write.

Answers and tapescript
Ruth
I'm having a holiday in Italy for a couple of weeks, staying in a villa in Tuscany. Then **I'm going to look** for a job. **I want to work** in the media – advertising or the BBC would be perfect. My sister and I **are going to buy** a flat together, somewhere central, so **we'll have** to start looking soon. I'm very excited about the future. And I'm also highly ambitious!

Henry
I'm not sure yet. Some friends have invited me to go to Long Island with them, so I might go to America. I'll have to earn some money, so I **might work** in a restaurant for a bit.
I don't know what I want to do. I love France, so I **might live** in Paris for a while. I could earn some money painting portraits in Montmartre. Who knows? I **might meet** a beautiful French girl and fall in love! Wouldn't that be wonderful!

2 This exercise revises future tenses in a controlled written exercise. Ask students to write sentences.

Answers
She's staying in a villa in Tuscany.
She's going to look for a job.
They are going to buy a flat together.
They'll have to start looking soon.

3 This exercise checks the contrasting use of *might* to express possibilities. Ask students to write sentences. Make sure they don't try to follow *might* with *to*.

Answers
He might work in a restaurant for a bit.
He might go to Paris for a while.
He might meet a beautiful French girl.

GRAMMAR SPOT (SB p97)

Read through the *Grammar Spot* as a class.

Answers
2 We do not add *-s* with *he/she/it*. *Might*, like all modal auxiliary verbs, remains the same in all persons.
We do not use *do/does* in the negative. We use *not* after the modal auxiliary verb.

Refer students to Grammar Reference 12.2 on p141.

PRACTICE (SB p97)

Discussing grammar

These exercises bring together all the grammar points in this unit.

1 You could do this as a quick oral reinforcement activity with the whole class, or you could ask your students to work on their own and underline the correct answers, then check with a partner before you conduct a feedback session.

Answers
1 We're having
2 It'll be
3 he might be
4 I'm having
5 I might

Possibilities

2 This aims to give further controlled practice of *might*. You could do it as a writing exercise, but it is best as a sort of prompt drill. Do the first as an example question and answer with your students. Then put students in pairs to make conversations with the other prompts.

Answers

1 What sort of car are you going to buy?
I don't know/I'm not sure. I might buy a Fiat, or I might buy a Toyota.
2 Where are you going on holiday?
I'm not sure. I/we might go to Scotland, or I/we might go to Spain.
3 What are you going to have to eat?
I'm not sure. I might have the streak, or I might have the fish.
4 Who are you going to the dance with?
I don't know. I might ask Tony, or I might ask Richard.

Get pairs of students to act out the questions and answers to the whole class.

3 This is a short and freer personalized activity. Students take it in turn to ask their partner.

What are you doing/going to do after the lesson? etc.

If the partner is sure the answer is: *I'm going to* ... or *I'm ... ing* ... .

If the partner is not sure the answer is: *I'm not sure/I don't know. I might* ... .

Check it

4 Ask students to work in pairs to correct the mistakes.

Answers

1 If I **had** a car. I'd give you a lift.
2 They **might** call their baby Lily, but they aren't sure yet.
3 I'd visit you more often if you **didn't** live so far away.
4 I **might** play tennis tomorrow, but I'm not sure.
5 If I **was/were** younger, **I'd (would)** learn to play the piano, but I'm too old now.

Check through the answers with the whole class. Ask students to say why the sentences are wrong.

Refer students to Grammar Reference 12.1–2 on p141.

ADDITIONAL MATERIAL

Workbook Unit 12
Exercises 6–9 practise *might*.

READING AND LISTENING (SB p98)

Ghost stories

In this unit the reading texts and listening text are integrated under the common theme of ghostly experiences.

1 In the lead-in, create as much interest in the topic of ghosts as you can. You could tell a short ghost story – and see if students have any 'ghost' experiences of their own. Try to gauge your students' interest in the topic – some students may not want things to get too scary. You could brainstorm vocabulary around the topic of ghosts here: *haunted house, scary, scream, tremble.*

Put students in small groups to discuss the questions in the Student's Book. In the feedback, find out which students really believe in ghosts.

2 Ask students to look at the picture of ghostbuster Aelwyn Roberts, and in pairs to predict the answers to the questions. Get feedback on their ideas.

Students read the text to find the answers to the questions.

Answers

Yes, he believes in ghosts, he says 'I don't think ghosts *might* exist. I know they *do* exist.' (line 16)
No, he doesn't try to find ghosts. He helps people who already have ghosts in their houses.
Yes, he tries to get rid of ghosts.

3 Students read the text to decide whether the statements are true or false. Ask students to correct any false statements.

Answers

1 False. Mr Roberts is retired. He describes himself as 'a kind of social worker for ghosts'. (line 8)
2 True.
3 True.
4 False. The boy didn't know it was his great-grandfather at the end of his bed. He described the ghost as 'an old man in a funny hat'. (line 30)
5 False. The old man was wearing 'a funny hat'. *Funny* means *strange* or *unusual* in this context.
6 True.
7 False. Mr Roberts tells us that eighty per cent of the time ghosts are members of the family.
8 False. Mr Roberts says you should talk to them firmly.

4 **T 12.5** Read the introduction, look at the photo of Alice Lester, and read the extract as a class. Check students understand the key words in the box. They will probably need to use dictionaries. Play the recording.

Tapescript
I = Interviewer A = Alice Lester

I When did you first hear these voices, Alice?
A Well, I was at home, sitting and reading.
I And what did they say?
A The first time, there was just one voice. It said, 'Don't be afraid, I just want to help you.'
I But it didn't say how it wanted to help you?
A No, it didn't. It just went away.
I And what about the second time?
A It was while I was away on holiday, but this time there were two voices. They told me to go back home immediately, because there was something wrong with me.
I So is that what you did?
A Yes. And when I was back in London, the voices gave me an address to go to.
I And what was the address?
A Well, now it starts to get very strange. The address was the brain scan department of St Mary's Hospital. I went there and I met Mr Abrahams, who is a consultant. As I was meeting him, the voices said to me, 'Tell him you have a tumour in your brain, and that you're in a lot of danger.' I said this to Mr Abrahams, but I know he didn't believe me. Anyway, he gave me a scan, and I did have a tumour!
I What an incredible story? Did you have an operation?
A Yes, I did. And after the operation, the voices came back again, and they said 'We're pleased we were able to help you. Goodbye.' And I've been in good health ever since. Now, what do you think of that?

5 Ask students to work in pairs to discuss and answer the questions. They may need to listen to the recording again.

Answers

1. No, she didn't.
2. She was at home reading.
3. 'Don't be afraid. I just want to help you.'
4. She heard two voices and they told her to go home.
5. The voices gave her an address to go to.
6. No, he didn't.
7. 'We're pleased we were able to help you. Goodbye.' She is in good health now.

What do you think?

It could be a ghost story. It is certainly strange that the voices in her head were so precise.

Mr Roberts claims to have got rid of ghosts, his story about the boy and the great-grandfather certainly sound convincing. Naturally, students may have very different interpretations.

Encourage a short class discussion. Have any students changed their mind?

Telling stories

This could be set for homework. Students could prepare a short ghost story to tell in the next class.

VOCABULARY (SB p100)

Phrasal verbs

Students will have already met quite a few phrasal verbs because they are so common in English. These four exercises are staged in such a way as to illustrate some of the different types of phrasal verbs and to show that they can have both literal and non-literal (idiomatic) meaning.

NOTE

Here for your information is a description of the types of phrasal verb. We do not suggest that you pass on this information to your students, but it is useful to remind yourself of the types so that you can deal with any queries that arise.

There are four types:

Type 1: verb + adverb (no direct object)

*The plane **took off**.*
*We **sat down**.*

(This type is not highlighted for students in these exercises although examples appear.)

Type 2: verb + adverb + direct object

*He **put on** his hat/**put** his hat **on**. He **put** it **on**.*
*She **looked up** the word/**up**. She looked it **up**.*
*I **turned off** the light/**turned** the light **off**. I **turned** it **off**.*

The adverb can change position, but not if the object is a pronoun.

(These are highlighted in exercise 3.)

Type 3: verb + preposition + object

*He **fell down** the stairs. He **fell down** them.*
*She's **looking for** her purse. She's **looking for** it.*
*He **looked after** the baby. He **looked after** her.*

The preposition cannot change position.

(These are highlighted in exercise 4.)

Type 4: verb + adverb + preposition + object

*Anna doesn't **get on with** her husband. She doesn't **get on with** him.*
*Billy's **looking forward to** Christmas. He's **looking forward to** it.*

(These also appear in exercise 4 because the adverb and preposition cannot change position.)

1 Read through the examples with your students to make sure they have an idea what is meant by a phrasal verb.

Ask them to do this exercise on their own. Stress that the words in this exercise are used literally and therefore they should be able to work out the answers quite logically and easily. Tell them that one of the words is used twice.

Ask students to check their answers with a partner, and then go through the answers quickly with the whole class.

Answers
1 on 2 out 3 up 4 out 5 back

Focus students on the phrasal verbs in the box. Put them in small groups to do or mime the actions. The other students must guess which words they are doing or miming.

2 Read through the introduction and make it clear that here the phrasal verbs have a non-literal, idiomatic meaning. In other words you cannot work out the meaning logically from the parts. The three examples should illustrate this.

Ask them to work in small groups to do or mime the actions. The other students must guess which words they are doing or miming. They may need to look up the verbs in a dictionary, but they should try to guess the meaning from the context of the whole phrase.

NOTE

Tell your students to be careful when looking up phrasal verbs, as many of them have more than one meaning, for example *put out* can also mean *cause inconvenience.*

Do not be tempted to start discussing all the uses! This would be very confusing. These exercises do not aim to 'tell all' about phrasal verbs, just to provide an introduction.

3 This and the next exercise aim to highlight and practise problems of word order with phrasal verbs.

Read through the introduction as a class and the instructions for the exercise. Put students in pairs to complete the sentences with phrasal verbs. They must use the correct pronoun and phrasal verbs in the boxes in exercises 1 and 2.

Answers
1 ... I threw **it away**.
2 ... Put **it out**.
3 ... Turn **them off**.
4 ... I'll look **after her**.
5 ... I'll fill **it in** later.

4 Ask students to work in pairs to complete the sentences. After you have checked that they have the answers correct, let them ask their partner the questions.

Answers
1 How do you **get on with** your parents?
2 Do you ever **fall out with** your brothers or sisters?
3 What are you **looking forward to** doing on holiday?
4 Are you **going out with** anyone at the moment?
5 Where did you **grow up**? Or have you always lived here?

ADDITIONAL MATERIAL

Workbook Unit 12
Exercise 10 is a vocabulary exercise which revises many of the phrasal verbs students have met in *New Headway Pre-Intermediate.*

EVERYDAY ENGLISH (SB p101)

Social expressions 2

1 Focus students on the illustrations. Ask them what they think the people are saying in each situation. Ask students to work in pairs to complete the conversations with expressions from the boxes.

Answers and tapescript
T 12.6

1 A **Excuse me**! Can I get past?
B **Pardon**?
A Can I get past, please?
B **I'm sorry**. I didn't hear you. Yes, **of course**.
A Thanks a lot.

2 A **I hear** you're going to get married soon. **Congratulations**!
B **That's right**, next July. July 21. Can you come to the wedding?
A **Oh, what a pity**! That's when we're away on holiday.
B **Never mind**. We'll send you some wedding cake.
A That's very kind.

3 A **Oh, dear**! Look at the time! **Hurry up**, or we'll miss the train.
B **Just a minute**! I can't find my umbrella. Do you know where it is?
A **I haven't a clue**. But you won't need it. It's a lovely day. Just look at the sky!
B Oh, **all right**. Let's go, then.

4 A **Good luck** in your exam!
B **Same to you**. I hope we both pass.
A Did you go out last night?
B **No, of course not**. I went to bed early. **What about you?**
A Me, too. **See you later** after the exam. Let's go out for a drink.
B **Good idea**.

2 **T 12.6** Play the dialogues and pause after each for students to check their answers. After each one ask the pairs to practise saying that dialogue together.

At the end of all four, allocate a pair for each dialogue to read and act it for the whole class. Ask the other students to comment on the pronunciation. You could play the recordings again at any point to establish a good model.

3 Round off the lesson by prompting some of the expressions from students.

Don't forget!

Workbook Unit 12

Exercises 11 and 12 are writing exercises: adverbs and writing a story

Pronunciation book Unit 12

Word list

Photocopy the Word list for Unit 12 (TB p159) for your students, and ask them to write in the translations, learn them at home, and/or write some of the words into their vocabulary notebook.

Video

Situation (Section 10) ***Introductions*** David takes Paola to meet his parents. Students practise meeting new people and making introductions.

EXTRA IDEAS UNITS 9–12

1 On p125 of the Teacher's Book there is a game, 'The dream game', to practise the skills of reading and speaking.

2 On p126 of the Teacher's Book there is a song, *I'll be there for you*, and suggested activities to exploit it. You will find the song after Unit 12 on the Class Cassette/CD.

If you have time and feel that your students would benefit from one or both of these activities, photocopy them and use them in class.

The answers to the activities are on p147 of the Teacher's Book.

Stop and check 3 (TB p134)

A suggestion for approaching the *Stop and check* tests is in the introduction on p5 of the Teacher's Book.

Present Perfect Continuous
Word formation
Adverbs • Telephoning

Earning a living

Introduction to the unit

The title of this unit is 'Earning a living'. The story of how Andy earns a living provides the context for contrasting the Present Perfect Simple and Present Perfect Continuous to talk about unfinished past. The unit also looks at the Present Perfect Continuous to express the present result of a past activity.

The *Reading and speaking* section contains texts about unusual ways in which people earn a living, and the listening is a conversation between a young man who has just started his first job, and his mother. It provides further practice of the Present Perfect Continuous.

Language aims

Grammar – Present Perfect Simple In Unit 7 several uses of the Present Perfect Simple were presented and practised.

Your students should be familiar with the form of the Present Perfect by now, but it is most unlikely that their production of the tense is accurate. This is for the reasons mentioned in the teaching notes to Unit 7. Although a similar form of *have* + the past participle exists in many other European languages, its use in English is dictated by aspect (i.e. how the speaker sees the event), not necessarily time. The Present Perfect is probably the most difficult tense form for learners to master, and it is not an exaggeration to say that this process takes years.

However, this is not to say that nothing can be done to help! If students can be shown how the tense is used in context, and where it is *not* used, their understanding will gradually increase. There is a case for saying that you are *always* teaching the Present Perfect. When a student makes a mistake, you might decide to remind your class of the rules. If an interesting example occurs in a reading or listening text, you might decide to draw their attention to it. This is not to say that you should correct *every* mistake. Students would become very frustrated! But seeing the tense in context, again and again and again, is the only way that their familiarity with this tense will increase.

Present Perfect Continuous Many of the above comments are true of the Present Perfect Continuous, too. This tense is sometimes introduced idiomatically in first-year courses, and in this unit of *New Headway Pre-Intermediate*, it is not examined in any great depth. This is because the subtleties of it are too complex for the level. There are two aspects which students have to perceive, the perfect aspect and the continuous aspect, and it is unreasonable to expect them to be able to do this immediately. As it is a continuous verb form, there are more 'bits' for students to get wrong.

Common mistakes
**I been learning English for three years.*
**I've learn English for three years.*
**I've been learn English for three years.*

The concepts expressed by the Present Perfect Continuous are often expressed by either a present tense verb form in other languages, or by a form of the Present Perfect Simple. Many languages (quite sensibly) dispense with the need to express the ideas inherent in the continuous aspect, but English has it, and where it is possible, prefers to use it. *I've been learning English for three years* sounds much more natural than *I've learned English for three years.* But *I've lived here all my life* sounds better than *I've been living here all my life*, because of the temporariness expressed by the continuous aspect.

When the Present Perfect is used to refer to an activity with a result in the present, it can be very difficult to know whether to use the simple or the continuous. *I've painted the bathroom* and *I've been painting the bathroom* refer to the same action, but mean very different things. The first refers to a completed action, but the second refers to a recent activity which may or may not be finished. The area is further complicated by the fact that, if a completed quantity is stated, the Present Perfect Simple must be used, not the Continuous. This is because of the idea of activity in progress expressed by the continuous aspect and the idea of completion expressed by the simple aspect: *I've written three letters today.*

Common mistakes

**I learn English for three years.*
**I've been knowing her for a long time.*
**I've been writing three letters today.*
**I'm hot because I've run.*

It is for the above reasons that the Present Perfect Continuous is not dealt with in too much detail in this unit!

Vocabulary There are exercises on word formation and shifting stress as a word changes class (for example, from noun to verb). There are two activities on *-ly* adverbs.

Everyday English In this section, using the telephone is practised in both formal and informal situations.

Notes on the unit

STARTER (SB p102)

This is a quick question and answer session to preview the new structure introduced in this unit.

1 Students work in pairs to ask and answer the questions.

2 Answer your students' questions.

STREET LIFE (SB p102)

Present Perfect Continuous

> **NOTE**
> Ask students to read the *Grammar Reference* on the Present Perfect Continuous for homework before beginning this presentation.
>
> As was explained in *Language aims*, the Present Perfect Continuous is dealt with relatively lightly in this unit. It is unrealistic to expect students to perceive all the differences of meaning between the simple and the continuous, and the perfect aspect will continue to present problems.

1 Focus students on the photograph of Andy. Ask questions.
Where is he? What is he doing? Why?
Ask students to read the text. Ask them why homeless people sell *The Big Issue.*

> **NOTE**
> *The Big Issue* is a street paper which was set up in 1991 to give homeless people the chance to have an income. Homeless people can often be seen selling the paper on street corners in Britain's major cities. It campaigns on behalf of homeless people and highlights the major social issues of the day. It allows homeless people to voice their views and opinions.

2 **T 13.1** Students work in pairs to match the questions and answers. Do the first as an example. Play the recording so that they can check their answers.

Answers and tapescript

1e 2f 3b 4c 5a 6d

T 13.1

1 How long have you been sleeping on the streets?
For a year. It was very cold at first, but you get used to it.
2 Why did you come to London?
I came here to look for work, and I never left.
3 How long have you been selling *The Big Issue*?
For six months. I'm in Covent Garden seven days a week selling the magazine.
4 Have you made many friends?
Lots. But I can't stand people who think I drink or take drugs. My problem is I'm homeless. I want a job, but I need somewhere to live before I can get a job. So I need money to get somewhere to live, but **I can't get money because I can't get a job, and I can't get a job because I haven't got somewhere to live. So I'm trapped.**
5 How many copies do you sell a day?
Usually about fifty.
6 How many copies have you sold today?
So far, ten. But it's still early.

3 Drill the Present Perfect questions round the class briefly. Model the conversation with a student then put students in pairs to practise. They should take it in turns to cover the questions then the answers and act out the conversation.

GRAMMAR SPOT (SB p102)

Answer the questions as a class.

1 **Answer**
Questions **b** and **e** are in the Present Perfect Continuous. The other tenses are the Present Simple (**a**), the Present Perfect (**c** and **d**), and the Past Simple (**f**).

Point out the form of the Present Perfect Continuous at this stage:

Question word + *have* + subject + *been* + *-ing … ?*

How long + *have* + *you* + *been* + *selling … ?*

2 *How long have you been selling The Big Issue?* asks about the *activity* of selling.
How many copies have you sold today? asks about the *number* of copies sold.

3 **Answers**
I **have been smoking** since I was 16.
I **have smoked** five cigarettes today.

The first sentence refers to an *activity* which started in the past and continues until now.

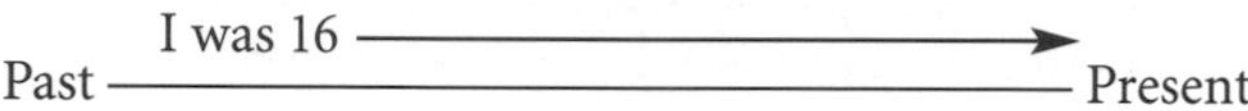

The second sentence refers to the *number* smoked during a period of time up to now.

x? x? x? x? x?
Past ——————————————— Present

Refer students to Grammar Reference 13.1 on p142.

4 **T 13.2** Ask students to work in pairs to make questions. Do the first two as an example with the class to show students that a number of different tenses are needed. When they are ready, play the recording so that they can check and correct their questions.

Answers and tapescript

- How long **have you been** trying to find a job?
- How many jobs **have you** had?
- How long **have you been** standing here today?
- How **did you** lose your business?
- How long **have you** had your dog?
- Who**'s your** best friend?
- Where **did you** meet him?
- How long **have you** known each other?

Play and pause the recording for students to repeat or drill the questions round the class. Pay close attention to the weak pronunciation of *have* /əv/ and *been* /bɪn/ in the Present Perfect questions.

5 **T 13.3** Students work in pairs to ask the questions and invent Andy's answers. Play the recording so that students can compare their answers.

Answers and tapescript

A How long have you been trying to find a job?
B **For three years. It's been really difficult.**
A How many jobs have you had?
B **About thirty, maybe more. I've done everything.**
A How long have you been standing here today?
B **Since 8.00 this morning, and I'm freezing.**
A How did you lose your business?
B **I owed a lot of money in tax, and I couldn't pay it.**
A How long have you had your dog?
B **I've had her for about two months, that's all.**
A Who's your best friend?
B **A chap called Robbie, who's also from Scotland, like me.**
A Where did you meet him?
B **I met him here in London.**
A How long have you known each other?
B **About ten months. I met him soon after I came to London.**

PRACTICE (SB p103)

Discussing grammar

1 Students work in pairs or small groups to choose the correct verb form. Do the first one as a class as an example. Expect students to make mistakes with this exercise, and tell them not to worry. As you correct, remind them of the rules.

Answers

1 **have you been living** (because the activity began in the past and continues to the present)
2 **has found** (because this is a completed activity – the action of *finding* doesn't last a long time, unlike *look for*)
3 **have been going out** (because the activity began in the past and continues to the present)
4 **bought** (because we have a definite time – a few months ago)
5 **have you had** (because *have* to express possession is a state verb, not an activity, so it cannot go into the continuous)
6 **has been working** (because he is still working as a postman)
7 **'ve been writing** (The sentence is stressing the continuous activity, not the fact that the essay is written. It may or may not be finished.)
8 **'ve written** (The continuous is not possible because the quantity (six) is stated.)

Talking about you

2 Ask students to work in pairs to do this exercise. Check the answers then drill the questions. Ask the questions round the class. Finally, put students in pairs to interview each other using the questions.

Answers
1 How long **have** you **been coming** to this school?
2 How long **have** you **used** this book?
3 Which book **did** you **have** before this one?
4 How long **have** you **known** your teacher?

What have they been doing?

3 This activity practises the other use of the Present Perfect Continuous to talk about present results of a past *activity*. It differs from the similar use of the Present Perfect Simple, practised in exercise 4, which is used to talk about results of a completed past *action*, and tends to be used when we say how many.

Read the introduction and look at the example sentence as a class. Students work in pairs to make a sentence about the people.

Sample answers
b His back hurts because he's been digging the garden.
c She's got paint on her clothes because she's been painting the bathroom.
d He's got dirty hands because he's been mending his car.
e They have no money because they've been shopping.
f They're tired because they've been playing tennis.
g Her eyes hurt because she's been studying.
h He's wet because he's been bathing the baby.
i He's got a red face because he's been cooking.

4 Students work in pairs to make sentences. Ask them why we use the Present Perfect here, (because we are talking about the completed action and we talk about how many).

Answers
1 He**'s run** five miles.
2 They**'ve spent** all their money.
3 She**'s read** five books today.
4 They**'ve played** six games.
5 He**'s made** a cake and a pie.

Getting information

5 In this information gap activity students must ask each other questions to find out about the famous Hollywood director, Steven Spielberg. In an activity of this kind the more preparation and setting up you do, the more likely that students will do it accurately and well.

Lead in by focusing students on the photograph of Spielberg and asking them questions to find out what they know about him.

Where is he from? Can you name any of his films? What are they about?

Photocopy the information cards on p127 of the Teacher's Book. Give half the class Student A cards, and half the class Student B cards. Ask them to read their information and check any words they don't know. Then ask them to work with a partner with the same card to prepare questions using the question word prompts. Monitor and help them prepare. When they are ready, change the pairs so that one Student A is with a Student B. Model the activity briefly by asking one or two questions, then let students ask and answer to complete their information.

COMPLETE TEXT
Steven Spielberg was born in Ohio. He is one of the most successful filmmakers of the late 20th century, and in his career he has earned millions of dollars. He has been making movies since 1961 when he made a war film, Escape to Nowhere. He was only 13. He studied English Literature at California State University then worked in the television division at Universal Studios in Hollywood for seven years. In 1975, he made Jaws, which was very successful, and made him rich and famous. Since then, he has made more than thirty films, including the box office hits Close Encounters of the Third Kind, Indiana Jones, ET, and Jurassic Park. He has also directed more serious movies, like Schindler's List and Saving Private Ryan, and he has produced a lot of hit films. In 1994, he formed a new Hollywood studio, Dreamworks.

Recently, Dreamworks has been working with Microsoft to produce interactive games and videos.

ADDITIONAL MATERIAL

Workbook Unit 13
Exercises 1–4 Present Perfect Simple
Exercises 5 and 6 Present Perfect Continuous
Exercises 7–9 Present Perfect Simple or Continuous?

VOCABULARY (SB p105)

Word formation

1 Ask students to work in pairs to complete the charts and mark the stress. Do one or two as an example. Ask students to guess what they think the missing word is before checking in the dictionary. These activities take longer to do than you might think because students have to use dictionaries to find the new word and its stress pattern.

Answers

Noun	**Verb**
death	**die**
waste	**waste**
be'lief	be'lieve
ad'vertisement	'advertise
'promise	**'promise**
'feeling	feel
ad'vice	**ad'vise**
de'scription	de'scribe
in'vention	**in'vent**
'government	**'govern**

Noun	**Adjective**
death	**dead**
'honesty	'honest
va'riety	**'various**
'madness	mad
'mystery	**my'sterious**
'beauty	'beautiful
wealth	'wealthy
suc'cess	**suc'cessful**
'comfort	'comfortable
peace	**'peaceful**

When you have the answers, ask several students to say the words, and correct any pronunciation mistakes.

POSSIBLE PROBLEMS

- In longer words, it is important to make the main stress strong, so that in comparison, the other syllables are unstressed. The most common sound in unstressed syllables is the schwa /ə/, of which there are many in the words in the box.
- Many learners of English find it hard to pronounce the word *ad'vertisement*. They want to put the stress on the third syllable. The situation is further confused by the stress on the verb (*'advertise*) being on the first syllable.

2 Ask students to work in pairs to complete the sentences.

Answers

1 Promise
2 dead
3 wealthy, successful
4 peace
5 advertisement
6 comfortable
7 description
8 advice
9 feeling

Students could follow up this activity by working in pairs to write sentences using some of the other words in the charts.

Adverbs

These two activities provide a further focus on adverbs, which were dealt with earlier in Unit 7.

Put students in pairs to complete the sentences.

1 **Answers**

1 Possibly
2 really
3 nearly
4 mainly

2 **Answers**

1 fluently
2 carefully
3 exactly
4 seriously

You could provide further practice by getting students to think of new sentences containing the adverbs.

READING AND SPEAKING (SB p106)

A funny way to earn a living

1 The aim of this game is to lead in to the topic and revise the vocabulary area of jobs. Do it as a class, or divide students into groups of five or six if you have a large class. If possible, get students to sit in a circle. One student says a job beginning with A, the next student repeats the same job beginning with A, and adds another beginning with B. It is a memory game. Be prepared to help with jobs for letters that students can't think of. Don't let this activity go on too long. If it begins to drag, stop it.

2 Discuss the questions as a class. This could lead to an interesting discussion in a multilingual class. It can be interesting to hear about other people's countries. You could extend this by writing some jobs on the board, for example, *doctor, teacher, nurse, coal miner, farmer, sales manager*, and asking students to discuss which jobs are most highly-paid, and which they think *should* be highly-paid and why.

NOTE

In Britain, the average salary is £20,000. Professional jobs such as doctors, dentists, and lawyers, are considered good jobs. Very highly-paid jobs exist in the financial sector, advertising and marketing. People working in the private sector often earn more than people working in the public sector.

3 Ask students to look at the pictures and headlines quickly and answer the questions. Discuss their answers briefly as a class. It doesn't matter if students don't have the right answers. The aim is to create context and raise interest.

Answers

1 Tom is really the only one who has a regular job with regular hours and a regular income.
2 All of them like their jobs.

3 *life* is a noun.
lively is an adjective meaning *full of life and energy.*
living is a noun which means *way of earning money with which to live.*

4 This is a jigsaw reading activity. Students decide which text they would like to read. Try to ensure that a more or less equal number of students read each text. Read through the questions with students, then let them read their text and answer the questions. Ask them to find somebody who has read the same text so that they can check their answers.

Answers
Life's a beach
1 Outdoors.
2 Seventeen years.
3 He's a beachcomber. He walks up and down beaches looking for things.
4 He was a policeman.
5 No. His life is rich in variety.
6 Not much. He doesn't need money.
7 His job allows him to live a simple, honest life, rich in variety. He has everything he wants.

Lively Tom skates for Tesco
1 Indoors.
2 Fifteen months.
3 He skates around the store fetching things for customers who have forgotten something.
4 He was a plumber.
5 No. Every day is different.
6 £4.50 an hour.
7 Because he likes helping and meeting people, and the job keeps him fit and busy.

Flying for a living
1 Outdoors.
2 Twelve years, (professionally).
3 She takes people on balloon trips.
4 She has only ever had one job.
5 No. She flies different balloons and never knows where she will land.
6 £25,000 a year.
7 She loves being in the countryside and hates routines, and she loves flying balloons.

5 Divide students into groups of three, each student having read a different text. They must work together to find the answers.

Answers
1 Cathy.
2 Probably Terry.
3 Chairs, tables, tins of food, a barrel of beer, and lots of bottles with messages in them.
4 Because they are more calm and authoritative when dealing with customers.
5 Since she was ten.
6 'You have to find a way to live a simple, honest life', and not chase money and things you don't need.
7 Because he thought they might not want older people, so he wanted to prove he was lively for his age.
8 Between 0 and 15 hours, depending on the weather.

In the feedback, ask students which of these jobs they would like and why.

What do you think?

Have a whole class discussion on this subject.Encourage students to give reasons for their answers.

Language work

Ask students to find five adverbs in the text about the beachcomber.

Answers
nearly (line 5)
mainly (line 8)
really (line 11)
actually (= in fact) (line 13)
possibly (line 19)

LISTENING AND SPEAKING (SB p108)

Giving news

This activity takes quite a while to do, as there are several parts to it. Students first listen to one side of a telephone conversation between Craig and his mother. They only hear Craig. Then they work in pairs to imagine what his mother said. Finally, they hear the complete conversation.

Because students have to think what the mother said, they need time to understand the nature of the activity. They then use the clues and their imagination to complete the conversation.

The conversation contains many examples of the Present Perfect Simple and Continuous.

This will provide students with further exposure to these two tenses, but when students are trying to imagine the mother's side of the conversation, it is not expected that they will always use the tenses accurately. When they have heard the complete conversation, you can draw their attention to the tenses.

Read the introduction together. If you have a multinational class, ask them if students in their country usually move to another part of the country when they go to university.

1 **T 13.4** Before they listen, ask students to read through the statements. Check that there are no problems of vocabulary. Students listen to Craig's side of the conversation.

Students work in pairs to decide if the statements are true or false. If they are false, ask students to say why.

Answers

1 We don't know. He doesn't say. He leaves work at eight o'clock every evening.
2 True.
3 False. He goes to the pub.
4 True (But Craig thinks he has told his mother about her.)
5 False. She lives near him.
6 True.
7 True.
8 False. He's been relaxing after his trip.
9 False. Next Tuesday.
10 False. They'll take her out for a meal.

Tapescript

T 13.4

C Hi Mum. It's me, Craig.
C Work's OK – I think. I'm just . . . so . . .
C I *am* tired, really tired. I've been working so hard and everything's so new to me. I'm in the office until eight o'clock every night.
C Yes, yes – I've been eating OK. After work, Tessa and I go out for a drink and something to eat in the pub round the corner. We're too tired to cook.
C Tessa? Yes, Tessa. I'm sure I've told you about Tessa. We work together in the same office – she's been working here for a while, so she's been helping me a lot. She's really nice. You'd like her mum, if you met her. She lives near me.
C Ah yes. Dad. How is he? What's he been doing recently?
C Oh, yes of course. He's been working in Amsterdam, hasn't he? Well, I'm glad he's relaxing now. And what about you, Mum?
C Next Tuesday. That's great! Of course you can stay at my flat. I'll try to leave work earlier that day and I'll meet you after the conference. You can meet Tessa, too. We'll go out for a meal.
C Me too. See you next week. Bye for now. Love to Dad!

2 **T 13.4** Play and pause the recording. Get a number of suggestions from various students as to what Craig's mother says after each sentence from Craig. Students should be trying to use the Present Perfect and the Present Perfect Continuous, so prompt this.

It is very important that you stop the recording at the right moment, so that students can work out from Craig's replies what his mother said. It doesn't matter whether they get the exact words, as long as their suggestions are logical.

Complete the first four or five gaps as a class, so that students see what they have to do. Stop the recording after *It's me, Craig.* and ask *What did his mother say?* (Something like *Hello*, or *How are you?*). Play the recording again, and stop after *I'm just … so …* . Ask *What did his mother say?* (It has to be *tired*). Continue to play and pause and take time to prompt answers. Once students have got the idea, you could ask them to write their answers then compare them in groups at the end.

If you think this activity might be too difficult for your class, you could give them a copy of the tapescript. Working from the written word would be easier than working from the spoken word. Make sure you give them the tapescript *without* the mother's words!

3 **T 13.5** Students listen to both sides of the conversation, and compare their ideas. This could be done as a class. You will need to be careful when accepting or rejecting students' suggestions. Try to correct their ideas for content and logic rather than language, as this is more of a fluency activity (both listening and speaking) than accuracy.

Tapescript

C Hi Mum. It's me, Craig.
M Craig! Hello! How lovely to hear from you. How are you? How's the new job going?
C Work's OK – I think. I'm just . . . so . . .
M Tired? You sound tired. Are you tired? What have you been doing?
C I *am* tired, really tired. I've been working so hard and everything's so new to me. I'm in the office until eight o'clock every night.
M Eight o'clock! Every night? That's terrible. And when do you eat? Have you been eating well?
C Yes, yes – I've been eating OK. After work, Tessa and I go out for a drink and something to eat in the pub round the corner. We're too tired to cook.
M Tessa? Who's Tessa?
C Tessa? Yes, Tessa. I'm sure I've told you about Tessa. We work together in the same office – she's been working here for a while, so she's been helping me a lot. She's really nice. You'd like her mum, if you met her. She lives near me.
M Mmm. Maybe you told your father about her, but not me. I've certainly never heard you talk about Tessa before.
C Ah yes. Dad. How is he? What's he been doing recently?
M Well, he's just returned from a business trip to Holland, so he hasn't been to work today, he's . . . he's been relaxing.
C Oh, yes of course. He's been working in Amsterdam, hasn't he? Well, I'm glad he's relaxing now. And what about you, Mum?
M Well, I was going to ring you actually. You see I'm coming to London next Tuesday. I'm going to a teachers' conference at the university, and I wondered if I could stay at your flat.
C Next Tuesday. That's great! Of course you can stay at my flat. I'll try to leave work earlier that day and I'll meet you after the conference. You can meet Tessa, too. We'll go out for a meal.
M Lovely! I'm looking forward to it already.
C Me too. See you next week. Bye for now. Love to Dad!
M Bye, Craig. Take care.

Language work

Students read the tapescript on p127 to find examples of the Present Perfect Simple and Continuous.

Roleplay

1 Depending on how you and your class feel after the listening activity, you might want this roleplay to last a short time or a long time, or you might decide to do it on another day. Here is a possible approach, which is best done on another day.

Photocopy the complete tapescript. (You could begin by using part of the recording as a dictation.)

Ask two students to start reading the text. Stop after *What have you been doing?* Ask students *What tense is this?* Ask the two readers to carry on, and ask the rest of the class to say *Stop!* when they find an example of the Present Perfect Simple or the Continuous.

Read the introduction to this activity in the Student's Book. Put the question *What have you been doing?* on the board. Remind students that it is Friday evening, and ask for some possible answers.

I've been watching TV.
We've been playing football.
I've been cooking.

Be careful with the suggestions you accept. The Present Perfect Continuous will not always be the right tense.

We've just had a meal.
I went to a party last night.

Ask for some other questions you might ask, and put them on the board.

What have your parents been doing?
What did you do last night? Did you go out?

2 Ask students to work in pairs to have a chat on the telephone. Finally, ask one or two pairs to have their conversation again so everyone can hear.

EVERYDAY ENGLISH (SB p109)

Telephoning

You need to photocopy tapescript **T 13.8** to do this section, and sufficient role cards for your class. They are on p128 of the Teacher's Book.

1 Tell students the following information about phone numbers in England.

Telephone numbers are said one by one. We don't put two together as many languages do. 71 is *seven one*, not *seventy-one*.

0 is pronounced /əʊ/.

Two numbers the same are usually said with *double*, for example, *double three*.

Practise the telephone numbers first as a class, then in pairs. This is to establish a correct model. Try to get a pause after each group of numbers.

Example

020 (pause) *7927* (pause) *4863*

T 13.6 Put students in pairs to practise the numbers then play the recording so that they can check. Play the recording a second time. Students listen and repeat.

2 **T 13.7** Students listen to the American phone numbers. The difference is that Americans say *zero*, *not O*, and say *two two*, etc, not *double two*.

Play the recording again. Students listen and repeat.

Tapescript
307 4922
1-800-878-5311
315 253 6031
517 592 2122
212 726 6390
1

3 **T 13.8** Students listen to the recording and answer the questions. Ask students to check their answers in pairs, then have the feedback.

Tapescript
P = Peter J = John
1 **P** Hello. 793422.
J Hello, Peter. This is John.
P Hi, John. How are you?
J Fine, thanks. And you?
P All right. Did you have a nice weekend? You went away, didn't you?
J Yes, we went to see some friends who live in the country. It was lovely. We had a good time.
P Ah, good.
J Peter, could you do me a favour? I'm playing squash tonight, but my racket's broken. Could I borrow yours?
P Sure, that's fine.
J Thanks a lot. I'll come and get it in half an hour, if that's OK.
P Yes, I'll be in.
J OK. Bye.
P Bye.
A = Receptionist B = Student C = Ann, a teacher
2 **A** Good morning. International School of English.
B Hello, could I speak to Ann Baker, please?
A Hold on. I'll connect you.
C Hello.
A Hello. Can I speak to Ann Baker, please?
C Speaking.
A Ah, hello. I saw your advertisement about English classes in a magazine. Could you send me some information, please?

C Certainly. Can I just take some details? Could you give me your name and address, please?

A = Mike's flatmate B = Jim

3 **A** Hello.
B Hello. Is that Mike?
A No, I'm afraid he's out at the moment. Can I take a message?
B Yes, please. Can you say that Jim phoned, and I'll try again later. Do you know what time he'll be back?
A In about an hour, I think.
B Thanks. Goodbye.
A Goodbye.

Answers

1 Peter is speaking to John.
John wants to borrow a squash racket.
They know each other well.

2 A Japanese boy speaks first to a telephonist, then to Ann Baker.
The boy wants some information about English classes.
They don't know each other.

3 Jim speaks to a friend of Mike's.
Jim wants to speak to Mike, but Mike isn't in.
Jim doesn't seem to know the man he talks to.

1 Read through the expressions in the Caution box as a class.

2 Complete the expressions as a class.

Answers
Could I **speak to** Ann Baker?
I'm afraid he's out at the moment.
Can I take **a message**?
I'll **call** later.

Drill the expressions around the class.

Answers

3 *Hold on. I'll connect you* is what a telephonist says when he or she is putting you through to the extension you want. *Hold on* means *Wait*.
We say *Speaking* when someone asks to speak to, say, Mrs Black, and *you* are Mrs Black.

4 Ask students to look at the tapescript on p128 of the Student's Book and practise the dialogues in pairs.

5 There are six role cards. **A** works with **B**, **C** with **D**, and **E** with **F**. Make sure you get your sums right when you are deciding how many copies to make! Every **A** needs a **B**, every **C** needs a **D**, and every **E** needs an **F**. If you have an odd number of students, you will have to take a role yourself. Give out the cards and let students prepare on their own. Say you will give them a role card which tells them who they are and who's phoning who. On each one, there are decisions to be made. Give an example from **A**'s card: *You are at home. It's 7.00 in the evening. What are you doing? Watching TV? Reading? Doing your homework?*

When you feel students are ready, ask the **A**s to find a **B**, the **C**s to find a **D**, and the **E**s to find an **F**. They can do the roleplay standing up. Remind them that **A**, **C**, and **E** must start the conversation.

When they have finished, ask two or three pairs to do their roleplay again in front of the class so everyone can hear. It's a nice idea to put two chairs back to back when doing this, so students can't see each other's lips and have to rely on what they hear.

Don't forget!

Workbook Unit 13

Exercise 10 is a vocabulary exercise which revises many of the phrasal verbs students have met in *New Headway Pre-Intermediate.*

Exercises 11 and 12 Students are asked to write a formal or informal letter.

Pronunciation book Unit 13

Word list

Photocopy the Word list for Unit 13 (TB p159) for your students, and ask them to write in the translations, learn them at home, and/or write some of the words into their vocabulary notebook.

Video

Report (Section 11) ***The Village*** This is a short documentary showing how life has changed in rural Britain over the last 50 years.

Past Perfect
Reported statements
Saying goodbye

Love you and leave you

Introduction to the unit

The theme of this unit is love. In the first presentation, students read an extract from a popular romance, and examine the Past Perfect in relation to the Past Simple. In the second presentation, reported statements are practised. The link between the Past Perfect and reported speech is that the Past Perfect is used in reporting past tense verb forms.

In the *Reading and speaking* section, students read an adaptation of a story by Arnold Bennett about two quarrelling brothers. In the *Vocabulary and listening* section, students listen to a Bruce Springsteen song, *Talk to me.*

Language aims

Grammar – Past Perfect All perfect tenses (Present Perfect, Past Perfect, and Future Perfect) express the idea of an action being completed before a certain time. The Present Perfect expresses an action which happened before now; the Past Perfect expresses an action which happened before another action in the past. Neither the form nor the concept of the Past Perfect present learners with any great difficulty, and there are equivalents in many European languages. There are none of the complexities of use that confront students with the Present Perfect.

However, students still need to perceive the relationship between the Past Simple and the Past Perfect, and to understand when the latter tense is needed to show one action finished before another one started. There is also the problem that *'d* is the contracted form of both *would* and *had*, and there are exercises to practise this in the Student's Book and the Pronunciation book.

Reported statements Tense usage in reported speech is relatively straightforward and logical, and comparable systems exist in many European languages. Students need to perceive the mechanics of 'one tense back'. This unit does not go into areas such as *here* changing to *there*, and *yesterday* changing to *the day before*, or any of the occasions when the verb form does not shift one tense back in reported speech. However, it does look at the difference between *say* and *tell*, which is often confused as this distinction does not exist in many languages.

Common mistake
**Hc said me that he loved me.*

Everyday English As this is the final activity in *New Headway Pre-Intermediate*, the *Everyday English* section practises different ways of saying goodbye.

Notes on the unit

STARTER (SB p110)

This starter is a chain story which aims to revise present and past tenses introduced on this course so far, and to contextualize and introduce the Past Perfect.

Ask students to work in pairs to match the lines.

Answers
They met each other a long time ago.
They've known each other for a long time.
They see each other every week.
They were living in New York when they met.
They had never been to New York before.

A LOVE STORY (SB p110)

Past Perfect

SUGGESTION

This is probably the first time your students have been formally introduced to the Past Perfect, although they may well have come across it in their reading, and it has been used occasionally in previous units of *New Headway Pre-Intermediate.* You might want to present the tense yourself before beginning this unit. Here is one possible deductive approach.

Write the following two sentences on the board.

When we arrived, Anna made some coffee.
When we arrived, Anna had made some coffee.

Ask students the following questions:

What are the tenses in the first sentence? (both Past Simple)
Which action happened first, ***we arrived*** *or* ***Anna made some coffee****?* (we arrived)

You could ask similar questions about the second sentence if you think students might know the answer, or you might choose to tell them.

In the second sentence, *had made* is the Past Perfect. It is used to show that one action happened before another action in the past. So in the second sentence, *Anna made some coffee before we arrived.*

The Past Perfect is formed with the auxiliary verb *had* and the past participle.

You could put the following on the board.

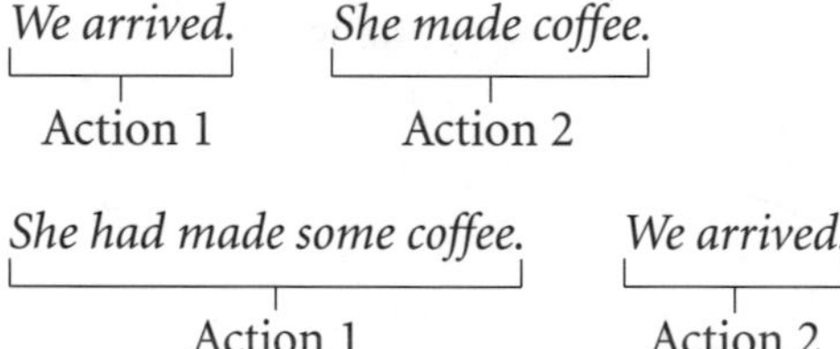
We arrived.
She made coffee.
Action 1
Action 2
She had made some coffee.
We arrived.
Action 1
Action 2

1 Ask students to look at the picture, and tell them they're going to read part of a popular romance. Ask *What sort of things happen in such stories?*

Read out or ask a student to read out version A, and then read version B. Ask students to work in pairs to compare the two versions. They might immediately spot that in version B the Past Perfect is used, or they might manage something such as *the order is different,* which is fine.

GRAMMAR SPOT (SB p111)

Answer the questions as a class. You might have to explain *chronological order.*

Answers

1 In the first text the story is in chronological order. All the verbs are in the Past Simple.

Answers

2 *They had met only one week earlier at a party and had fallen in love.*
Both the Past Simple and the Past Perfect are used.

Answers

3 *When we arrived, they were leaving.* (*was/were* + the present participle)
An activity in progress interrupted by a shorter event.

When we arrived, they left. (Past Simple)
A finished action in the past.
We arrived *then* they left. It happened in chronological order. (Perhaps they left because we arrived.)

When we arrived, they had left. (*had* + the past participle)
An action which happened before another action in the past.

Refer students to Grammar Reference 14.1 on p142.

2 **T 14.1** Ask students to underline examples of the Past Perfect as they listen to the recording. In the feedback, point out that the reader on the recording contracted *had* to *They'd* /ðeɪd/ and *Bradley had* /'brædli:(ə)d/.

Ask individual students to read out the text paying attention to contracted forms.

3 The aim of this exercise is to show students how the Past Perfect can be used to change the order in which events are given in a story. They must use the Past Perfect to explain the false statements.

Ask students to work in pairs to correct the statements.

Answers

1 False. When they got married, they had known each other for **a week**.
2 True.
3 False. They were angry because she **had got married before telling them** and Bradley **had moved into her flat**.
4 False. Bradley **had begun to behave strangely before** the marriage began to go wrong.

PRACTICE (SB p111)

Speaking

1 Students work in pairs to tell the story in the pictures. Stress the fact that they must do this first in chronological order. Ask *What tense will you use?* The answer is the Past Simple.

Sample answer
Bradley packed his suitcase. Then he wrote Saskia a note and left the flat. Saskia arrived home and saw the note on the mantelpiece.

2 Discuss this as a class.

Answer
The 'true' sentence is *When Saskia arrived home, Bradley had packed.* This is because Bradley packed the suitcase *before* she arrived home.

3 Now ask students to tell the story again, beginning at picture 4.

Sample answer
When Saskia arrived home, Bradley had already packed his case. He had written Saskia a note and had left the flat. She saw the note on the mantelpiece.

Grammar and pronunciation

4 Students work in pairs to make sentences from the chart. Do one or two as a class as an example.

Sample answers and tapescript
I was delighted because I'd passed all my exams.
I was hungry because I hadn't had any breakfast.
I went to bed early because I'd had a busy day.
Our teacher was angry because we hadn't done the homework.
My leg hurt because I'd fallen over playing football.
The plants died because I'd forgotten to water them.
The house was in a mess because we'd had a party the night before.

T 14.2 Play the recording so that students can check their answers. Then play and pause and ask students to repeat, paying attention to the contracted forms of *had ('d)* and *had not (hadn't)* /hædnt/.

5 **T 14.3** Read the introduction as a class. Ask students to listen and tick the sentences with *had*. Let them check in pairs before feedback. They may need to listen twice.

Answers and tapescript
1 ✗ 2 ✔ 3 ✗ (would) 4 ✔ 5 ✗ 6 ✗ (would) 7 ✔ 8 ✗
9 ✔ 10 ✗ (would)

T 14.3
1 When we arrived she left.
2 When we arrived she'd left.
3 She'd like to leave now.
4 We'd stopped playing when the rain started.
5 We stopped playing when the rain started.
6 We'd play tennis if the rain stopped.
7 He checked that he'd turned off his mobile phone.
8 He turned off the television and went to bed.
9 I couldn't believe that I'd lost my passport again.
10 If I lost my passport, I'd be very upset.

6 Ask students to work in pairs to put the verbs in brackets into the correct tense. They can complete the story in class or for homework.

Answer

1 read	6 had been
2 walked	7 had laughed
3 had bought	8 felt
4 threw	9 rang
5 had . . . done	

7 Read the happy ending as a class. Then put students in small groups to write what happened before. Stress that they must start their story with the happy ending which means that they will have to use the Past Perfect to refer back.

When students are ready, listen to the stories as a class and decide which stories they like.

Refer students to Grammar Reference 14.1 on p142 for homework.

ADDITIONAL MATERIAL

Workbook Unit 14
Exercises 1–4 practise the Past Perfect.

SUGGESTION
Your students might be tired of doing accuracy work, and might prefer to do some fluency work before beginning the second presentation. You could do the reading activity on p114.

WHAT DID SHE SAY? (SB p113)

Reported statements

1 **T 14.4** Ask students to listen and complete what Mary says. In the feedback, read them out one by one, and ask students to identify the tense.

Answers and tapescript
'I **love** John very much.'
'We **met** six months ago.'
'**I've never been** in love before.'
'We**'re** very happy.'
'**I'll love** him forever.'
'**I'm seeing** him this evening.'

2 **T 14.5** Play the recording. Students listen.

Tapescript
Mary told me that she loved John very much. She said that they'd met six months ago and that she'd never been in love before. She told me that they were very happy and that she'd love him forever. She said that she was seeing him that evening.

GRAMMAR SPOT (SB p113)

Answer the questions as a class.

Answers
1 Tenses move 'one back'.
2 *Say* is used *without* an object:
She said that she loved him.
Tell is used *with* an object:
She told me that she loved him.

Refer students to Grammar Reference 14.2 on p142.

3 Students practise the sentences. Insist that they use contracted forms.

SUGGESTION
Your students might enjoy some freer practice. Put students in groups of three. Give them three or four minutes to write down as many 'secrets' as they can think of. They don't have to be real. Give them a few ideas to start: *I love my teacher*, *I've met the Queen*, etc. Model the activity by whispering a 'secret' in a student's ear. They must pass on your secret using *He/She said …* or *He/She told me that …* Once they have the idea, let them take it in turns to pass on 'secrets'. In the feedback, find out what secrets they heard and correct any errors involving reported statements.

PRACTICE (SB p113)

An interview

1 **T 14.6** Look at the photograph of Carmen Day with students. Ask them to think of some questions they would like to ask Carmen. Read the introduction and play the recording. In the feedback, find out if students heard the answers to any of their questions.

Tapescript
I = Interviewer CD = Carmen Day
I Carmen, why have you written another romantic novel?
CD Because I find romantic fiction easy to write, but my next novel won't be a romance. I'm hoping to write something different, perhaps a detective story.
I In *One Short Hot Summer*, who is the character of Bradley based on?
CD Ah, well, he's based on my first husband, Clive Maingay, the actor. Clive made me very unhappy, very unhappy indeed.
I You say 'your first husband' – have you then remarried?
CD Yes, indeed. I've been married for nearly ten years to Tony Marsh, you know, the politician.
I Yes, I know him. And are you happy now?
CD Oh, yes. I can honestly say that I've found happiness again. Tony and I are very happy indeed.
I Carmen, how many novels have you written so far?
CD Well, I've written five novels now, and three stories for children.
I And when do you think you'll stop writing?
CD Never. I'll never stop. I'll continue to write even when I'm an old lady.

2 Ask students to work in pairs to complete the report of the interview. They may need to listen again or, if they find it difficult, they may need to look at the tapescript on p128 of the Student's Book.

T 14.7 Play the recording so that students can listen and check.

Answers and tapescript
In an interview Carmen said she (1) **had written** another romantic novel because she (2) **found** romantic fiction easy to write, but that her next novel (3) **would be** something different, possibly a detective story.
Carmen said that the character of Bradley (4) **was based** on her first husband, Clive Maingay, the actor, who (5) **had made** her very unhappy. But she added that she (6) **was** now married to Tony Marsh, the politician. She said that they (7) **had been** married for nearly ten years and that they (8) **were** very happy together.
She told me that she (9) **had** now **written** five novels, and also that she (10) **had written** three stories for children. She said she (11) **would** never stop writing, not even when she (12) **was** an old lady.

Check it

3 Ask students to work in pairs to report the statements. Alternatively, you could set this for homework.

Answers

1 Jim said (that) he liked Anna.
2 Anna said (that) she was staying with her aunt.
3 Sue said (that) Mr Walker had phoned before lunch. She said (added)(that) he hadn't left a message.
4 Ken said he didn't think it would rain.
5 Sue said (that) Ken had gone home. She said (added) (that) he had gone early.
6 Anna told Jim (that) she would ring him *that* evening.

Refer students to Grammar Reference 14.2 on p142 for homework.

ADDITIONAL MATERIAL

Workbook Unit 14
Exercises 5 and 6 practise reported speech.
Exercises 7 practises the verbs *say* and *tell*.

READING AND SPEAKING (SB p114)

The tale of two silent brothers

1 Lead in to the topic by reading the introduction in Student's Book and asking the question. You could extend this by asking students to think of reasons why family feuds might start: *two people in love with the same person, an argument over money, a disagreement over a will, something hurtful that someone said.*

You could brainstorm the interesting vocabulary area involved here: *argue, quarrel, row; have a quarrel/ argument/row; take revenge, (kiss and) make up; a family feud.*

2 Ask students to work in pairs to match the verbs and phrases.

Answers

get revenge
make a will
have a quarrel
see a solicitor about something
remain a bachelor all his life
toss a coin
kiss and make up

3 Ask students to look at the picture. Ask them why they think the two old men aren't speaking, thus creating a prediction task for the reading. Students read the first part of the story. (They aren't speaking because they had had a quarrel ten years earlier.)

What do you think?

Ask students to discuss the questions with a partner. Get feedback, but don't tell them the answers, of course.

Answers

The brothers quarrelled about a woman, Annie Emery, and, in the will, their sister leaves the money to the brother who will marry Annie.

Discuss the questions as a class. Try to get as many different potential solutions as you can.

4 Ask students to read part two and find out which students were correct.

What do you think?

Discuss the questions as a class.

5 Ask students to read part three and find out which students were closest to the actual story. Check that they understand *toss a coin* and *heads or tails.*

Answer

The brothers made up and tossed a coin to decide who would marry Annie. But in the end Annie married somebody else.

What do you think?

Ask students to work in pairs or small groups to discuss the questions. In the feedback, get students' ideas, then read out what actually happened (printed below), and find out which students were closest to the actual story.

What actually happened

Annie refuses to marry either of the brothers because they treated her so badly and behaved so stupidly by not talking to each other. She married the solicitor Mr Powell Liversage, but she did not keep the £12,000 that Mary left her. She gave it to John and Robert to share.

Language work

Ask students to work in pairs to complete the sentences. Make sure they are using the Past Perfect correctly.

Sample answers

1 . . . they had had an argument.
2 . . . their older sister Mary had died.
3 . . . had left a will.
4 . . . they had both behaved stupidly and had been cruel and unfair to Annie.
5 . . . had been in love with her.
6 . . . they had waited so long to make up their minds.

LISTENING AND VOCABULARY (SB p116)

A song – *Talk to me*

Exploit this song for fun. It is by the popular American singer/songwriter Bruce Springsteen.

1 **T 14.8** Ask students to guess what they think the song might be about from the title, *Talk to me*. Play the recording and ask students what they think it is about.

2 Ask students to complete the song in pairs. Do the first couple of lines as a class to get them started.

Answers and tapescript

Well every night I see a **light** up in your window
But every night you won't **answer** the door
But although you won't **ever** let me in
From the street I can see your **silhouette** sitting close to him

What must I do?
What does it take
To get you to
Talk to me
Until the night is over
Talk to me

Well until the night is over, yeah yeah yeah
I got a full week's **pay**
And baby I've been working hard **all** day
I'm not **asking** for the world, you see
I'm just asking, girl
Talk to me

Well late at night I hear music that you're playing **soft** and low
Yes and late at night I see the two of you **swaying,** so close
I don't understand darling, what was my **sin?**
Why am I down here below **while** you're up there with him?

What did I do?
What did I say?
What must I pay
to get you to
to talk to me . . .

3 When they are ready play the song again so that they can check their answers. If your students like singing you could play it one more time for them to sing along.

EVERYDAY ENGLISH (SB p117)

Saying goodbye

1 Ask students to work together to match the sentences with the photos.

Answers

1c 2h 3e 4b 5g 6d 7a 8f

2 **T 14.9** Students listen to the sentences and check their answers. Ask students to work in pairs to practise saying the sentences.

3 In pairs, ask students to prepare short conversations for the situations. Let some pairs act out one of their conversations for the class.

SUGGESTED IDEAS

- Goodbye. Make sure you keep in touch. Look after yourself.
- Goodbye. I've really enjoyed the holiday.
- Goodbye. Have a nice weekend.
- Goodbye. Thank you for everything. /Keep in touch.

Don't forget!

Workbook Unit 14

Exercise 8 is a vocabulary exercise on words that are often confused, e.g. *say* and *tell*, *lend* and *borrow*.

Exercise 9 Students are given the beginning and ending of a story, and are asked to write the middle.

Pronunciation book Unit 14

Word list

Photocopy the Word list for Unit 14 (TB p159) for your students, and ask them to write in the translations, learn them at home, and/or write some of the words into their vocabulary notebook.

Video

Situation (Section 12) ***Farewell*** Paola and David say goodbye to David's parents, and then go to Padstow harbour for an emotional farewell scene. Students practise saying goodbye.

Progress test 3

There is a Progress test for Units 11–14 on p144 of the Teacher's Book.

EXTRA IDEAS UNITS 13–14

On p129 of the Teacher's Book there is a song, *Sitting on the dock of the bay*, and suggested activities to exploit it. If you have time and feel that your students would benefit from it, photocopy the song and use it in class. You will find the song after Unit 14 on the Class Cassette/CD. The answers to the activities are on p147 of the Teacher's Book.

Stop and check 4 (TB p136)
It's time for the final revision.

A suggestion for approaching the *Stop and check* tests is in the introduction on p5 of the Teacher's Book.

Photocopiable material

UNITS 1–14

Unit 1 **Getting information** (SB p8)

Student A

Joy Darling started working as a postwoman ... *(When?)*. She drives a van because she delivers letters to a lot of small villages.

She gets up at ... *(What time?)* and starts work at 5.00. Every day she drives about ... miles *(How many miles?)*. She finishes work at 2.00 in the afternoon.

After work she goes ... *(Where?)* and has lunch with her husband, Jim. He has a part-time job. He works ... *(Where?)*. They like gardening, so they spend the afternoon outside in their garden.

They have ... children *(How many?)*, who both live in California. Last year Joy and Jim went ... *(Where?)* and visited their children and four grandchildren. They stayed for ... *(How long?)*.

They're going to Australia next month because ... *(Why?)*. It's their friends' wedding anniversary, and they want everyone to be there.

Student B

Joy Darling started working as a postwoman thirty years ago, when she was 22. She drives a van because ... *(Why?)*.

She gets up at 3.30 in the morning and starts work at ... *(When?)*. Every day she drives about 150 miles. She finishes work at ... *(What time?)*.

After work she goes home and has lunch with ... *(Who ... with?)*. He has a part-time job. He works in a shop. They like ... *(What ... like doing?)*, so they spend the afternoon outside in their garden.

They have two children, who both live in ... *(Where?)*. Last year Joy and Jim went to Los Angeles and visited ... *(Who?)*. They stayed for a month.

They're going ... *(Where?)* next month because some friends are having a big party. ... *(Why?)*

Unit 2 **Getting information** (SB p16)

Student B

Name and age	Town and country	Family	Occupation	Free time/holiday	Present activity
Mike, 26	Vancouver, Canada	a sister	works for a computer company	• skiing, ice hockey • Europe	playing ice hockey
Lucy, 38	Perth, Scotland	a son and a daughter	part-time teacher	• reading, going to the cinema • Spain or Greece	washing the dishes
Nicole, 15					
Jeff, 54, and **Wendy**, 53					

Student B

Name and age	Town and country	Family	Occupation	Free time/holiday	Present activity
Mike, 26	Vancouver, Canada	a sister	works for a computer company	• skiing, ice hockey • Europe	playing ice hockey
Lucy, 38	Perth, Scotland	a son and a daughter	part-time teacher	• reading, going to the cinema • Spain or Greece	washing the dishes
Nicole, 15					
Jeff, 54, and **Wendy**, 53					

Unit 3 **Getting information** (SB p25)

Student A

Mr and Mrs Harman arrived home at … *(When?)*. Zoë was staying with friends. She felt … *(How?)* because her parents would be furious with her.

Her parents started to … *(What?)*. Then they phoned Zoë and told her … *(What?)*.

Zoë got back home at two in the morning. She said … *(What?)* and she promised that she would never have another party.

Student B

Mr and Mrs Harman arrived home at 10.30 in the evening. Zoë was staying … *(Where?)*. She felt terrible because … *(Why?)*.

Her parents started to clean the house. Then they phoned … *(Who?)* and told her to come home immediately.

Zoë got back home at … *(What time?)*. She said she was very sorry and she promised … *(What?)*.

Student A

Mr and Mrs Harman arrived home at … *(When?)*. Zoë was staying with friends. She felt … *(How?)* because her parents would be furious with her.

Her parents started to … *(What?)*. Then they phoned Zoë and told her … *(What?)*.

Zoë got back home at two in the morning. She said … *(What?)* and she promised that she would never have another party.

Student B

Mr and Mrs Harman arrived home at 10.30 in the evening. Zoë was staying … *(Where?)*. She felt terrible because … *(Why?)*.

Her parents started to clean the house. Then they phoned … *(Who?)* and told her to come home immediately.

Zoë got back home at … *(What time?)*. She said she was very sorry and she promised … *(What?)*.

Student A

Mr and Mrs Harman arrived home at … *(When?)*. Zoë was staying with friends. She felt … *(How?)* because her parents would be furious with her.

Her parents started to … *(What?)*. Then they phoned Zoë and told her … *(What?)*.

Zoë got back home at two in the morning. She said … *(What?)* and she promised that she would never have another party.

Student B

Mr and Mrs Harman arrived home at 10.30 in the evening. Zoë was staying … *(Where?)*. She felt terrible because … *(Why?)*.

Her parents started to clean the house. Then they phoned … *(Who?)* and told her to come home immediately.

Zoë got back home at … *(What time?)*. She said she was very sorry and she promised … *(What?)*.

Extra ideas Units 1–4

Song

1 You are going to read and listen to a song called *Sailing*. It is a love song. Look at the words below, which come from the song, and guess what the song is about.

stormy waters	*high clouds*
dark night	*to be with you*

2 Match the four phrases on the left with the three phrases on the right.

I am sailing I am trying I am flying I am dying	across the sea to be near you to be with you

3 Read the song and complete the lines with *-ing* forms of the verbs below.

die   sail   fly   pass   try

4 Listen to the song and check your answers to exercises 1, 2, and 3.

5 Write your own song. Use the prompts below.

I am driving …	I am cycling …
I am driving …	I am cycling …
… to be …	… to be …
… to be…	… to be …

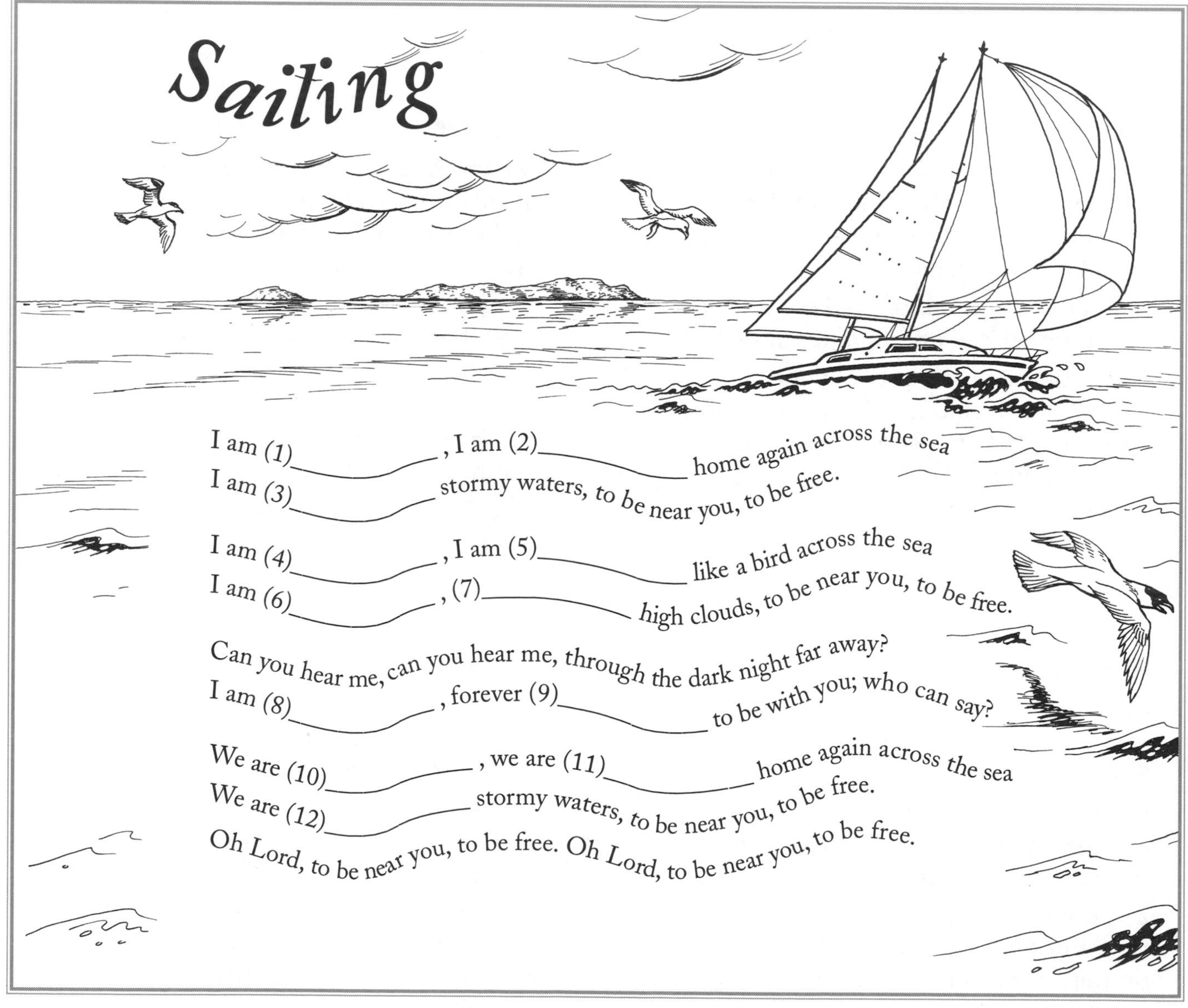

Sailing
I am (1)________, I am (2)________ home again across the sea
I am (3)________ stormy waters, to be near you, to be free.
I am (4)________, I am (5)________ like a bird across the sea
I am (6)________, (7)________ high clouds, to be near you, to be free.
Can you hear me, can you hear me, through the dark night far away?
I am (8)________, forever (9)________ to be with you; who can say?
We are (10)________, we are (11)________ home again across the sea
We are (12)________ stormy waters, to be near you, to be free.
Oh Lord, to be near you, to be free. Oh Lord, to be near you, to be free.

Unit 6 Comparing four capital cities (SB p48)

Student A

Paris (Île de France)

Founded	990	
Population	10,500,000	
Area	12,012 km2	
Temperatures	Jan: 4°C	July: 20°C
Rainfall	Jan: 56 mm	July: 59 mm
Km from the sea	150	

Beijing

Founded	1272 BC	
Population	10,819,000	
Area	16,808 km2	
Temperatures	Jan: –4°C	July: 26°C
Rainfall	Jan: 4 mm	July: 250 mm
Km from the sea	180	

Stockholm

Founded	________	
Population	________	
Area	________	
Temperatures	________	________
Rainfall	________	________
Km from the sea	________	

Brasilia

Founded	________	
Population	________	
Area	________	
Temperatures	________	________
Rainfall	________	________
Km from the sea	________	

Student B

Paris (Île de France)

Founded	________	
Population	________	
Area	________	
Temperatures	________	________
Rainfall	________	________
Km from the sea	________	

Beijing

Founded	________	
Population	________	
Area	________	
Temperatures	________	________
Rainfall	________	________
Km from the sea	________	

Stockholm

Founded	1250	
Population	880,100	
Area	6,488 km2	
Temperatures	Jan: –3°C	July: 18°C
Rainfall	Jan: 43 mm	July: 61 mm
Km from the sea	0	

Brasilia

Founded	1960	
Population	1,492,500	
Area	5,814 km2	
Temperatures	Jan: 20°C	July: 19°C
Rainfall	Jan: 94 mm	July: 46 mm
Km from the sea	600	

Find someone who . . . (SB p55)

Find someone who has been to China.	Find someone who has been to Portugal.	Find someone who has written a love letter.
Find someone who has been to Australia.	Fine someone who has been skiing.	Find someone who has had a party for more than thirty people.
Find someone who has tried Thai food.	Find someone who has flown in a balloon.	Find someone who has been horse-riding.
Find someone who has climbed a mountain.	Find someone who has won a competition.	Find someone who has been sailing.
Find someone who has read a book by a British author.	Find someone who has broken a bone.	Find someone who has been wind-surfing.
Find someone who has had an adventure holiday.	Find someone who has been to university.	Find someone who has lost something important.
Find someone who has been to Ireland.	Find someone who has worked on a farm.	Find someone who has never failed an exam.

Extra ideas Units 5–8

Reading and speaking

How ambitious are you?

1 Answer the questions from the questionnaire below and add up your score to find out how ambitious you are! Use your dictionary if necessary.

2 Do you agree with the interpretations?

3 Choose one of the questions.
Stand up and ask all the other students your question.
Then report back to the class.

Everybody thinks …
Nobody wants …
Most of us would like …
Some people hope … but others don't want …

How ambitious are you?

1 In ten years do you hope to
- a be married with a family?
- b have an interesting but not very well-paid job?
- c have a well-paid job that isn't very interesting?

2 In twenty years' time do you hope to
- a have enough money to pay your bills?
- b have quite a lot of money?
- c have a lot of money?

3 Here is a list of ten jobs. Which would you like to do? Put 1 next to your favourite, 2 next to your next favourite, etc.

nurse builder accountant journalist teacher artist politician engineer policeman/woman actor/actress/pop star

4 Is improving your standard of living important to you?

5 Do you think people who have money should help people who don't have money?

6 How old do you want to be when you have children?
- a 18–22
- b 23–26
- c 27–30
- d over 30

7 When you are playing a game, do you always want to win?

8 Can you tell a white lie?

9 Do you think that rich people are happier and more interesting than other people?

10 Do you work hard because you want to be successful?

11 If you have a job to do, do you do it immediately, or do you wait until the last moment?

12 Would you like to have more money than your parents?

13 Do you agree with the philosophy 'Every man for himself'?

14 Do you like hard work?

15 Which of the following is most important to you?
love happiness money health

Answers

1 a 0 b 5 c 10
2 a 0 b 5 c 10
3 0 nurse/artist first
2 builder/policeman or policewoman teacher/journalist first
5 engineer/actor or actress/pop star first
10 politician/accountant first
4 Yes 10 No 0
5 Yes 0 No 10
6 a 0 b 2 c 5 d 10
7 Yes 10 No 0
8 Yes 10 No 0
9 Yes 10 No 0
10 Yes 10 No 0
11 Immediately 10 Last moment 0
12 Yes 10 No 0
13 Yes 10 No 0
14 Yes 10 No 0
15 Love 0 Happiness 5 Money 10 Health 0

0–50 **You aren't very ambitious! You're happy with a quiet life.**
50–100 **You're quite ambitious, but you don't want to work too hard!**
Over 100 **You're very ambitious! Good luck, and try to be nice to people …**

Extra ideas Units 5–8

Song

1 You are going to read and listen to a song called *Killing me softly with his song*. Look at the picture, the title, and the opening lines of the song.

Strumming my pain with his fingers,
singing my life with his words,
killing me softly with his song …

What do you think the song is about? Do you think it is a romantic song? Is it a sad song?

2 Match the verbs and nouns.

1	strum	a	a story
2	sing	b	a song
3	tell	c	a prayer
4	read	d	a guitar
5	say	e	a letter

3 Look at the three verses of the song and put the lines in the correct order. The first line of each verse is given to you.

Killing me softly with his song

[1] *I heard he sang a good song,*
[ ] *to listen for a while.*
[ ] *A stranger to my eyes*
[ ] *I heard he had a style.*
[ ] *And so I came to see him*
[ ] *And there he was this young boy,*

[1] *I felt all flushed with fever,*
[ ] *and read each one out loud.*
[ ] *embarrassed by the crowd.*
[ ] *I felt he'd found my letters*
[ ] *but he just kept right on*
[ ] *I prayed that he would finish*

[1] *He sang as if he knew me*
[ ] *singing clear and strong*
[ ] *and then he looked right through me*
[ ] *as if I wasn't there.*
[ ] *in all my dark despair,*
[ ] *But he just kept on singing,*

4 Listen to the song and check your answers.

5 The singer and the song spoke directly to the woman. It said something about her life and her feelings. What do you think it was? Can you think of a song that has meant a lot to you?

Extra ideas Units 9–12

Reading and speaking

The dream game

1 Work in small groups and discuss the following:
   1 Did you dream last night? Can you remember what you dreamt about?
   2 Do you often dream? Do you often have the same dream? Describe your memorable dreams.
   3 Do you think dreams are important? If so, why?

2 Playing the dream game
   1 Play the dream game in pairs or small groups. Take turns to read the questions aloud. Make a note of your answers, then compare them. Use a dictionary if necessary.
   2 Read the interpretation.

3 Discuss with the whole class. Do you agree or disagree with the interpretation of your personality?

Play the dream game

1 You are asleep and you are dreaming. In your dream you find yourself in your perfect house. What is it like? Describe it in detail.

2 Now you are walking along a narrow path. Suddenly you find a cup/glass/drinking vessel on the ground in front of you. What is it like? What is in it?

3 Now the path ends and you are walking in a wood. You walk quite a long way until you find a clearing. In the middle of the clearing is a building. What sort of building is it?

4 Around the building is a garden. Describe the garden.

5 You walk out of the garden and through the wood. At the edge of the wood there is a wall. The wall is too high to climb over, and it is too long to walk round. Suddenly you notice a small door in the wall. It slowly opens as you watch. What do you do? Do you go through the door?

6 On the other side of the wall is water. What does it look like? Do you want to swim in it?

Interpretation

Now read about what the images represent and try to analyse your answers.

★ The house
The house is your idea of yourself. If your house is old, you probably do not like change, you like traditional things. If your house is large, it means you are quite confident, with a high opinion of yourself. If it is filled with light, you are optimistic. If it is dark, you are pessimistic. The number of rooms is the number of people you want in your life.

★ The cup
The cup is your idea of love. The more beautiful and valuable the cup, the more important love is in your life. You are a romantic person. The contents of the cup show what your experience of love has been so far.

★ The building
The building is your idea of religion and God. A strong building is a strong belief. A ruin would mean a lack of belief.

★ The garden
This is your idea of the world around you, your country, or the whole world. If the plants and flowers in your garden are dying, this might mean that you are worried about the environment and pollution in the world.

★ The wall
This is your idea of death. Is it the end or is there something after it? Do you go straight through the little door? Do you look and check before you go? Or don't you want to go through at all?

★ The water
The water is your idea of your future. If there is a sea with big waves, you feel positive and excited about your future. If you want to swim, you feel confident and want to take risks. If the water is a stagnant pool, you might fear your future and the future of the world.

Extra ideas Units 9–12

Song

1 You are going to read and listen to a song called *I'll be there for you*. It is a song about friendship. Which is the best synonym for the phrase *I'll be there for you*?

1 I will go to a place instead of you
2 I will always love and support you
3 I will be there on time and waiting for you to arrive

2 Match these other words and phrases from the song with their synonyms.

1	you're broke	a	it has defeated you
2	you're stuck in second gear	b	nothing has gone right for you
3	it hasn't been your day	c	you're not making any progress
4	it has brought you down to your knees	d	you haven't got any money

3 Read the song then look at the words in *italics*. Underline the words in the song that you think the words in *italics* could replace. Listen to the song and check your answers.

I'll be there for you

So no one told you work was gonna be this way. (1) *life*
Your job's a disaster, you're broke, (2) *joke*
Your social life's gone away. (3) *love*
It's like you're always stuck in second gear,
Now it hasn't been your day, your week, (4) *when*
Your month, or even your year.

But I'll be there for you,
When the rain starts to fall, (5) *pour*
I'll be there for you.
You know I've been around before (6) *there*
I'll be there for you,
'Cause you're there for me as well. (7) *too*

You're still at home at ten, and work began at eight, (8) *in bed*
You've burned your toast, (9) *breakfast*
So far, things aren't going well, (10) *great*
Your mother warned you, 'There'll be moments like these,' (11) *days*
But she didn't tell you when
Life has brought you down to your knees. (12) *the world*

Unit 13 **Getting information** (SB p104)

Student A

Steven Spielberg was born in ... (*Where?*). He is one of the most successful filmmakers of the late 20th century, and in his career he has earned millions of dollars. He has been making movies since ...(*How long?*) when he made a war film, *Escape to Nowhere*. He was only 13. He studied English Literature at California State University then worked ... (*Where?*) for seven years.

In 1975, he made *Jaws*, which was very successful, and made him rich and famous. Since then, he has made more than thirty films, including the box office hits *Close Encounters of the Third Kind*, *Indiana Jones*, *ET*, and *Jurassic Park*. He has also directed more serious movies, like ... (*Which movies?*), and he has produced a lot of hit films. In 1994, he formed ... (*What?*). Recently, *Dreamworks* has been working with Microsoft to produce interactive games and videos.

Student B

Steven Spielberg was born in Ohio. He is one of the most successful filmmakers of the late 20th century, and in his career he has earned ... (*How much?*). He has been making movies since 1961 when he made a war film, *Escape to Nowhere*. He was only 13. He studied ... (*What?*) at California State University then worked in the television division at Universal Studios in Hollywood for seven years.

In 1975, he made *Jaws*, which was very successful, and made him rich and famous. Since then, he has made ... (*How many?*) films, including the box office hits *Close Encounters of the Third Kind*, *Indiana Jones*, *ET*, and *Jurassic Park*. He has also directed more serious movies, like *Schindler's List* and *Saving Private Ryan*, and he has produced ... (*How many hit films?*). In 1994, he formed a new Hollywood studio, *Dreamworks*. Recently, *Dreamworks* has been working with ... (*Who...with?*) to produce interactive games and videos.

Student A

Steven Spielberg was born in ... (*Where?*). He is one of the most successful filmmakers of the late 20th century, and in his career he has earned millions of dollars. He has been making movies since ...(*How long?*) when he made a war film, *Escape to Nowhere*. He was only 13. He studied English Literature at California State University then worked ... (*Where?*) for seven years.

In 1975, he made *Jaws*, which was very successful, and made him rich and famous. Since then, he has made more than thirty films, including the box office hits *Close Encounters of the Third Kind*, *Indiana Jones*, *ET*, and *Jurassic Park*. He has also directed more serious movies, like ... (*Which movies?*), and he has produced a lot of hit films. In 1994, he formed ... (*What?*). Recently, *Dreamworks* has been working with Microsoft to produce interactive games and videos.

Student B

Steven Spielberg was born in Ohio. He is one of the most successful filmmakers of the late 20th century, and in his career he has earned ... (*How much?*). He has been making movies since 1961 when he made a war film, *Escape to Nowhere*. He was only 13. He studied ... (*What?*) at California State University then worked in the television division at Universal Studios in Hollywood for seven years.

In 1975, he made *Jaws*, which was very successful, and made him rich and famous. Since then, he has made ... (*How many?*) films, including the box office hits *Close Encounters of the Third Kind*, *Indiana Jones*, *ET*, and *Jurassic Park*. He has also directed more serious movies, like *Schindler's List* and *Saving Private Ryan*, and he has produced ... (*How many hit films?*). In 1994, he formed a new Hollywood studio, *Dreamworks*. Recently, *Dreamworks* has been working with ... (*Who...with?*) to produce interactive games and videos.

Student A

Phone number 322 4987

Information You're at home. It's 7.00 in the evening. You're watching TV. You've already done your homework. It was the vocabulary exercise on page 105 of *Headway Pre-Intermediate.*

Decision What are you doing for the rest of the evening? Going out? Staying in?

The phone call Your friend **B**, who's in the same class as you, is going to phone. When the phone rings, pick it up and say your number.

Student B

Information You're at home. It's 7.00 in the evening. It's time to do tonight's English homework, but you have a problem. You've forgotten what it is, and you've left your copy of *Headway Pre-Intermediate* at school. You're going to phone your friend **A**, who's in the same class.

Decision What are you doing for the rest of the evening? If you need to borrow a copy of *Headway Pre-Intermediate*, could you go round to **A**'s house? What time?

The phone call Phone **A**. **A** will start the conversation. Ask *How are you?* and have a little chat before you ask about the homework. Say *I've forgotten what tonight's homework is. Do **you** know?*

Student C

Phone number 899 0452

Information You're Mr/Mrs Carr, and you're English. You live in London. Your address is 22, Hill Road, and your house is about ten minutes from Highgate tube station, which is on the Northern Line. It's 7.00 in the evening. You're at home. Today is the 18th. Next week, on the 25th, Student **D**, Daniel/Denise, from France, is coming to stay at your house while he/she learns English for a month, but you don't know how he/she is travelling to London, or what time he/she expects to arrive.

Decision Are you going to meet **D** if he/she comes by plane? What about if he/she comes by train?

The phone call **D** is going to phone you. When the phone rings, pick it up and say your number. Ask questions such as *How are you?, Have you packed yet?* At the end of the conversation, say *We're looking forward to meeting you.*

Student D

Information You're French, and your name is Daniel/Denise. You live in Paris. Today is the 18th. Next week, on the 25th, you're going to England for a month to learn English. You're going to stay with Mr and Mrs Carr, who are English. They live in Highgate, which is in North London, but you don't know the exact address. You're going to phone them to tell them how you're travelling, and what time you expect to arrive.

Decision How are you going to travel? By plane? By boat and train? What time does the plane/train arrive? Do you want Mr/Mrs Carr to meet you? If you are going to get the tube to their house, you need to ask *Which is the nearest tube station?*

The phone call Phone **C**. **C** will start the conversation. Say *I'm phoning to tell you how I'm coming to London.* Don't forget to ask for the address.

Student E

Phone number 622 9087

Information You're at home in your flat, which you share with a girl called Marion. It's 7.00 in the evening. Marion is out at the moment.

Decision Where is Marion? When will she be back? Do you know what she's doing tonight, or not?

The phone call Someone is going to call. When the phone rings, pick it up and say your number. If it's for Marion, Say *Can I take a message?*

Student F

Information It's 7.00 in the evening. You want to talk to a friend of yours called Marion. It's very important, You've found a second-hand car that you think she'd like to buy.

Decision If she isn't in, are you going to leave a message? Are you going to phone back later, or do you want Marion to phone you? Are you in for the rest of the evening, or are you going out?

The phone call Phone Marion. The other person starts the conversation.

Extra ideas Units 13–14

Song

1 You are going to read and listen to a song called *Sitting on the dock of the bay.* Describe this man. Use your imagination. Where is he? What is he doing? Why is he there? What is he thinking about? Is he happy? Is he lonely? Why? Why not?

2 Do you know these words? *tide* *moon* *dock* *bay*

Where are Georgia and San Francisco ('Frisco) Bay?

3 Read the words of the first verse and choose the best word in *italics* to fill each gap. Listen to the song and check your answers then do the same with the other verses.

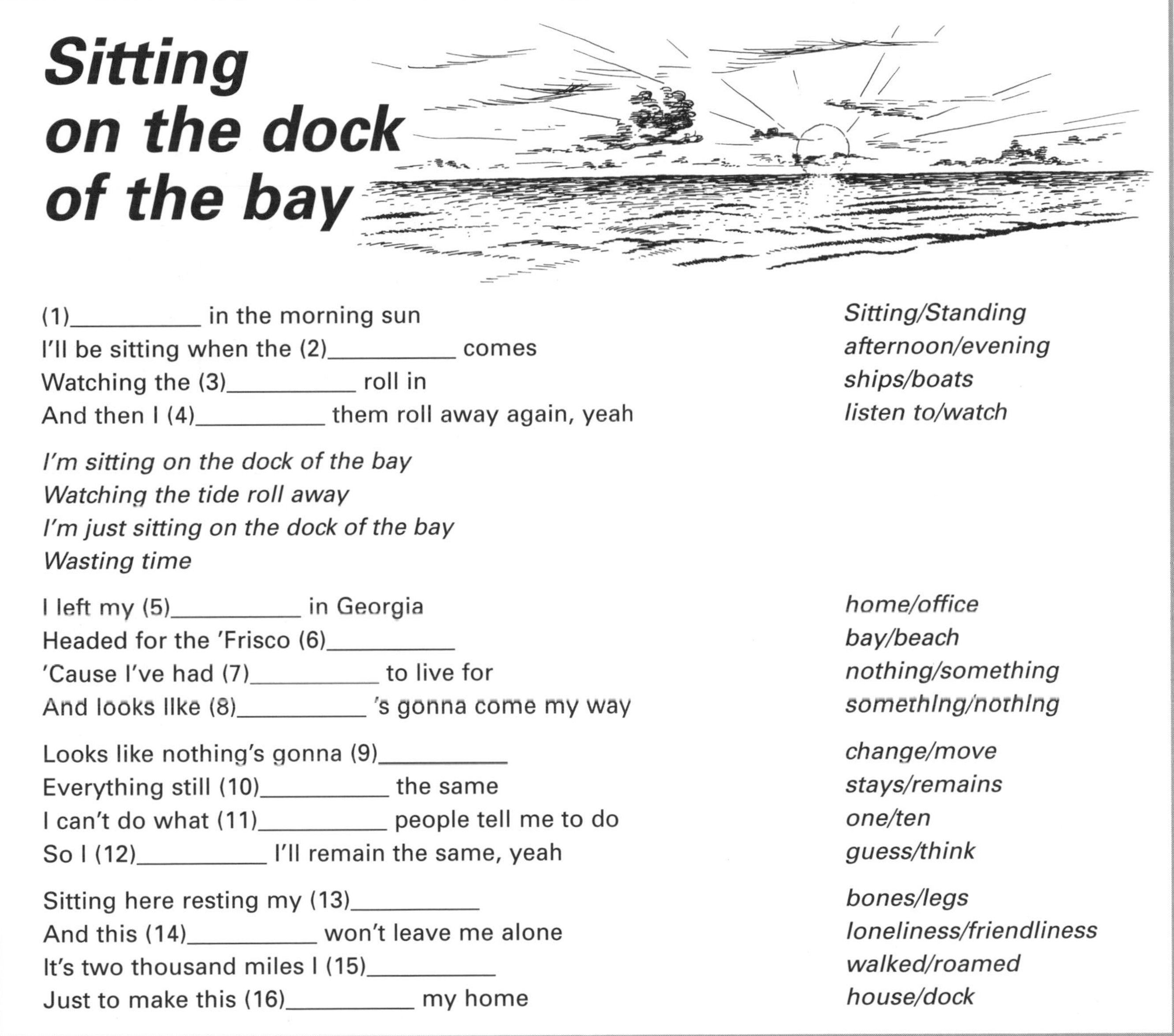

Sitting on the dock of the bay

(1)__________ in the morning sun	*Sitting/Standing*
I'll be sitting when the (2)__________ comes	*afternoon/evening*
Watching the (3)__________ roll in	*ships/boats*
And then I (4)__________ them roll away again, yeah	*listen to/watch*
I'm sitting on the dock of the bay	
Watching the tide roll away	
I'm just sitting on the dock of the bay	
Wasting time	
I left my (5)__________ in Georgia	*home/office*
Headed for the 'Frisco (6)__________	*bay/beach*
'Cause I've had (7)__________ to live for	*nothing/something*
And looks like (8)__________ 's gonna come my way	*something/nothing*
Looks like nothing's gonna (9)__________	*change/move*
Everything still (10)__________ the same	*stays/remains*
I can't do what (11)__________ people tell me to do	*one/ten*
So I (12)__________ I'll remain the same, yeah	*guess/think*
Sitting here resting my (13)__________	*bones/legs*
And this (14)__________ won't leave me alone	*loneliness/friendliness*
It's two thousand miles I (15)__________	*walked/roamed*
Just to make this (16)__________ my home	*house/dock*

4 What do you think the singer means when he says the following.

1 I'm wasting time.
2 I have nothing to live for.
3 I can't do what ten people tell me to do.
4 I guess I'll remain the same.

5 What advice would you give to this man?

Stop and check 1

UNITS 1–4

Questions

Make questions about the missing information.

Example
She earns ____ a year. ***How much does she earn a year?***

1 Peter has ____ children. (Two? Three?)

____

2 I'm reading ____ at the moment.

____

3 They went to ____ on holiday last year.

____

4 She works in the ____ shop. (Shoe shop? Book shop?)

____

5 I got up early this morning because ____ .

____

6 The supermarket closes at ____ .

____

7 I go swimming ____ . (Once a week? Once a month?)

____

8 I borrowed ____ car. (Tom's? Ann's?)

____

	8

Tenses

Complete the sentences with the correct form of the verb in brackets.

1 Emma __________ (spend) every school holiday in Scotland.
2 Why are you under the table? __________ you __________ (look) for something?
3 In my country we __________ (not have) lessons on Saturday.
4 My wife __________ (not like) football, but I __________ (love) it.
5 I __________ (buy) a new pair of shoes yesterday. __________ you __________ (like) them?
6 My grandfather __________ (live) in Belgium when the Second World War __________ (start).
7 Yuet Tung __________ (live) in the United States. She __________ (meet) her husband while she __________ (work) for a publisher on Madison Avenue.

	12

have/have got

1 Make ten sentences about the two people in the pictures. Say what they *have/have got* and what they *don't have/haven't got.*

Examples
He's got a cat.
He doesn't have a house.

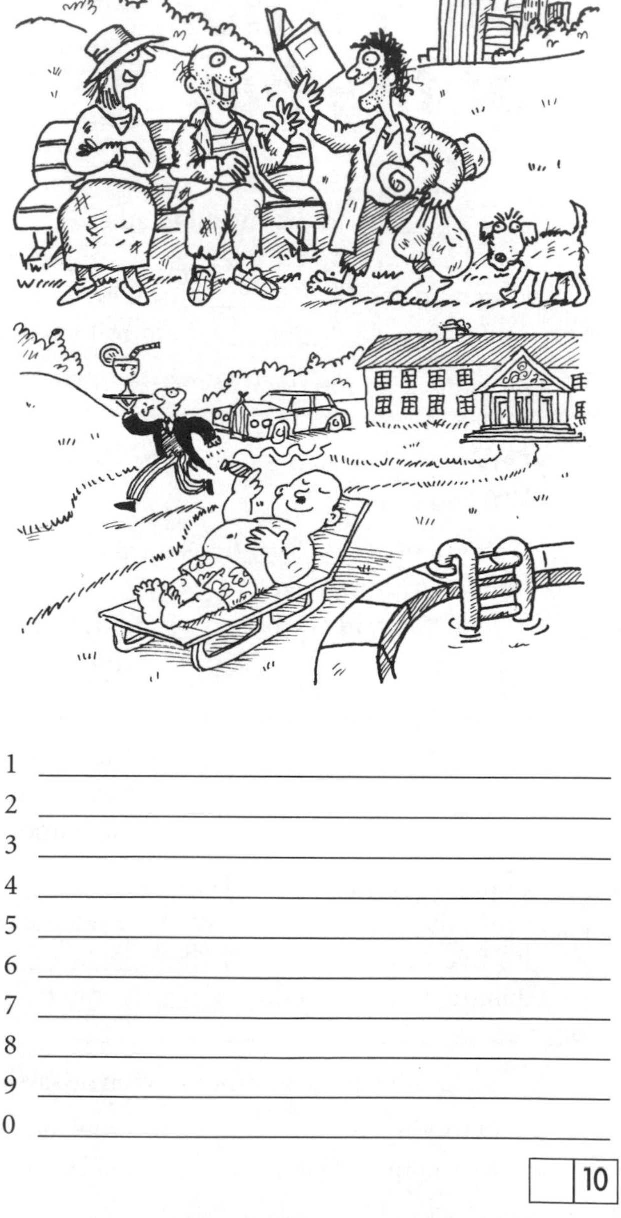

1 ______________________________
2 ______________________________
3 ______________________________
4 ______________________________
5 ______________________________
6 ______________________________
7 ______________________________
8 ______________________________
9 ______________________________
10 ______________________________

	10

2 Ask and answer five questions about the two people.

Examples

Does he have a car? **Yes, he does.**
Has he got a car? **Yes, he has.**

1 ______
2 ______
3 ______
4 ______
5 ______

| | 10 |

Past tense forms

What is the past tense of the following verbs? Some are irregular, and some are regular.

hear ______	can ______	break ______
phone ______	put ______	catch ______
live ______	begin ______	hit ______
try ______	leave ______	fall ______
make ______	feel ______	build ______

| | 15 |

Prepositions

Complete the sentences with the correct preposition. If *no* preposition is necessary, write nothing.

1 I listened ______ the news ______ the radio.
2 I'll see you ______ 9.00 ______ the morning.
3 I'm looking ______ my neighbour's car while she's on holiday.
4 What are you doing ______ this evening?
5 She arrived ______ England two years ago.
6 I'm going ______ home.
7 I spoke ______ Mary a few days ago.
8 My sister's coming to stay ______ 19 December.

| | 10 |

Expressions of quantity

1 Complete the sentences with *some* or *any*.

1 I'd like ______ tea, but I don't want ______ biscuits.
2 Is there ______ sugar? I can't see ______ .
3 I bought ______ sugar yesterday.
4 I didn't buy ______ coffee, because I thought we had ______.
5 We need ______ bread. I'll get it later.

| | 8 |

2 There is one mistake in each of the following sentences. Find it and correct it.

1 How many money have you got?
2 I only have a little potatoes.
3 I don't have many time, so I can't help you. Sorry.
4 In *Nowy Świat* there are a lot shops.
5 Close your eyes. I've got anything for you.
6 John lives anywhere near Bournemouth.
7 Anybody told me you're getting married. Is it true?

| | 7 |

Articles

Complete the sentences with *a*, *an*, *the*, or nothing.

1 China has ______ biggest population in ______ world.
2 ______ Yangtze River flows into ______ East China Sea.
3 Do you like ______ Chinese food?
4 We had some for ______ lunch ______ few days ago.
5 I come to ______ school by bus, but I get ______ lift home with ______ friend.

| | 10 |

Vocabulary

Match the verbs in A with phrases in B.

A	B
put on	a part-time job
do	a van
make	milk
drive	make-up
call	a decision
run out of	sorry
say	my money
wash	her wedding anniversary
lose	my hair
forget	the police

| | 10 |

| TOTAL | | 100 |

Stop and check 2

UNITS 5–8

Verb patterns

Put the verb in brackets in the infinitive or the *-ing* form.

John Frantz is American. He has a wonderful lifestyle and he wants (1)__________ (share) it with an English girl. He enjoys (2)__________ (go) on exotic holidays, but he wouldn't like (3)__________ (live) outside the United States. He hopes (4)__________ (find) an English wife through the English Rose dating agency. He'd like (5)__________ (meet) someone who likes (6)__________ (travel).

| | 6 |

going to and *will*

Complete the sentences with a form of *going to* or *will*.

1 'Why have you got so much food?'
'Because I __________ (cook) a meal for ten people.'
2 'Someone told me you've got a place at university.'
'That's right. I __________ (study) maths at St Andrews, in Scotland.'
3 'My car isn't working.'
'Ask Joe to look at it. He __________ (help) you.'
4 'I passed my driving test!'
'That's great! I __________ (buy) some champagne to celebrate!'
5 'Why have you got your old clothes on?'
'Because I __________ (cut) the grass.'

| | 5 |

Descriptions

1 Match a line in **A** with a line in **B**.

A	B
What's the weather like?	Horse riding.
What's Ann like?	They're a bit strict.
What was the film like?	OK, but boring near the end.
What does she like doing?	It's quite hot.
What are her parents like?	She's very nice.

| | 5 |

2 Write the comparative and superlative form of the adjective.

fast __________ __________
funny __________ __________
expensive __________ __________
rich __________ __________
hot __________ __________
interesting __________ __________
good __________ __________
bad __________ __________

| | 16 |

Past Simple and past participle

What is the Past Simple and the past participle of the following verbs? Some are regular and some are irregular.

make __________ __________
drink __________ __________
see __________ __________
travel __________ __________
act __________ __________
try __________ __________
eat __________ __________
break __________ __________
know __________ __________
spend __________ __________
have __________ __________
read __________ __________
write __________ __________
speak __________ __________

| | 28 |

Present Perfect or Past Simple?

1 Complete the sentences with the correct form of the verb in brackets: the Present Perfect or Past Simple.

1 Joanna Trollope __________ (write) a lot of books. She __________ (write) her first in 1980.
2 __________ you ever __________ (try) Indian food?
3 I__________ never __________ (be) to Russia. When __________ you __________ (go) there?
4 I __________ (live) in London for eight years, and I don't want to move.
5 He __________ (live) in Oxford for two years, and then in 1994 he __________ (move) to London.
6 We __________ (meet) Tim and Maureen three years ago. How long __________ you __________ (know) them?

| | 10 |

2 Complete the sentences with *ever*, *never*, *for*, or *since*.

1 He's worked there __________ many years, __________1983, I believe.
2 I have __________ loved anyone as much as I love you.
3 We've known Paul __________ two years. Have you __________ met him?
4 I've known him __________ we went to school together, but I've __________ met his parents.

| | 7 |

3 Make questions with the verb in brackets. Then answer the questions about you.

1 How long __________ you __________ (live) in your town?
2 __________ you ever __________ (drink) champagne?
3 How many foreign countries __________ you __________ (visit)?
4 Where __________ you __________ (go) on holiday last year?
5 What __________ you __________ (do) there?

| | 5 |

have to and *should*

The following sentences are all about visiting America. Complete them with *have to*, *don't have to*, or *should*.

When you go to America,
1 you __________ book a hotel room before you go, because there are usually a lot of vacancies.
2 you __________ get a work permit if you want to work there.
3 you __________ visit San Francisco, because many people think it is the most beautiful city in America.
4 you __________ change your money before you go, because there are a lot of 24-hour banks.
5 you __________ hire a car, because it's the easiest way to travel, and petrol is cheap.

| | 5 |

Vocabulary

1 Find the opposites.

come first	tell the truth
fed up	generous
messy	kind
mean	tidy
noisy	quiet
tell a lie	interested
cruel	stay at home
sensitive	come last
go abroad	tough

| | 8 |

2 Complete the sentences with words or phrases from exercise 1.

1 Sometimes you have to be __________ to be __________.
2 Anne was upset because she didn't __________ in the race. She really wanted to win.
3 We always __________ for our holidays.
4 I'm __________. There's nothing to do.

| | 5 |

| TOTAL | | 100 |

Stop and check 3

UNITS 9–12

Time and conditional clauses

1 Complete the sentences with *will* + the correct form of the verb in brackets, or the Present Simple.

1 If you __________ (eat) another cake, you __________ (be) sick.
2 You __________ (fail) your exam if you __________ (not study) hard.
3 What __________ you __________ (do) if you __________ (fail)?
4 Our children and grandchildren __________ (suffer) if we __________ (not look after) our planet.
5 I __________ (do) my homework as soon as this programme __________ (finish).
6 When she __________ (read) my letter, she __________ (understand) my problem.
7 Where __________ he __________ (stay) when he __________ (go) to New York?
8 We __________ (stay) in the classroom until the teacher __________ (tell) us to leave.

| | 16 |

2 Match a line in **A** with a line in **B**.

A	B
If I pass my driving test,	will you pay for the meal?
You'll learn English more easily if	we find somewhere to live.
Will you give her these when	you study a little every day.
If they don't give him the job,	you don't water them.
I'll marry you as soon as	we'll send them to you.
Your plants won't grow well if	I'll buy a car.
As soon as we get the tickets,	I don't know what he'll do.
If I buy the champagne,	you see her?

| | 8 |

Verb patterns and infinitives

1 Complete the sentences with the correct tense of the verb in brackets: the infinitive or the *-ing* form.

1 I enjoy __________ (swim) in the sea very much.
2 John managed __________ (tidy) his room before his mother came home.
3 There were no taxis so he decided __________ (walk) home.
4 I'd like __________ (go) to India.
5 It's very difficult __________ (learn) how to ski.

| | 5 |

2 Underline the correct verb form.

1 Sad films always make me *to cry/cry/crying.*
2 Please stop *make/to make/making* that awful noise!
3 I used *live/to live/living* in London.
4 I was lost. I didn't know where *go/to go/going.*
5 Please let me *to go/going/go* to the concert on Saturday!
6 I tried *explain/to explain* why I was late, but she didn't listen.
7 I walked into the town centre *for find/to find/for to find* a taxi.

| | 7 |

Passives

1 Underline the correct verb form: active or passive.

Example
Nylon *invented/was invented* in the 1930s.

1 Walt Disney *created/was created* the character of Mickey Mouse sixty years ago.
2 Mickey *calls/is called* 'Topolino' in Italian and 'Mi Lo Shu' in Chinese.
3 At first he *called/was called* Mortimer Mouse.
4 He *gave/was given* the name Mickey by Walt Disney's wife, Lillian.
5 Disney *made/was made* the first full-length cartoon, 'Snow White', in 1937.
6 Mickey Mouse cartoons *have translated/have been translated* into sixty languages.
7 Since 1928, 120 cartoons *have made/have been made.*

| | 7 |

2 Put the verbs in brackets in the correct tense. They are all in the passive.

1 The Volkswagen Beetle ______________ (design) by Ferdinand Porsche.
2 He __________ (ask) to design it by the German Government.
3 VWs __________ (take) to America by American soldiers who were returning home after the war.
4 The first VW __________ (make) in 1938.
5 They __________ (not make) in Europe any more.

| | 10 |

Second conditional

1 Complete the sentences with the correct form of the verbs in brackets: Past Simple or *would*.

1 If I _______________ (live) in the country, I _______________ (have) a dog.
2 If I _______________ (have) a lot of money, I _______________ (not work).
3 I _______________ (go) to the party if I _______________ (not be) so busy.
4 What _____________ you _____________ (do) if someone _____________ (give) you a million pounds?
5 If I _______________ (be) you, I _______________ (look) for another job.

| | 10 |

2 Rewrite the following sentences using the second conditional.

Example
I'm not rich. I don't live in a big house.
If I were rich, I'd live in a big house.

1 She spends a lot of money. She's poor.

____

2 She smokes forty cigarettes a day. She coughs a lot.

____

3 He doesn't understand Portuguese. He won't work in Brazil.

____

4 They don't have a garden. They don't grow vegetables.

____

5 I don't have a boat. I won't sail around the world.

____

| | 10 |

might

Complete the sentences using *might*.

Example
Take your umbrella because … (rain)
Take your umbrella because it might rain.

1 She's not sure what to do when she leaves university … (have a holiday/look for a job).

____

2 They don't know where to have a holiday … (Spain/stay at home).

____

3 Write my phone number in your book. … (forget it).

____

4 I'll try to arrive at 8.00, but … (be late) if the traffic is bad.

____

5 I'm going to Paris for a meeting next week … (stay the night/come back the same day). It depends how long the meeting goes on.

____

| | 10 |

Vocabulary

1 Complete the story with the correct tense of *take*, *get*, *do*, or *make*.

Yesterday morning, I (1)________ up, (2)________ the bed, (3)__________ dressed, and went downstairs. I (4)_________ breakfast. After that, I (5)________ the bus into town and (6)________ some shopping. I (7)_______ tired so I went home and (8)________ my homework, which (9)________ me a long time. Later, I felt ill, so I (10)________ a tablet and (11)_________ into bed.

| | 11 |

2 Complete the sentences using the verbs in the box.

grow carry tell give lose keep

1 In England, the police don't usually __________ a gun.
2 Don't tell Sue. She can't ____________ a secret.
3 Anne __________ me a lift to the party.
4 United __________ the match 2–0.
5 Frank decided to __________ a beard.
6 Martyn _________ a very funny joke.

| | 6 |

| TOTAL | | 100 |

Stop and check 4

UNITS 13–14

Present Perfect Simple and Continuous

Rewrite the sentences with the word or words in brackets. Make any necessary changes to the word order. Sometimes it is necessary to add another word.

Example
He's lived in that house. (1994)
He's lived in that house since 1994.

1 I've finished. (not yet)

____

2 They've booked the restaurant. (yet?)

____

3 We've ordered the champagne. (already)

____

4 Anna's been studying hard. (five hours)

____

5 Jim's been cleaning his bike. (How long?)

____

6 I've seen Jim. (just)

____

7 We've been helping Mary. (five o'clock)

____

8 They haven't spoken to each other. (four years)

____

9 Nobody has sent me a letter. (a long time)

____

10 It hasn't rained here. (June)

____

	10

Tenses

Complete the text with the correct form of the verb in brackets.

Marie-Thérèse

I (1)__________ (come) from Switzerland. I (2)__________ (come) to London six months ago to learn English. I (3)__________ (not meet) many English people yet, only my teachers. I (4)__________ (start) learning English at school in Switzerland when I (5)__________ (be) eleven, so I (6)__________ (learn) it for nearly ten years. At first in London, I (7)__________ (not understand) anything, but now my English (8)__________ (improve). I (9)__________ just __________ (take) an exam. If I (10)__________ (pass), I (11)__________ (move) into the next class. I'm excited today because my parents (12)__________ (come) tomorrow to stay with me for a few days and I (13)__________ (not see) them for a long time. They (14)__________ (never be) to England and they (15)__________ (not speak) English.

	15

Reported statements

Report what Marie-Thérèse said.

1 She told me that she __________ many English people.
2 She said that she __________ an exam.
3 She told me that her parents __________ to stay with her.
4 She said that she __________ her parents for a long time.
5 She told me that her parents __________ English.

	10

Past Perfect

Underline the correct verb form.

1 The view was wonderful. I *never saw/have never seen/had never seen* such a beautiful view before.
2 Peter picked up the ball and *threw/had thrown* it as far as he could.
3 When I was a child, I *lived/have lived/had lived* in New York.
4 I didn't need to tell Ann because Jane *already told/had already told* her.
5 I was hungry because I *didn't have/haven't had/hadn't had* any breakfast.

	5

Vocabulary

Complete the sentences. Use an *adjective* from the box in the correct form: *noun*, *verb* or *adverb*.

various honest possible successful comfortable real believable peaceful careful near

1 I like Chinese food because of the ___________ of ingredients.
2 The film was ___________ exciting. You must see it!
3 John eventually ___________ in passing his driving test after failing three times.
4 After winning the lottery, he lived the rest of his life in ___________.
5 I'm very lucky. I ___________ missed the bus.
6 I love my house in the country because of the ___________ and quiet.
7 He can't come from another planet. It's ___________.
8 Open the parcel with ___________. It's got glass in it.
9 I don't agree with his ___________ but I respect them.
10 Tell me ___________. Have you really asked her to marry you?

	10

TOTAL		50

Progress test 1

UNITS 1–5

Exercise 1 Questions and verb forms

Put the words in the right order to make a question.

Example
job / learning / for / English / your / you / are?
Are you learning English for your job?

1 English / you / start / did / learning / when?

____

2 tennis / often / play / how / does / she?

____

3 do / doing / what / at / you / like / weekend / the?

____

4 weekend / do / what / you / would / to / this / like?

____

5 dictionary / why / got / you / haven't / a?

____

6 much / put / my / coffee / sugar / how / did / in / you?

____

7 phoned / doing / John / when / what / you / were?

____

8 sandwiches / make / is / who / to / going / the?

____

9 radio / listening / does / enjoy / to / mother / the / your?

____

10 live / Anna / where / was / child / a / did / when / she?

____

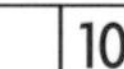

10

Exercise 2 Questions and tenses

Look at the chart.

Name	Xavier	Mr and Mrs Ramsey
Nationality	French	Australian
Town	London	Melbourne
Age	26	In their sixties
Family	one younger brother	no children
Occupation	chef	retired
Holiday last year	home to Paris for two weeks	two months in Scotland – visiting relatives
Holiday next year	drive to Morocco with friends	tour New Zealand for two weeks

Use the information in the chart and write the correct questions to the following answers.

Example
Where does Xavier come from?
He comes from France.

1 ______________________________
They come from Australia.

2 ______________________________
They live in Melbourne.

3 ______________________________
He's 26.

4 ______________________________
Yes, he does. He has one younger brother.

5 ______________________________
No, they haven't got any.

6 ______________________________
He's a chef.

7 ______________________________
He went home to Paris for two weeks.

8 ______________________________
They stayed there for two months.

9 ______________________________
They're going to tour New Zealand.

10 ______________________________
He's going to drive to Morocco.

10

Exercise 3 Tenses and verb forms

Put the verb in brackets into the correct tense or verb form.

Example
A Why _did_ you _go_ (go) to the seaside last weekend?
B Because we like _sailing_ (sail).

A (1)__________ you __________ (know) Brian Bailey?
B Yes, I (2)__________ (meet) him two years ago while I (3)__________ (work) in Germany. (4)__________ he still __________ (live) there?
A Yes, he does. He (5)__________ (live) in Frankfurt. He (6)__________ (have got) a good job there but at the moment he (7)__________ (work) in London. He's here for a few days and I'd like (8)__________ (invite) him and you for dinner. Can you (9)__________ (come)?
B Yes, I hope so. I'd love (10)__________ (see) Brian again! When I was in Germany we (11)__________ (see) each other quite often because his office was near the school where I (12)__________ (teach) and so we sometimes (13)__________ (have) lunch together. I always enjoyed (14)__________ (talk) to him. I wanted (15)__________ (write) to him but he moved and I (16)__________ (not have) his new address.
A Well, what about dinner on Friday?
B That's fine. What time?
A Is 8 o'clock OK? I (17)__________ (ring) Brian yesterday to check the day, and I (18)__________ (ring) him again tomorrow to check the time.
B Well, 8 o'clock is fine for me. I (19)__________ (come) at about 8 and I (20)__________ (bring) a bottle of wine.
A See you on Friday then!

| | 20 |

Exercise 4 Irregular past tenses

Here are twenty verbs. Ten are regular and ten are irregular. Write the past tense form of the *irregular* verbs only.

buy	put
cook	speak
do	start
happen	take
have	talk
hear	visit
laugh	wait
leave	watch
listen	whisper
make	write

| | 10 |

Exercise 5 Count and uncount nouns

Underline the uncount noun in the following pairs of words.

Example
cheese/egg

money/pound	rice/potato	meat/hamburger
flower/flour	loaf/bread	song/music
job/homework	luggage/suitcase	food/meal
furniture/desk		

| | 5 |

Exercise 6 Articles

Complete the text with *a*, *an*, *the* or nothing.

Example
I had _____ dinner with _the_ Queen.

My Aunt Vanessa is (1)_____ artist. She lives in (2)_____ beautiful old cottage by (3)_____ sea and she paints (4)_____ small pictures of wild flowers and birds. She doesn't like leaving (5)_____ cottage, but once (6)_____ year she travels by (7)_____ train to London and has (8)_____ tea with me at (9)_____ Savoy Hotel. At the moment I'm quite worried about her because she's in (10)_____ hospital, but I'm sure she'll be better soon. I'm going to visit her next week.

| | 10 |

Exercise 7 Expressions of quantity

Tick (✓) the correct sentence.

1 Is there any milk? I can't see one.
Is there any milk? I can't see any.
Are there any milks? I can't see them.

2 There's some potatoes, but only a little.
There's some potatoes, but only few.
There are some potatoes, but only a few.

3 There's much cars parked in the street.
There are a lot of cars parked in the street.
There are lots cars parked in the street.

4 Have you got much unemployment in your town?
Have you got the unemployment in your town?
Have you got much unemployed people in your town?

5 Only a few people believes his story.
Only a little people believes his story.
Only a few people believe his story.

6 How much homeworks do you have tonight?
How much homework do you have tonight?
How many homeworks do you have tonight?

7 There aren't many rice and there aren't any eggs.
There isn't much rice and there isn't any eggs.
There isn't much rice and there aren't any eggs.

8 There was much snow last winter.
There was a little snow last winter but not many.
There was some snow last winter but not much.

9 How lovely! Somebody gave you some flowers.
How lovely! Anybody gave you some flowers.
How lovely! Somebody gave you any flowers.

10 I went anywhere very interesting for my holiday.
I didn't go anywhere very interesting for my holiday.
I didn't do anywhere very interesting for my holiday.

| | 10 |

Exercise 8 Which one is different?

Underline the one word in each group that is different.

Example
castle <u>cathedral</u> cottage house
(You can't live in a cathedral.)

1 language translator dictionary art
2 poem story joke sing
3 handbag wallet suitcase purse
4 mobile phone fax photography e-mail
5 video iron Walkman CD player
6 make-up soap toothpaste towel
7 untidy messy dirty clean
8 break smash mend destroy
9 hairdresser shopkeeper customer banker
10 tomorrow morning yesterday evening the day after tomorrow in two weeks' time
11 worried nervous friendly excited
12 impossible careful unemployed illegal
13 speak talk print tell
14 posters magazines books newspapers
15 butcher's greengrocer's chemist's baker's

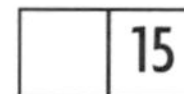

Exercise 9 Words that go together

Match a line in **A** with a line in **B**.

A	B
tell	driver
spend	work
hard	abroad
say	a bill
make	money
take	sorry
sore	a joke
taxi	throat
pay	a photograph
go	a promise

| | 10 |

| TOTAL | | 100 |

Progress test 2

UNITS 6–10

Exercise 1 Descriptions

Complete the dialogues with words from the box.

worst latest more as (×2) funniest funnier than friendlier tastier like was what the most

1 **A** I started a new job today, working in an office.
B Really! How did it go?
A It was OK. I was a bit nervous.
B What are the other people (1)__________?
A They're very nice. They seem (2)__________ than the people in my old job, and the job is much (3)__________ interesting.
B You worked in a shop before, didn't you?
A Yes. Working in an office is better (4)__________ working in a shop, I'll tell you! That was the (5)__________ job I've ever had. I hated it.

2 **C** We went out for a meal to Luigi's last night – you know, that new Italian restaurant.
D Mm, I know. What (6)__________ it like?
C It was (7)__________ best Italian meal I've ever had, and it wasn't as expensive (8)__________ Giovanni's, so I think we'll go there again.
D Yes. Giovanni's used to be the (9)__________ popular restaurant around here, but then it started getting very expensive.
C And the service isn't (10)__________ good as it used to be.
D What did you have?
C Paul and I both had veal, but mine was cooked in wine and herbs, and it was (11)__________ than Paul's. But *he* liked it.
D It sounds great.

3 **E** Have your read John Harrison's (12)__________ book, *Going Round the World*?
F No. (13) __________'s it like?
E I think it's the (14) __________ book he's written. I laughed out loud all the way through.
F I didn't like *The Truth and the Light*, the one that came out last year.
E Neither did I. This one's much (15)__________.
F Can I borrow it?

	15

Exercise 2 Correct the mistakes

Tick (✓) the correct sentence.

Example
I have watched TV last night.
I watched TV last night. ✓

1 I have lived in Chesswood for five years.
I live in Chesswood for five years.

2 We moved here after my daughter was born.
We have moved here after my daughter was born.

3 Before that we have lived in London.
Before that we lived in London.

4 I am a teacher since I left university.
I have been a teacher since I left university.

5 I went to Bristol University in 1994.
I have been to Bristol University in 1994.

6 We have studied English since three years.
We have studied English for three years.

7 I never went to Russia, but I'd like to go.
I have never been to Russia, but I'd like to go.

	7

Exercise 3 Tenses

Complete the text with the correct form of the verbs in brackets: the Present Simple, the Past Simple, or the Present Perfect.

Example
I *got* (get) up at 7.00 this morning.

Carla Brown has a job in advertising. It's a good job, and she (1)__________ (earn) over £30,000 a year. She (2)__________ (study) marketing at college, and then (3)__________ (find) a job with a small advertising agency in Manchester. Since then she (4)__________ (change) her job several times. Now she (5)__________ (work) for Jerome and Jerome, which is a big company with offices all over the world. She (6)__________ (be) with the company for three years.

The company has clients in America, and she (7)__________ (be) there several times on business. Last year she (8)__________ (spend) six months there.

	8

Exercise 4 *have to* or *should*?

Complete the sentences with a form of *have to*, *don't have to*, *should*, or *shouldn't*.

Example
If you feel ill, you **should** go to bed.

1 When you catch a plane, you __________ check in before you board the plane.
2 You __________ have too much hand luggage.
3 You __________ wear comfortable clothing.
4 A pilot __________ train for many years.
5 People who want to smoke __________ sit in certain seats.
6 You __________ wear your seat belt all the time. You can take it off.
7 But you __________ wear it at take-off and landing.
8 You __________ drink too much alcohol because you might be ill.
9 There is often a film on a long flight, but you __________ watch it. You can go to sleep.
10 When you've got your luggage, you __________ go through Customs.

| | 10 |

Exercise 5 Time clauses

Put the words in the right order.

Example
bath / I / when / home / will / get / have / a / I
I will have a bath when I get home.

1 hear / if / I / news / any / you / I / phone / will
____
2 pay / as / you / I / back / soon / can / I / as / will
____
3 you / feel / stop / better / if / will / you / smoking
____
4 car / Peter / enough / when / he / buy / a / has / will / money
____
5 problem / help / I / you / have / you / a / will / if
____

| | 5 |

Exercise 6 Tenses

Complete the sentences with the correct form of the verbs in brackets: the Present Simple or the *will* future.

1 I __________ (call) you when lunch __________ (be) ready.
2 If you __________ (be) late, I __________ (go) without you.
3 If she __________ (pass) her driving test, she __________ (buy) a car.
4 I __________ (go) home as soon as I __________ (finish) work.
5 If my neighbours __________ (not stop) making a noise, I __________ (go) round and complain.

| | 5 |

Exercise 7 *used to* or the Past Simple?

Look at the profile of the singer, Andy Goodchild. Complete the sentences, using *used to* where possible, or the Past Simple.

Example
He ***used to*** live with his parents in Leeds.
He **had** his first guitar when he was six.

FACTFILE ON ANDY GOODCHILD

Andy's highly successful solo career began in 1984. He now lives in London with his wife, Suzy, and their daughter, Trixie. Andy tells us about his background.

1969–90	Lived in Leeds with my parents
1975	Got my first guitar!
1980–90	Went to Bradford School
1981–85	Wrote songs with a friend called Keith
1986–93	Played with a band called *The Forwards*
1989–92	Played in pubs and clubs
1990	Started going out with a girl called Mandy
June 1991	Had a number one record, *She's mine*
1992	Toured the United States
1995	Broke up with Mandy
1997	Went solo
April 2000	Played at a pop festival in Los Angeles

1 He ______________ Bradford School.
2 He ______________ football for the school.
3 He ______________ songs with a friend called Keith.
4 He ______________ with *The Forwards*.
5 *The Forwards* ______________ in pubs and clubs.

6 In 1991 he ______________ a number one record.
7 He ______________ with a girl called Mandy.
8 *The Forwards* ______________ the United States in 1992.
9 Andy ______________ in 1997.
10 He ______________ a pop festival in Los Angeles three years later.

| | 10 |

Exercise 8 Verb patterns and infinitives

Underline the correct verb form.

1 The police managed *catch/to catch/catching* the burglar.
2 My parents let me *open/to open/opening* my birthday present early.
3 I tried *stop/to stop* her but she ran away.
4 Would you like something *drink/to drink/drinking?*
5 They go *ski/to ski/skiing* every winter.
6 It was wonderful *see/to see* you again!
7 He didn't have anything *say/to say/saying.*
8 I started *learn/learning* Chinese when I was at University.
9 I never know when *shut up/to shut up/shutting up.* I'm sorry.
10 I've decided *marry/to marry/marrying* Helen.

| | 10 |

Exercise 9 Words that go together

Match a line in **A** with a line in **B**.

A	B
open	work
regular	post
tell	a bank account
part-time	responsibility
alarm	ring
ear	hour
sign	hours
sun	clock
rush	a story
take	glasses

| | 10 |

Exercise 10 Homophones

In the following sentences, the word in *italics* is the wrong homophone. The word *sounds* right, but the spelling is wrong. Correct the spelling.

Example
I *new* Peter when we were at school. → ***knew***

1 Can you *cheque* this for me?
2 We *red* about the accident in the newspaper.
3 How much is the *fair* to Manchester?
4 Do you like my shirt? I bought it in a *sail.*
5 I didn't mean to *brake* your bike. Sorry.

| | 5 |

Exercise 11 Adverbs

Complete the sentences with an adverb from the box.

too exactly only just especially

1 I'm hungry. I ___________ had a piece of toast this morning.
2 I like the Impressionists, ___________ Monet.
3 It is ___________ three fifty-five and twenty seconds.
4 Paul plays the guitar and sings, ___________ .
5 He went abroad on the 5th, ___________ before my birthday.

| | 5 |

Exercise 12 Opposites

Match each adjective with its opposite from the box.

Example
cheap – ***expensive***

generous well-behaved pleased tidy quiet
beautiful interesting modern poor miserable

1 ugly ___________
2 annoyed ___________
3 noisy ___________
4 mean ___________
5 old ___________
6 wealthy ___________
7 happy ___________
8 naughty ___________
9 boring ___________
10 messy ___________

| | 10 |

| TOTAL | | 100 |

Progress test 3

UNITS 11–14

Exercise 1 Irregular past tenses

Here are twenty verbs. Ten are regular and ten are irregular. Write in the Past Simple and Past Participle for the irregular verbs only.

	Past Simple	Past participle
appear	________	________
bring	________	________
climb	________	________
fall	________	________
feel	________	________
forget	________	________
improve	________	________
invent	________	________
know	________	________
let	________	________
lose	________	________
manage	________	________
pass	________	________
pick	________	________
speak	________	________
start	________	________
tell	________	________
understand	________	________
use	________	________
want	________	________

10

Exercise 2 Active or passive?

Underline the correct verb form.

Example
Portuguese *speaks/is spoken* in Brazil.

1. That's the third time he *has failed/has been failed* the exam.
2. 'Hot lips' *wrote/was written* by Celia Young.
3. A lot of trees *cut down/were cut down* to build that house.
4. They *don't grow/aren't grown* bananas in Scotland.
5. Some pictures *have taken/have been taken* from the museum.

5

Exercise 3 Passives

Put the words in the correct order.

1. world / is / English / the / all / spoken / over
   ____
2. since / has / nylon / 1932 / made / been
   ____
3. Mary's / invited / I / to / wasn't / party / why?
   ____
4. will / when / be / new / the / bridge / built?
   ____
5. asked / car / design / were / they / to / new / a
   ____

5

Exercise 4 Second conditional

Make five sentences from the chart. Use each verb in **B** once only.

A	B	C	D	E
If I	lived earned knew had were	a dictionary you in Brazil more money Maria's address	I'd I wouldn't	go to see her. look up the word. marry George. learn Portuguese. save it.

____
____
____
____
____

5

Exercise 5 Second conditional and *might*

Read the text about Jane. Then complete the sentences.

> Jane's unhappy at home and unhappy at work. She has a boring job and she doesn't earn much money. Her boss says that he will perhaps give her a pay rise next month, but he isn't sure yet. She doesn't have a car and she goes to work on crowded buses every day. She doesn't have a flat, she lives in a small room above a noisy restaurant in the centre of town. She finds it difficult to sleep because the restaurant doesn't close until after midnight. She thinks that she will perhaps go and live with her friend Wendy but she isn't sure yet because she likes living on her own.

Example
Jane **wouldn't be** unhappy if she lived in a quiet flat.

1 Jane ____________ happier if she ____________ a more interesting job.
2 Her boss might ____________ .
3 If she ____________ a car, she ____________ to work by bus.
4 If she ____________ live above a restaurant, she ____________ it easier to sleep.
5 She might ____________ her friend Wendy.

| | 5 |

Exercise 6 Present Perfect Simple and Continuous

Tick (✓) the correct sentence.

1 I saw her five minutes ago.
I've seen her five minutes ago.
2 We are here since last Saturday.
We've been here since last Saturday.
3 How long have you known Wendy?
How long have you been knowing Wendy?
4 We haven't made coffee yet.
We didn't make coffee yet.
5 He is waiting to see the doctor since nine o'clock.
He has been waiting to see the doctor since nine o'clock.
6 When did you buy your new car?
When have you bought your new car?
7 Mary isn't home. She's been to work.
Mary isn't home. She's gone to work.
8 I've run in the park, so I'm tired.
I've been running in the park, so I'm tired.
9 I've run round the park three times.
I've been running round the park three times.
10 They already had their dinner.
They've already had their dinner.

| | 10 |

Exercise 7 Present Perfect Continuous

Ask questions to find out *How long … ?*

Example
'I'm learning English.'
'How long have you been learning English?'

1 'I'm waiting for a bus.'
'____________________________________?'
2 'Tom's saving up to buy a boat.'
'____________________________________?'
3 I'm having driving lessons.'
'____________________________________?'
4 'Alice is working in the library.'
'____________________________________?'
5 'The Greens are trying to sell their house.'
'____________________________________?'

| | 5 |

Exercise 8 Reported statements

Put the following sentences into reported speech.

Example
'They live in Oxford,' She said.
She said (that) **they lived in Oxford.**

1 'I love you very much,' she said.
She told him ____________________________
2 'I visit her every Sunday,' he said.
He said that ____________________________
3 'I took her some flowers for her birthday,' he said.
He said that ____________________________
4 'I'm leaving you forever,' he said.
He told her ____________________________
5 'I've forgotten,' she said.
She said that ____________________________

| | 5 |

Exercise 9 *had* or *would*?

Decide whether *'d* in these sentences means *had* or *would*.

Example
He*'d* left before I arrived. = **had**

1 I told him that I*'d* like to come.
2 When we*'d* had tea, we went for a walk.
3 Why did you tell her that I*'d* broken the vase?
4 If I had a car, I*'d* drive you there with pleasure.
5 She said that he*'d* just given it to her.

| | 5 |

Exercise 10 Tenses and verb forms

Complete the newspaper article. Put the verb in brackets in the correct form, active or passive.

Example
I asked John ***to do*** (do) the shopping but he ***hasn't done*** (not do) it yet.

£200M ART STOLEN

Paintings by Monet, Rembrandt, and Degas (1)____________ (steal) from the Boston Museum.

Yesterday afternoon two thieves wearing police uniforms arrived at the museum and asked the guard (2)__________ (show) them Monet's paintings. They said that they (3)__________ (receive) a telephone call at the police station that morning telling them that the paintings were in danger. The guard immediately let them (4)__________ (see) the paintings. The thieves told him (5)__________ (turn off) the alarm system and then suddenly they made him (6)__________ (lie) on the ground and they tied his arms and legs. They worked very quickly and carefully and when they (7)__________ (collect) the best paintings they (8)__________ (leave) the museum quietly and calmly through the front door. The director of the museum, Karen Haas said:

'The thieves (9)__________ (take) our best pictures. I (10)__________ (work) here for 12 years and I can't believe that this (11)__________ (happen). How did they manage (12)__________ (take) them so easily? They might (13)__________ (try) (14)__________ (sell) them to an art collector in Europe, but this will be difficult because the paintings are so well known. If they (15)__________ (not be) so well known, it would (16)__________ (be) easier (17)__________ (sell) them. We have decided (18)__________ (employ) more guards, and a new alarm system (19)__________ already __________ (put) in. I'm sure the police will find the thieves and our paintings, but they think it might (20)__________ (take) a long time.'

	20

Exercise 11 Multi-word verbs

Match a line in **A** with a line in **B**.

A	B
I didn't know the word,	but I picked it up quite easily.
I used to enjoy smoking,	I'll look after it.
People say French is difficult,	so I looked it up.
Don't worry about the cat,	but I gave it up.

	4

Exercise 12 Prepositions

Complete the sentences with the correct preposition.

1 I've been reading a story __________ two girls who travelled round the world.
2 I sold my car __________ £2,000.
3 If that machine weren't __________ of order, I'd get you a drink.
4 Do you believe __________ UFOs?
5 He said that she was too young to buy alcohol and that it was __________ the law.
6 Let me pay __________ the drinks.

	6

Exercise 13 Words that go together

Match a line in **A** with a line in **B**.

A	B
never	story
wear	a lift
wait	the truth
drive	patiently
tell	weight
detective	a uniform
lose	carefully
give someone	mind

A	B
narrow	concert
get	glasses
sun	in computers
pop	forecast
rain	path
interested	heavily
weather	ready

	15

TOTAL		100

Answer keys

Extra ideas Units 1–4

Song – Sailing

2 I am sailing across the sea
I am trying to be with you
I am flying across the sea
I am dying to be near you

3
1	sailing	7	passing
2	sailing	8	dying
3	sailing	9	trying
4	flying	10	sailing
5	flying	11	sailing
6	flying	12	sailing

Tapescript

I am sailing, I am sailing home again across the sea
I am sailing stormy waters, to be near you, to be free.

I am flying, I am flying like a bird across the sea
I am flying, passing high clouds, to be near you, to be free.

Can you hear me, can you hear me, through the dark night far away?
I am dying, forever trying to be with you; who can say?

We are sailing, we are sailing home again across the sea
We are sailing stormy waters, to be near you, to be free.
Oh Lord, to be near you, to be free.
Oh Lord, to be near you, to be free.

Extra ideas Units 5–8

Song – Killing me softly with his song

1 The song is about a woman who goes to listen to a young singer, and finds that his songs have great meaning for her.

2 1d 2b 3a 4e 5c

3 **Answers and tapescript**

1 4 6 2 3 5
1 4 2 3 6 5
1 6 3 4 2 5

Strumming my pain with his fingers,
Singing my life with his words,
Killing me softly with his song,
Killing me softly with his song,
Telling my whole life with his words,
Killing me softly with his song.

I heard he sang a good song, I heard he had a style
And so I came to see him to listen for a while
And there he was this young boy, a stranger to my eyes
(Strumming my pain, etc.)
I felt all flushed with fever, embarrassed by the crowd
I felt he'd found my letters and read each one out loud
I prayed that he would finish but he just kept right on
(Strumming my pain, etc.)
He sang as if he knew me in all my dark despair
And then he looked right through me as if I wasn't there
But he just kept on singing, singing clear and strong
(Strumming my pain, etc.)

Extra ideas Units 9–12

Song – I'll be there for you

1 *I'll be there for you* means *I will always love and support you.*

2 1d 2c 3b 4a

3
1	*work*	7	*as well*
2	*disaster*	8	*at home*
3	*social*	9	*toast*
4	*Now*	10	*well*
5	*fall*	11	*moments*
6	*around*	12	*Life*

Tapescript

So no one told you life was gonna be this way,
Your job's a joke, you're broke,
Your love life's gone away.
It's like you're always stuck in second gear,
When it hasn't been your day, your week,
Your month, or even your year.

But I'll be there for you,
When the rain starts to pour,
I'll be there for you.
You know I've been there before.
I'll be there for you,
'Cause you're there for me too.

You're still in bed at ten, and work began at eight,
You've burned your breakfast,
So far, things aren't going great,
Your mother warned you, 'There'll be days like these,'
But she didn't tell you when
The world has brought you down to your knees.

But I'll be there for you, etc.

Extra ideas Units 13–14

Song – Sitting on the dock of the bay

2 The *tide* is the regular rise and fall in the level of the sea, caused by the gravitational pull of the *moon* and the sun.
A *dock* is the part of a port where ships go to have their cargo removed.
A *bay* is a part of the sea enclosed by a wide curve of the shore.
Georgia is a state in the south east of the United States.
San Francisco is a city on the west coast of the United States.

3
1	Sitting	9	change
2	evening	10	remains
3	ships	11	ten
4	watch	12	guess
5	home	13	bones
6	bay	14	loneliness
7	nothing	15	roamed
8	nothing's	16	dock

Tapescript

Sitting in the morning sun
I'll be sitting when the evening comes
Watching the ships roll in
And then I watch them roll away again, yeah
I'm sitting on the dock of the bay
Watching the tide roll away
I'm just sitting on the dock of the bay
Wasting time
I left my home in Georgia
Headed for the 'Frisco bay
'Cause I've had nothing to live for
And looks like nothing's gonna come my way
So I'm just gonna sit on the dock of the bay
Watching the tide roll away
I'm sitting on the dock of the bay
Wasting time
Looks like nothing's gonna change
Everything still remains the same
I can't do what ten people tell me to do
So I guess I'll remain the same, yeah

Sitting here resting my bones
And this loneliness won't leave me alone
It's two thousand miles I roamed
Just to make this dock my home
Now, I'm just gonna sit at the dock of the bay
Watching the tide roll away
Sitting on the dock of the bay
Wasting time …

Stop and check 1

Questions

1 How many children has Peter got/does Peter have?
2 What are you reading?
3 Where did they go (to) on holiday last year?
4 Which shop does she work in?
5 Why did you get up early this morning?
6 When/What time does the supermarket close?
7 How often do you go swimming?
8 Whose car did you borrow?

Tenses

1 spends
2 Are … looking
3 don't have
4 doesn't like love
5 bought Do … like
6 was living started
7 lives met was working

have/have got

Sample answers

1 He has/He's got a dog, friends, a bag, a sleeping bag, a book.
He doesn't have/He hasn't got a car, a house, any money, shoes.
He has/He's got a big house, a car, a garden, a swimming pool, a servant.
He doesn't have/He hasn't got a dog, friends.

2 Has he got a dog? Yes, he has.
Does he have a car? No, he doesn't.
Has he got a big house? Yes, he has.
Does he have a dog? No, he doesn't.
Has he got a swimming pool? Yes, he has.

Past tense forms

heard	could	broke
phoned	put	caught
lived	began	hit
tried	left	fell
made	felt	built

Prepositions

1 to on	5 in
2 at in	6 nothing
3 after	7 to
4 nothing	8 on/until

Expressions of quantity

1 some any
any any
some
any some
some

2 1 How much money
2 a few potatoes
3 much time
4 a lot of shops
5 I've got something
6 John lives somewhere
7 Somebody told me

Articles

1 the the
2 The the
3 nothing
4 nothing a
5 nothing a a

Vocabulary

put on make-up
do a part-time job
make a decision
drive a van
call the police
run out of milk
say sorry
wash my hair
lose my money
forget her wedding anniversary

Stop and check 2

Verb patterns

1 to share	4 to find
2 going	5 to meet
3 to live	6 travelling

going to and *will*

1 I'm going to cook
2 I'm going to study
3 He'll help
4 I'll buy
5 I'm going to cut

Descriptions

1 What's the weather like? – It's quite hot.
What's Ann like? – She's very nice.
What was the film like? – OK, but boring near the end.
What does she like doing? – Horse riding.
What are her parents like? – They're a bit strict.

2

faster	fastest
funnier	funniest
more expensive	most expensive
richer	richest
hotter	hottest
more interesting	most interesting
better	best
worse	worst

Past Simple and past participle

made made
drank drunk
saw seen
travelled travelled
acted acted
tried tried
ate eaten
broke broken
knew known
spent spent
had had
read read
wrote written
spoke spoken

Present Perfect or Past Simple?

1 1 has written wrote
2 Have … tried
3 have … been, did … go
4 have lived
5 lived moved
6 met have … known

2 1 for since
2 never
3 for ever
4 since never

3 Sample answers
1 have … lived
For ten years.
2 Have … drunk
Yes, I have.
3 have … visited
Five.
4 did … go
To Italy.
5 did … do
We went sightseeing

have to and *should*

1 don't have to	4 don't have to
2 have to	5 should
3 should	

Vocabulary

1
fed up	interested
messy	tidy
mean	generous
noisy	quiet
tell a lie	tell the truth
cruel	kind
sensitive	tough
go abroad	stay at home

2
1 cruel kind
2 come first
3 go abroad/stay at home
4 fed up

Stop and check 3

Time and conditional clauses

1
1	eat	will be
2	will fail	don't study
3	will … do	fail
4	will suffer	don't look after
5	will do	finishes
6	reads	will understand
7	will … stay	goes
8	will stay	tells

2 If I pass my driving test, I'll buy a car.
You'll learn English more easily if you study a little every day.
Will you give her these when you see her?
If they don't give him the job, I don't know what he'll do.
I'll marry you as soon as we find somewhere to live.
Your plants won't grow well if you don't water them.
As soon as we get the tickets, we'll send them to you.
If I buy the champagne, will you pay for the meal?

Verb patterns and infinitives

1
1 swimming
2 to tidy
3 to walk
4 to go
5 to learn

2
1 cry
2 making
3 to live
4 to go
5 go
6 to explain
7 to find

Passives

Correct forms

1
1 created
2 is called
3 was called
4 was given
5 made
6 have been translated
7 have been made

2
1 was designed
2 was asked
3 were taken
4 was made
5 are not made

Second conditional

1
1 lived, would have
2 had, wouldn't work
3 would go, wasn't/weren't
4 would … do, gave
5 were, would look

2
1 She wouldn't be poor if she didn't spend a lot of money.
2 She wouldn't cough if she didn't smoke.
3 If he understood Portuguese, he'd work in Brazil.
4 If they had a garden, they'd grow vegetables.
5 If I had a boat, I'd sail around the world.

might

1 She might have a holiday or she might look for a job.
2 They might go to Spain or they might stay at home.
3 You might forget it.
4 I might be late.
5 I might stay the night or I might come back the same day.

Vocabulary

1
1 got
2 made
3 got
4 made
5 got
6 did
7 got
8 did
9 took
10 took
11 got

2
1 carry
2 keep
3 gave
4 lost
5 grow
6 told

Stop and check 4

Present Perfect Simple and Continuous

1 I haven't finished yet.
2 Have they booked the restaurant yet?
3 We've already ordered the champagne.
4 Anna's been studying hard for five hours.
5 How long has Jim been cleaning his bike?
6 I've just seen Jim.
7 We've been helping Mary since five o'clock.
8 They haven't spoken to each other for four years.
9 Nobody has sent me a letter for a long time.
10 It hasn't rained here since June.

Tenses

1 come
2 came
3 haven't met
4 started
5 was
6 have been learning
7 didn't understand
8 has improved
9 have just taken
10 pass
11 will move
12 are coming
13 haven't seen
14 have never been
15 don't speak

Reported statements

1 hadn't met
2 had just taken
3 were coming
4 hadn't seen
5 didn't speak

Past Perfect

1 had never seen
2 threw
3 lived
4 had already told
5 hadn't had

Vocabulary

1 variety
2 really
3 succeeded
4 comfort
5 nearly
6 peace
7 impossible
8 care
9 beliefs
10 honestly

Progress test 1

Exercise 1

1 When did you start learning English?
2 How often does she play tennis?
3 What do you like doing at the weekend?
4 What would you like to do this weekend?
5 Why haven't you got a dictionary?
6 How much sugar did you put in my coffee?
7 What were you doing when John phoned?
8 Who is going to make the sandwiches?
9 Does your mother enjoy listening to the radio?
10 Where did Anna live when she was a child?

Exercise 2

1 Where do Mr and Mrs Ramsey come from?
2 Where do they live?
3 How old is Xavier?
4 Does he have/Has he got any brothers or sisters?
5 Have Mr and Mrs Ramsey got/Do Mr and Mrs Ramsey have any children?
6 What does Xavier do/What's Xavier's job?
7 Where did he go on holiday last year?
8 How long did Mr and Mrs Ramsey stay in Scotland?
9 What are they going to do on holiday next year?
10 What is Xavier going to do on holiday next year?

Exercise 3

1 Do … know
2 met
3 was working
4 Does … live
5 lives
6 has got
7 is working
8 to invite
9 come
10 to see
11 saw
12 was teaching
13 had
14 talking
15 to write
16 don't have/haven't got
17 rang
18 am going to ring/will ring
19 'll come
20 'll bring

Exercise 4

bought, did, had, heard, left, made, put, spoke, took, wrote

Exercise 5

Uncount nouns

money, flour, homework, furniture, rice, bread, luggage, meat, music, food

Exercise 6

1 an
2 a
3 the
4 nothing
5 the
6 a
7 nothing
8 nothing
9 the
10 nothing

Exercise 7

Correct sentences

1 Is there any milk? I can't see any.
2 There are some potatoes, but only a few.
3 There are a lot of cars parked in the street.
4 Have you got much unemployment in your town?
5 Only a few people believe his story.
6 How much homework do you have tonight?
7 There isn't much rice and there aren't any eggs.
8 There was some snow last winter but not much.
9 How lovely! Somebody gave you some flowers.
10 I didn't go anywhere very interesting for my holiday.

Exercise 8

1 art (The others are to do with learning a language.)
2 sing (The others are nouns.)
3 suitcase (The others are everyday objects.)
4 photography (The others are to do with communication.)
5 iron (The others are to do with entertainment.)
6 towel (The others are products you put on your face or teeth.)
7 clean (The others mean the opposite of *clean*.)
8 mend (The others are the opposite of *mend*.)
9 customer (The others all give a service to the customer.)
10 yesterday evening (The others refer to the future.)
11 friendly (The others are feelings.)
12 careful (The others are adjectives with a negative prefix.)
13 print (The others are to do with speaking.)
14 posters (The others are things that you have to open to read.)
15 chemist's (The others sell food.)

Exercise 9

tell a joke
spend money
hard work
say sorry
make a promise
take a photograph
sore throat
taxi driver
pay a bill
go abroad

Progress test 2

Exercise 1

1 like
2 friendlier
3 more
4 than
5 worst
6 was
7 the
8 as
9 most
10 as
11 tastier
12 latest
13 What
14 funniest
15 funnier

Exercise 2

Correct sentences

1 I have lived in Chesswood for five years.
2 We moved here after my daughter was born.
3 Before that we lived in London.
4 I have been a teacher since I left university.
5 I went to Bristol University in 1994.
6 We have studied English for three years.
7 I have never been to Russia, but I'd like to go.

Exercise 3

1 earns
2 studied
3 found
4 has changed
5 works
6 has been
7 has been
8 spent

Exercise 4

1 have to
2 shouldn't
3 should
4 has to
5 have to
6 don't have to
7 have to
8 shouldn't
9 don't have to
10 have to

Exercise 5

1 If I hear any news, I will phone you.
2 I will pay you back as soon as I can.
3 You will feel better if you stop smoking.
4 Peter will buy a car when he has enough money.
5 I will help you if you have a problem.

Exercise 6

1 'll call, is
2 are late, 'll go
3 passes, 'll buy
4 'll go, finish
5 don't stop, 'll go

Exercise 7

1 He used to go to Bradford School.
2 He used to play football for the school.
3 He used to write songs with a friend called Keith.
4 He used to play with *The Forwards*.

5 *The Forwards* used to play in pubs and clubs.
6 In 1991 he had a number one record.
7 He used to go out with a girl called Mandy.
8 *The Forwards* toured the United States in 1992.
9 Andy went solo in 1997.
10 He played at a pop festival in Los Angeles three years later.

Exercise 8

1	to catch	6	to see
2	open	7	to say
3	to stop	8	learning
4	to drink	9	to shut up
5	skiing	10	to marry

Exercise 9

open a bank account
regular hours
tell a story
part-time work
alarm clock
ear-ring
signpost
sun-glasses
rush hour
take responsibility

Exercise 10

1	check	4	sale
2	read	5	break
3	fare		

Exercise 11

1	only	4	too
2	especially	5	just
3	exactly		

Exercise 12

1	beautiful	6	poor
2	pleased	7	miserable
3	quiet	8	well-behaved
4	generous	9	interesting
5	modern	10	tidy

Progress test 3

Exercise 1

brought	brought
fell	fallen
felt	felt
forgot	forgotten
knew	known
let	let
lost	lost
spoke	spoken
told	told
understood	understood

Exercise 2

Correct forms

1	has failed	4	don't grow
2	was written	5	have been taken
3	were cut down		

Exercise 3

1 English is spoken all over the world.
2 Nylon has been made since 1932.
3 Why wasn't I invited to Mary's party?
4 When will the new bridge be built?
5 They were asked to design a new car.

Exercise 4

If I lived in Brazil, I'd/I wouldn't learn Portuguese.
If I earned more money, I'd/I wouldn't save it.
If I knew Maria's address, I'd/I wouldn't go to see her.
If I had a dictionary, I'd/I wouldn't look up the word.
If I were you, I'd/I wouldn't marry George.

Exercise 5

1 would be, had
2 give her a pay rise next month.
3 had, wouldn't go
4 didn't live, would find
5 go and live with

Exercise 6

Correct sentences

1 I saw her five minutes ago.
2 We've been here since last Saturday.
3 How long have you known Wendy?
4 We haven't made coffee yet.
5 He has been waiting to see the doctor since nine o'clock.
6 When did you buy your new car?
7 Mary isn't home. She's gone to work.
8 I've been running in the park, so I'm tired.
9 I've run round the park three times.
10 They've already had their dinner.

Exercise 7

1 How long have you been waiting for a bus?
2 How long has he been saving up to buy a boat?
3 How long have you been having driving lessons?
4 How long has she been working in the library?
5 How long have they been trying to sell their house?

Exercise 8

1 She told him she loved him very much.
2 He said that he visited her every Sunday.
3 He said that he'd taken her some flowers for her birthday.
4 He told her he was leaving her forever.
5 She said that she'd forgotten.

Exercise 9

1	would	4	would
2	had	5	had
3	had		

Exercise 10

1 have been stolen
2 to show
3 had received
4 see
5 to turn off
6 lie
7 had collected
8 left
9 have taken
10 have worked/have been working
11 has happened
12 to take
13 try
14 to sell
15 weren't
16 be
17 to sell
18 to employ
19 has already been put
20 take

Exercise 11

I didn't know the word, so I looked it up.
I used to enjoy smoking, but I gave it up.
People say French is difficult, but I picked it up quite easily.
Don't worry about the cat. I'll look after it.

Exercise 12

1	about	4	in
2	for	5	against
3	out	6	for

Exercise 13

never mind	narrow path
wear a uniform	get ready
wait patiently	sun-glasses
drive carefully	pop concert
tell the truth	rain heavily
detective story	interested in computers
lose weight	weather forecast
give someone a lift	

Word list

Here is a list of most of the new words in the units of New Headway Pre-intermediate Student's Book.

adj = adjective
adv = adverb
US = American English
coll = colloquial
conj = conjunction
pl = plural
prep = preposition
pron = pronoun
pp = past participle
n = noun
v = verb

Unit 1

advertising *n* /'ædvətaɪzɪŋ/
alphabet *n* /'ælfəbet/
ancient society *n* /'eɪnʃənt sə'saɪəti/
anger *n* /'æŋgə/
architect *n* /'ɑ:kɪtekt/
art gallery *n* /'ɑ:t ˌgæləri/
as usual /'æz 'ju:ʒʊəl/, /əz 'ju:ʒəl/

bee *n* /bi:/
book *v* /bʊk/
born (*Where were you born?*) *pp* /bɔ:n/
borrow *v* /'bɒrəʊ/
builder *n* /bɪldə/

can *v* /kæn/, /kən/
Chinese meal *n* /'tʃaɪˌni:z 'mi:l/
come round (= visit) *v* /ˌkʌm 'raʊnd/
communicate *v* /kə'mju:nɪkeɪt/
communication *n* /kəˌmju:nɪ'keɪʃn/
compared to /kəm'peəd tə/
course *n* /kɔ:s/

depend *v* /dɪ'pend/
development *n* /dɪ'veləpmənt/
drama *n* /'drɑ:mə/

(know) each other *v* /ˌi:tʃ 'ʌðə/
e-mail *n* /'i:meɪl/
Egyptian *adj* /ɪ'dʒɪpʃn/
elephant *n* /'elɪfənt/
enjoy *v* /ɪn'dʒɔɪ/
essay *n* /'eseɪ/
exchange *v* /ɪks'tʃeɪndʒ/
explain *v* /ɪks'pleɪn/

face *n* /feɪs/
fax *n* /fæks/
flat *adj, n* /flæt/
future *n* /'fju:tʃə/

generation gap *n* /ˌdʒenə'reɪʃn ˌgæp/
government *n* /'gʌvənmənt/
graduate *v* /'grædʒʊeɪt/

hard (work) *adj* /hɑ:d/
hieroglyphics *n pl* /ˌhaɪrə'glɪfɪks/
history *n* /'hɪstəri/
How many ... ? /ˌhaʊ 'meni/
How much ... ? /ˌhaʊ 'mʌtʃ/
huge *adj* /hju:dʒ/
human *n* /'hju:mən/

idea *n* /aɪ'dɪə/
ideal *adj* /aɪ'di:əl/
infinite *adj* /'ɪnfɪnət/
influence *n* /'ɪnflʊəns/
Internet *n* /'ɪntənet/
introduce *v* /ɪntrə'dju:s/
invite *v* /ɪn'vaɪt/

kind *adj, n* /kaɪnd/

last *adj* /lɑ:st/

make a promise *v* /ˌmeɪk ə 'prɒmɪs/
make yourself at home *v* /ˌmeɪk jɔ:ˌself ət 'həʊm/
married *pp* /'mærɪd/
mean *adj, v* /mi:n/
media *n* /'mi:dɪə/
message *n* /'mesɪdʒ/
mobile phone *n* /ˌməʊbaɪl 'fəʊn/
modern *adj* /'mɒdən/
monkey *n* /'mʌŋki/
museum *n* /mju:'zɪəm/

neighbour *n* /'neɪbə/
nobody *pron* /'nəʊbɒdi/
noise *n* /nɔɪz/
north *n* /nɔ:θ/

painting *n* /'peɪntɪŋ/
paper *n* /'peɪpə/
part-time (job) *adj* /ˌpɑ:t 'taɪm/
party *n* /'pɑ:ti/
past *n* /pɑ:st/
persuade *v* /pə'sweɪd/
philosophy *n* /fɪ'lɒsəfi/
photography *n* /fə'tɒgrəfi/
play *n, v* /pleɪ/
pleased to meet you /'pli:zd tə 'mi:t ju:/
poetry *n* /'pəʊətri/
postlady *n* /'pəʊstleɪdi/
present *n* /'preznt/
probably *adv* /'prɒbəbli/
public speaking *n* /'pʌblɪk 'spi:kɪŋ/

quiet *adj* /'kwaɪət/

ring *n, v* /rɪŋ/
Russian *adj* /'rʌʃən/

send *v* /send/
sense *n* /sens/
show *v* /ʃəʊ/
single *adj* /'sɪŋgl/
sound *n* /saʊnd/
speak (a language) *v* /spi:k/
special *adj* /'speʃl/
spoken word *n* /'spəʊkən 'wɜ:d/
strange *adj* /streɪndʒ/
system *n* /'sɪstəm/

T-shirt *n* /'ti:ˌʃɜ:t/
technology *n* /tek'nɒlədʒi/
tell a joke *v* /ˌtel ə 'dʒəʊk/
tell lies *v* /ˌtel 'laɪz/
tell the truth *v* /ˌtel ðə 'tru:θ/
together *adv* /tə'geðə/
train *n, v* /treɪn/
transform *v* /træns'fɔ:m/
translator *n* /trænz'leɪtə/

unique *adj* /ju:'ni:k/
until *conj* /ʌn'tɪl/
unusual *adj* /ʌn'ju:ʒʊəl/

van *n* /væn/

wall *n* /wɔ:l/
wear *v* /weə/
well-paid *adj* /ˌwel'peɪd/
whale *n* /weɪl/
Which ... ? /wɪtʃ/
Whose ... ? /hu:z/

Unit 2

aborigine *n* /ˌæbə'rɪdʒni:/
annoy *v* /ə'nɔɪ/
annoying habit *n* /əˌnɔɪŋ 'hæbɪt/
architect *n* /'ɑ:kɪtekt/

barbecue *n* /'bɑ:bɪkju:/
baseball *n* /'beɪsbɔ:l/
bungalow *n* /'bʌŋgələʊ/

certainly *adv* /'sɜ:tənli/
change gears *v* /'tʃeɪndz 'gɪəz/
clear up *v* /ˌklɪə(r) 'ʌp/
climate *n* /'klaɪmət/
coast *n* /kəʊst/
complain *v* /kəm'pleɪn/
computer *n* /kəm'pju:tə/
cosmopolitan *adj* /ˌkɒzmə'pɒlɪtən/
couple *n* /'kʌpl/
credit card *n* /'kredɪt ˌkɑ:d/
cricket *n* /'krɪkɪt/
crowded *adj* /'kraʊdɪd/
culture *n* /'kʌltʃə/

descent (of European descent) *n* /dɪ'sent/
diamonds *n pl* /'daɪəməndz/
drive (sb) mad *v* /ˌdraɪv 'mæd/

electrician *n* /ɪlek'trɪʃn/
exciting *adj* /ik'saɪtɪŋ/
export *v* /ek'spɔ:t/

fast *adj* /fɑ:st/
fine art *n* /ˌfaɪn 'ɑ:t/
fish *v* /fɪʃ/
flag *n* /flæg/
free time *n* /ˌfri: 'taɪm/
fries (French fries) *n pl* /fraɪz/

game reserve *n* /'geɪm rɪˌzɜ:v/
gear (change gear) *n* /gɪə/
get used to (sth) *v* /get 'ju:st tu:/
giraffe *n* /dʒɪ'rɑ:f/
go jogging *v* /ˌgeʊ 'dʒɒgɪŋ/
gold *adj* /gəʊld/
grape *n* /greɪp/

habit *n* /'hæbɪt/
have in common *v* /ˌhæv ɪn 'kɒmən/
hesitation *n* /hezɪ'teɪʃn/

ice hockey *n* /'aɪs ˌhɒki/
immigrant *n* /'ɪmɪgrənt/
in control *adj* /ˌɪn kən'trəʊl/
independence *n* /ɪndɪ'pendəns/
inhabitants *n pl* /ɪn'hæbɪtənts/
inland *adj* /ɪn'lænd/
island *n* /'aɪlənd/

join *v* /dʒɔɪn/

lake *n* /leɪk/
light *n* /laɪt/
lion *n* /'laɪən/

mainly *adv* /'meɪnli/
make a decision *v* /ˌmeɪk ə dɪ'sɪʒn/
make-up (put on make-up) *n* /'meɪkʌp/
Maori *n* /'maʊri/
marriage *n* /'mærɪdʒ/
mathematician *n* /mæθmə'tɪʃn/
mess *n* /mes/
miserable *adj* /'mɪzrəbl/
miss (miss home) *v* /mɪs/
miss (miss the match) *v* /mɪs/
motorbike *n* /'məʊtəˌbaɪk/

nearly *adv* /'nɪəli/
northern *adj* /'nɔ:ðən/

old-fashioned *adj* /ˌəʊld 'fæʃnd/
on time *adv* /ˌɒn 'taɪm/
only *adj* /'əʊnli/
opportunity *n* /ɒpə'tju:nɪti/
organized *adj* /'ɔ:gənaɪzd/
original *adj* /ə'rɪdʒənl/
outdoors *adv* /aʊt'dɔ:z/

parliament *n* /'pɑ:ləmənt/
partner *n* /'pɑ:tnə/
pear *n* /peə/
pet (= animal) *n* /pet/
population *n* /ˌpɒpjʊ'leɪʃn/
poster *n* /'pəʊstə/
professional *adj* /prə'feʃənl/
pub lunch *n* /ˌpʌb 'lʌntʃ/
publisher *n* /'pʌblɪʃə/
put up with *v* /pʊt 'ʌp wɪð/

relative *n* /'relətɪv/
relax *v* /rɪ'læks/
remote control *n* /rɪ'məʊt kən'trəʊl/
romantic *adj* /rəʊ'mæntɪk/
rugby *n* /'rʌgbi/

salmon *n* /'sæmən/
scruffy (= untidy) *adj, coll* /'skrʌfi/
sheep *n* /ʃi:p/
shout *v* /ʃaʊt/
similar to *adj* /'sɪmələ tu:/
soap (a soap opera) *n* /'səʊp/
soccer store *n US* /'sɒkə ˌstɔ:(r)/
sofa *n* /'səʊfə/
south-east Asian *adj* /ˌsaʊθi:st 'eɪʒn/
space (in your home) *n* /speɪs/
strange *adj* /streɪndʒ/
successful *adj* /sək'sesfl/
sunshine *n* /'sʌnʃaɪn/

talk loudly *v* /ˌtɔ:k 'laʊdli/
tidy *v* /'taɪdi/
train (train a dog) *v* /treɪn/
transportation *n* /ˌtrænspɔ:'teɪʃn/

uniform *n* /'ju:nɪfɔ:m/
untidy *adj* /ʌn'taɪdi/

variety *n* /və'raɪəti/
Vietnamese *adj* /viˌetnə'mi:z/

Walkman *n* /wɔ:kmən/
way of life *n* /ˌweɪ əv 'laɪf/
whisky *n* /'wɪski/
wildlife *n* /'waɪldlaɪf/
wool *n* /wʊl/

yard (Brit. Eng. = garden) *n* /jɑ:d/

zebra *n* /'zebrə/, /'zi:brə/

Unit 3

adore *v* /ə'dɔ:/
advice *n* /əd'vaɪs/
agree *v* /ə'gri:/
alone *adj* /ə'ləʊn/
ambition *n* /æm'bɪʃŋ/
angry *adj* /'æŋgri/
appear *v* /ə'pɪə/
arm *n* /ɑ:m/
armed (with a gun) *pp* /ɑ:md/
awful *adj* /ɔ:fl/

back door *n* /ˌbæk 'dɔ:/
be in love *v* /ˌbi: ɪn 'lʌv/
believe *v* /bɪ'li:v/
birthday *n* /'bɜ:θdeɪ/
bit (= small piece) *n* /bɪt/
bomb *n* /bɒm/
brandy *n* /'brændi/
break *v* /breɪk/
broken *pp* /'brəʊkən/
burglar *n* /'bɜ:glə/
burglary *n* /'bɜ:gləri/
business *n* /'bɪznəs/

call (the police) *v* /kɔ:l/
care *v* /keə/
carry *v* /'kæri/
catch (a criminal) *v* /kætʃ/
catch a plane *v* /ˌkætʃ ə 'pleɪn/
CD player *n* /'si: 'di: ˌpleɪə/
central heating *n* /ˌsentrəl 'hi:tɪŋ/
clean your teeth *v* /ˌkli:n jɔ: 'ti:θ/
clearly *adv* /'klɪəli/
comfort *v* /'kʌmfət/
cook *v* /kʊk/
crime *n* /kraɪm/
cry (= with tears) *v* /kraɪ/
cut *v* /kʌt/

danger *n* /'deɪndʒə/
dead *pp* /ded/
decide *v* /dɪ'saɪd/
detective *n* /dɪ'tektɪv/
develop *v* /dɪ'veləp/
discuss *v* /dɪs'kʌs/
distinct *adj* /dɪs'tɪŋkt/
do an exam *v* /ˌdu: ən ig'zæm/
downstairs *adv* /ˌdaʊn'steəz/
drawer *n* /drɔ:/
dream *n* /dri:m/
drive *v* /draɪv/
drop *v* /drɒp/

education *n* /ˌedʒʊ'keɪʃn/
employ *v* /ɪm'plɔɪ/
employed *pp* /ɪm'plɔɪd/
enjoy *v* /ɪn'dʒɔɪ/
enter *v* /'entə/
escape *v* /ɪ'skeɪp/
even so /ˌi:vn 'səʊ/
explanation *n* /ˌeksplə'neɪʃn/

factory *n* /'fæktri/
fair *adj* /feə/
fall *v* /fɔ:l/
famous *adj* /'feɪməs/
fast asleep *adj* /ˌfɑ:st ə'sli:p/
feel ill *v* /ˌfi:l 'ɪl/
finally *adv* /'faɪnəli/
find *v* /faɪnd/
floor *n* /flɔ:/
forget *v* /fə'get/
fortunately *adv* /'fɔ:tʃənətli/
friend *n* /'frend/
furniture *n* /'fɜ:nɪtʃə/

get hot *v* /ˌget 'hɒt/
get ready *v* /ˌget 'redi/
go away (on holiday) *v*
/ˌgəʊ ə'weɪ/
go wrong *v* /ˌgəʊ 'rɒŋ/
govern *v* /'gʌvən/
government *n* /'gʌvənmənt/
guest *n* /gest/

habit *n* /'hæbɪt/
hand *v* /hænd/
happy *adj* /'hæpi/
have a shower *v* /ˌhæv ə 'ʃaʊə/
hear *v* /hɪə/
help *v* /'help/
help yourselves *v* /ˌhelp jɔ:'selvz/
hit *n, v* /hɪt/
hold *v* /həʊld/
however *adv* /haʊ'evə/

ice *n* /aɪs/
immediately *adv* /ɪ'mi:dɪətli/
improvement *n* /ɪm'pru:vmənt/
industry *n* /'ɪndʌstri/
invitation *n* /ɪnvɪ'teɪʃn/

jewellery *n* /'dʒu:əlri/

kill *v* /kɪl/
knife *n* /naɪf/

laugh *v* /lɑ:f/
leave (sb/sth somewhere) *v* /li:v/
legal *adj* /'li:gl/
listen (to the radio) *v* /'lɪsn/
look forward to *v*
/ˌlʊk 'fɔ:wəd tu:/
lose *v* /lu:z/

mask *n* /mɑ:sk/
meet *v* /mi:t/
melt *v* /melt/
mend *v* /mend/
motor racing *n* /'məʊtə ˌreɪsɪŋ/
murder weapon *n*
/'mɜ:də ˌwepən/

noise *n* /nɔɪz/
note *n* /nəʊt/

odour *n* /'əʊdə/
organize *v* /'ɔ:gənaɪz/

pack *v* /pæk/
pay day *n* /'peɪ deɪ/
perfect *adj* /'pɜ:fekt/
petrol *n* /'petrəl/
pick up (the phone) *v* /ˌpɪk 'ʌp/
pocket money *n* /'pɒkɪt ˌmʌni/
polite *adj* /pə'laɪt/
pool *n* /pu:l/
present *n* /'preznt/
purse *n* /pɜ:s/
put on make-up *v*
/ˌpʊt ɒn 'meɪk ʌp/

revise (for an exam) *v* /rɪ'vaɪz/
robber *n* /'rɒbə/
routine *n* /ru:'ti:n/
run out of (coffee) *v* /rʌn 'aʊt əv/

say sorry *v* /ˌseɪ 'sɒri/
science *n* /'saɪəns/
scream *v* /skri:m/
search *v* /sɜ:tʃ/
shock *n* /ʃɒk/
show *v* /ʃəʊ/
similar *adj* /'sɪmələ/
smash *n* /smæʃ/
smile *v* /smaɪl/
snow *n* /snəʊ/
sob *v* /sɒb/
special *adj* /'speʃl/
statue *n* /'stætju:/
steal *v* /sti:l/
stereo *n* /'steriəʊ/

tears (= cry) *n* /tɪəz/
teenage daughter *n*
/'ti:neɪdʒ 'dɔ:tə/
teller (in a bank) *n* /'telə/
thief *n* /θi:f/
thirsty *adj* /'θɜ:sti/
tidy *adj* /'taɪdi/
toilet *n* /'tɔɪlət/
turn up (the heating) *v* /ˌtɜ:n 'ʌp/

umbrella *n* /ʌm'brelə/
unfortunately *adv* /ʌn'fɔ:tʃənətli/
uninvited *adj* /ˌʌnɪn'vaɪtɪd/
use *v* /ju:z/

video recorder *n*
/'vɪdiəʊ rɪ'kɔ:də/

wait *v* /weɪt/
wake up *v* /ˌweɪk 'ʌp/
wedding anniversary *n*
/'wedɪŋ ænɪˌvɜ:səri/
whole *adj* /həʊl/
wonder *v* /'wʌndə/

Unit 4

a dozen eggs /ə ˌdʌzən 'egz/
a loaf of bread *n* /ə ˌləʊf əv 'bred/
a pint of milk /ə ˌpaɪnt əv 'mɪlk/
a pound of cheese
/ə ˌpaʊnd əv 'tʃi:z/
accountant *n* /ə'kaʊntənt/
assistant *n* /ə'sɪstənt/
atmosphere *n* /'ætməsfɪə/
attractive *adj* /ə'træktɪv/

belt *n* /belt/
billboards *n pl* /'bɪlbɔ:dz/
boutique *n* /bu:'ti:k/
brand *n* /brænd/
busiest *adj* /'bɪziəst/
butter *n* /'bʌtə/
by the way /ˌbaɪ ðə 'weɪ/

carrot *n* /'kærət/
cashier *n* /kæ'ʃɪə/
changing rooms *n pl*
/'tʃeɪndʒɪŋ ˌru:mz/
chic *adj* /ʃi:k/
coat *n* /kəʊt/
cold (*I've got a cold*) *n* /kəʊld/
conditioner *n* /kən'dɪʃənə/
consumption *n* /kən'sʌmpʃn/
crisps *n pl* /krɪsps/

delicious *adj* /dɪ'lɪʃəs/
deodorant *n* /di'əʊdərənt/
department store *n*
/dɪ'pɑ:tmənt ˌstɔ:/
desk *n* /desk/
doughnut *n* /'dəʊnʌt/

edition *n* /ɪ'dɪʃn/
exclusive *adj* /ɪks'klu:sɪv/
exquisite *adj*
/'ekskwɪzɪt/, /ɪks'kwɪzɪt/

fantastic *adj* /fæn'tæstɪk/
fashionable *adj* /'fæʃnəbl/
folk art *n* /'fəʊk ˌɑ:t/
for sale /fə'seɪl/
frozen yoghurt *n*
/ˌfrəʊzən 'jɒgət/

glasses (to see) *n pl* /'glɑ:sɪz/

hairbrush *n* /'heəbrʌʃ/
hand-made suit *n*
/ˌhænd meɪd 'su:t/
handbag *n* /'hændbæg/
high-class *adj* /ˌhaɪ 'klɑ:s/

icon *n* /'aɪkɒn/
incredible *adj* /ɪn'kredəbl/

jumper *n* /'dʒʌmpə/

leather goods *n pl* /'leðə ˌgʊdz/
lively *adj* /'laɪvli/

manufacturer *n*
/ˌmænjʊ'fæktʃərə/
mass produced *adj*
/ˌmæs prə'dju:st/
medium (size) *adj* /'mi:dɪəm/
middle shelf *n* /ˌmɪdl 'ʃelf/
millionaire *n* /mɪljə'neə/
mineral water *n*
/'mɪnərəl ˌwɔ:tə/

need *v* /ni:d/
neon lights *n pl* /ˌni:ɒn 'laɪts/
nephew *n* /'nefju:/

olive oil *n* /ˌɒlɪv 'ɔɪl/
onion *n* /'ʌnjən/
owe (money) *v* /əʊ/

packet *n* /'pækɪt/
palace *n* /'pæləs/
paradise *n* /'pærədaɪs/
pavement *n* /'peɪvmənt/
perfume *n* /'pɜ:fju:m/
picnic *n* /'pɪknɪk/
pleasant *adj* /'pleznt/
post office *n* /'pəʊst ˌɒfɪs/
postman *n* /'pəʊstmən/
product *n* /'prɒdʌkt/

rebuild *v* /ri:'bɪld/
record shop *n* /'rekɔ:d ˌʃɒp/
roll (= bread) *n* /rəʊl/

sausages *n pl* /'sɒsɪdʒɪz/
shampoo *n* /ʃæm'pu:/
share *v* /ʃeə/
shaving foam *n* /'ʃeɪvɪŋ ˌfəʊm/
shopkeeper *n* /'ʃɒpki:pə/
shopping list *n* /'ʃɒpɪŋ ˌlɪst/
shorts *n pl* /ʃɔ:ts/
soap *n* /səʊp/
sore throat *n* /ˌsɔ: 'θrəʊt/
sparkling (mineral water) *adj*
/'spɑ:klɪŋ/
spoonful *n* /'spu:nfʊl/
still (mineral water) *adj* /stɪl/
stomach ache *n* /'stʌmək ˌeɪk/
survey *n* /'sɜ:veɪ/
sweets *n pl* /swi:ts/

tie (to wear) /taɪ/
tissues *n pl* /'tɪʃu:z/
toilet paper *n* /'tɔɪlət ˌpeɪpə/
toothbrush *n* /'tu:θbrʌʃ/
toothpaste *n* /'tu:θpeɪst/
towel *n* /'taʊəl/
traffic *n* /'træfɪk/
trainers *n pl* /'treɪnəz/

underwear *n* /'ʌndəweə/
unique *adj* /ju:'ni:k/

village *n* /'vɪlɪdʒ/

well-known *adj* /ˌwel 'nəʊn/
wide *adj* /waɪd/

Unit 5

A levels *n pl* /'eɪ ˌlevəlz/
a day off (= not at work) *n*
/ə ˌdeɪ 'ɒf/
abroad *adv* /ə'brɔ:d/
adult *n* /'ædʌlt/
ambition *n* /æm'bɪʃn/
astronaut *n* /'æstrənɔ:t/
atmosphere *n* /'ætməsfɪə/
attention *n* /ə'tenʃn/

beautician *n* /bju:'tɪʃn/
boast *v* /bəʊst/
bodyguard *n* /'bɒdigɑ:d/
boot *n* /bu:t/
brighten *v* /'braɪtən/

call *v* /kɔ:l/
cash *n* /kæʃ/
chauffeur *n* /'ʃəʊfə/
Cheer up! /'tʃɪə(r) 'ʌp/
childhood *n* /'tʃaɪldhʊd/
close *v* /kləʊz/
cloud *n* /klaʊd/
club *n* /klʌb/
coach (= trainer) *n* /kəʊtʃ/
complain *v* /kəm'pleɪn/
cool *adj* /ku:l/
cost *v* /kɒst/
counsellor *n* /'kaʊnsələ/
crazy *adj* /'kreɪzi/

dentist *n* /'dentɪst/
depressed *adj* /dɪ'prest/
desert *v* /dɪ'zɜ:t/
designer clothes *n pl*
/dɪ'zaɪnə ˌkləʊðz/
down (= upset) *adj* /daʊn/
drop *v* /drɒp/
drug *n* /drʌg/

easily *adv* /'i:zəli/
ex-girlfriend *n*
/ˌeks 'gɜ:lfrend/
extravagant *adj* /ɪk'strævəgənt/

fall (= autumn) *n US* /fɔ:l/
fantastic *adj* /fæn'tæstɪk/
fed up *adj* /ˌfed 'ʌp/
fish *v* /fɪʃ/
fit (= healthy) *adj* /fɪt/
flu *n* /flu:/
flying school *n* /'flaɪɪŋ ˌsku:l/
forever *adv* /fə'revə/
freshman *n US* /'freʃmən/

get my nose done *v*
/ˌget maɪ 'nəʊz ˌdʌn/
glamorous *adj* /'glæmərəs/
go far (in life) *v* /ˌgəʊ 'fɑ:/
Good luck! /ˌgʊd 'lʌk/
grandfather *n* /'grænfɑ:ðə/
grow up *v* /ˌgrəʊ 'ʌp/
guilty *adj* /'gɪlti/
gun *n* /gʌn/

headache *n* /'hedeɪk/
health club *n* /'helθ ˌklʌb/
heavy *adj* /'hevi/
hobby *n* /'hɒbi/
hope *n, v* /həʊp/

in a rush *n* /ˌɪn ə 'rʌʃ/
it was worth it /ˌɪt wəz 'wɜ:θ ˌɪt/

kid *n* /kɪd/
knock *v* /nɒk/

lads *n pl* /lædz/
lend *v* /lend/
liposuction *n* /'laɪpoˌsʌkʃn/
lonely *adj* /'ləʊnli/
lucky *adj* /'lʌki/

mad about (sth) (= passionate)
/'mæd əˌbaʊt/
mirror *n* /'mɪrə/
miserable *adj* /'mɪzrəbl/
model *n* /'mɒdəl/
move (house) *v* /mu:v/
movies *n pl US* /'mu:viz/

need *n* /ni:d/
nervous *adj* /'nɜ:vəs/
normal *adj* /'nɔ:məl/
nutritionist *n* /nju:'trɪʃənɪst/

organize *v* /'ɔ:gənaɪz/

passion *n* /'pæʃn/
perform (a play) *v* /pə'fɔ:m/
personally *adv* /'pɜ:sənəli/
pick (sth) up (from the floor)
/ˌpɪk 'ʌp/
plastic surgery *n*
/ˌplæstɪk 'sɜ:dʒəri/
play (in the theatre) *n* /pleɪ/
pleasure *n* /'pleʒə/
poor *adj* /pɔ:, pʊə/
pose *v* /pəʊz/
post *v* /pəʊst/
project (at work) *n* /'prɒdʒekt/

relationship *n* /rɪ'leɪʃnʃɪp/
remember *v* /rɪ'membə/
responsibility *n* /rɪspɒnsə'bɪləti/
retire *v* /rɪ'taɪə/
rocket *n* /'rɒkɪt/

secret *n* /'si:krət/
sky *n* /skaɪ/
social life *n* /'səʊʃl ˌlaɪf/
soul *n* /səʊl/
spoilt *adj* /spɔɪlt/
stage (in a theatre) /steɪdʒ/

terrible *adj* /'terəbl/
tests (in hospital) *n pl* /tests/
trainer (= person) *n* /'treɪnə/
troubled *adj* /'trʌbəld/

unknown *adj* /ʌn'nəʊn/
unlimited *adj* /ʌn'lɪmɪtɪd/
unreal *adj* /ʌn'ri:əl/
unwell *adj* /ʌn'wel/

value *n* /'vælju:/
violence *n* /'vaɪələns/

wedding *n* /'wedɪŋ/
with a bit of luck
/wɪð ə ˌbɪt əv 'lʌk/
worried *adj* /'wʌrɪd/
worry *v* /'wʌri/

Unit 6

amputate *v* /'æmpjʊteɪt/
arrest *v* /ə'rest/
baker('s) /'beɪkə(z)/
bank account *n* /'bænk ə,kaʊnt/
behind *prep* /bɪ'haɪnd/
between *prep* /bɪ'twi:n/
bone *n* /bəʊn/
break up (a relationship) *v* /,breɪk 'ʌp/
brilliant (very good) *adj* /'brɪlɪənt/
building *n* /'bɪldɪŋ/
championship *n* /'tʃæmpɪənʃɪp/
chemist('s) *n* /'kemɪst(s)/
cookies (Brit Eng = biscuits) *n pl US* /'kʊkiz/
cosmopolitan *adj* /,kɒzmə'pɒlɪtən/
cottage *n* /'kɒtɪdʒ/
crowded *adj* /'kraʊdɪd/
darkness *n* /'dɑ:knəs/
daylight *n* /'deɪlaɪt/
depressing *adj* /dɪ'presɪŋ/
disaster *n* /dɪ'zɑ:stə/
dry *adj* /draɪ/
especially *adv* /ɪ'speʃəli/
farm *n* /fɑ:m/
fed up *adj* /,fed 'ʌp/
financial *adj* /faɪ'nænʃl/
flower shop *n* /'flaʊə ,ʃɒp/
founded (*the city was founded in 1177*) *pp* /'faʊndɪd/
funeral *n* /'fju:nərəl/
gate *n* /geɪt/
generosity *n* /dʒenə'rɒsɪti/
generous *adj* /'dʒenərəs/
greengrocer('s) *n* /'gri:ngrəʊsə(z)/
heating *n* /'hi:tɪŋ/
high *adj* /haɪ/
hill *n* /hɪl/
horrible *adj* /'hɒrəbl/
imagine *v* /ɪ'mædʒɪn/
in front of *prep* /ɪn 'frʌnt əv/
inherit *v* /ɪn'herɪt/
injure *v* /'ɪndʒə/
insulated *adj* /'ɪnsjʊleɪtɪd/
invest money in st *v* /ɪn,vest 'mʌni ɪn/
kind *adj* /kaɪnd/
kind-hearted *adj* /kaɪnd'hɑ:tɪd/
knee *n* /ni:/
legendary *adj* /'ledʒəndri/
library *n* /'laɪbrəri/, /laɪbri/
look forward to *v* /,lʊk 'fɔ:wəd tu:/
luxurious *adj* /lʌg'ʒʊərɪəs/
make a will *v* /,meɪk ə 'wɪl/
meanness *n* /'mi:nnəs/
mixture *n* /'mɪkstʃə/
model *n* /'mɒdəl/
nature *n* /'neɪtʃə/
next to *prep* /'nekst tu:/
noisy *adj* /'nɔɪzi/
on the corner /,ɒn ðə 'kɔ:nə/
opposite *prep* /'ɒpəzɪt/
path *n* /pɑ:θ/
penny *n* /'peni/
polluted *adj* /pə'lu:tɪd/
pond *n* /pɒnd/
poverty *n* /'pɒvəti/
primitive *adj* /'prɪmətɪv/
ragged *adj* /'rægɪd/
railway bridge *n* /'reɪlweɪ ,brɪdʒ/
river *n* /'rɪvə/
romantic *adj* /rəʊ'mæntɪk/
running water *n* /,rʌnɪŋ 'wɔ:tə/
sauna *n* /'sɔ:nə/
save *v* /seɪv/
second hand *adj* /,sekənd 'hænd/
spoil (a child) *v* /spɔɪl/
stocks and shares *n pl* /,stɒks ənd 'ʃeəz/
successful *adj* /sək'sesfl/
supermarket *n* /'su:pə,mɑ:kɪt/
take five minutes *v* /'teɪk 'faɪv 'mɪnɪts/
tall *adj* /tɔ:l/
thief *n* /θi:f/
wealthy *adj* /'welθi/
wet *adj* /wet/
widow *n* /'wɪdeʊ/
will *n* /wɪl/
windy *adj* /'wɪndi/
witch *n* /wɪtʃ/
wood *n* /wʊd/
wrap up (= put on warm clothes) *v* /,ræp 'ʌp/

Unit 7

a whole load (= lots) *coll* /ə ,həʊl 'ləʊd/
accuse *v* /ə'kju:z/
adore *v* /ə'dɔ:/
afraid of *adj* /ə'freɪd əv/
album (= record) *n* /'ælbəm/
appear *v* /ə'pɪə/
at last /ət 'lɑ:st/
award *n* /ə'wɔ:d/
away from (sb) (= not together) *adv* /ə'weɪ frəm/
background *n* /'bækgraʊnd/
backing group *n* /'bækɪŋ ,gru:p/
band (of musicians) *n* /bænd/
be prepared *v* /,bi: prɪ'peəd/
biography *n* /baɪ'ɒgrəfi/
break (= rest) *n* /breɪk/
by hand *adv* /,baɪ 'hænd/
career *n* /kə'rɪə/
celebrity *n* /sə'lebrəti/
copy (of a book) *n* /'kɒpi/
couple (= two people) *n* /'kʌpl/
drum *n* /drʌm/
especially *adv* /ɪ'speʃəli/
exactly *adv* /ɪg'zæktli/
football match *n* /'fʊtbɔ:l ,mætʃ/
freedom *n* /'fri:dəm/
fussy *adj* /'fʌsi/
gardener *n* /gɑ:dnə/
go camping *n* /,gəʊ 'kæmpɪŋ/
good taste *n* /,gʊd 'teɪst/
Gran *n coll* /græn/
guitar *n* /gɪ'tɑ:/
hard (person) *adj* /hɑ:d/
harmonica *n* /hɑ:'mɒnɪkə/
in her thirties /,ɪn hə 'θɜ:tiz/
ironing *n* /'aɪənɪŋ/
jazz *n* /dʒæz/
keyboards *n pl* /'ki:bɔ:dz/
last *v* /lɑ:st/
love at first sight /,lʌv ət ,fɜ:st 'saɪt/
mate (= friend) *n coll* /meɪt/
naturally *adv* /'nætʃrəli/
nearly *adv* /'nɪəli/
novel *n* /'nɒvəl/
novelist *n* /'nɒvəlɪst/
number one record *n* /,nʌmbə ,wʌn 'rekɔ:d/
obviously *adv* /'ɒbvɪəsli/
on tour /,ɒn tʊə/, /,ɒn 'tɔ:/
only *adj* /'əʊnli/
opposite *adj* /'ɒpəzɪt/
painter *n* /'peɪntə/
peace *n* /pi:s/
pen *n* /pen/
penny *n* /'peni/
pepper *n* /'pepə/
prefer *v* /prɪ'fɜ:/
recording studio *n* /rɪ'kɔ:dɪŋ ,stju:dɪəʊ/
related (to sb) *pp* /rɪ'leɪtɪd/
ride *v* /raɪd/
rock concert *n* /'rɒk ,kɒnsət/
rubbish (= no good) *adj coll* /'rʌbɪʃ/
salt *n* /sɔ:lt, sɒlt/
score a goal *v* /,skɔ:(r) ə 'gəʊl/
sensitive *adj* /'sensətɪv/
several (books) /'sevrəl/
short story *n* /,ʃɔ:t 'stɔ:ri/
shy *adj* /ʃaɪ/
spend time *v* /,spend 'taɪm/
split up *v* /,splɪt 'ʌp/
spoil *v* /spɔɪl/
strict *adj* /strɪkt/
superstar *n* /'su:pə,stɑ:/
take-away meal *n* /,teɪkəweɪ 'mi:l/
team up with (sb) *v* /,ti:m 'ʌp wɪð/
term (school) *n* /tɜ:m/
tour *v* /tʊə/, /tɔ:/
travel book *n* /'trævl ,bʊk/
trust *v* /trʌst/
usually *adv* /'ju:ʒəli/
vocalist *n* /'vəʊkəlɪst/
watch (to tell the time) *n* /wɒtʃ/
west *n* /west/

Unit 8

accommodation *n* /əˌkɒmə'deɪʃn/
act your age *v* /ˌækt jə(r) 'eɪdʒ/
adventurous *adj* /əd'ventʃərəs/
advice *n* /əd'vaɪs/
alarm clock *n* /ə'lɑ:m ˌklɒk/
ambulance driver *n* /'æmbjʊləns ˌdraɪvə/
anniversary *n* /ˌænɪ'vɜ:səri/
antibiotics *n pl* /ˌæntibaɪ'ɒtɪks/
appointment *n* /ə'pɔɪntmənt/
argue *v* /'ɑ:gju:/
arrangement *n* /ə'reɪndʒmənt/
artist *n* /'ɑ:tɪst/
available *adj* /ə'veɪləbl/

be sick (= vomit) *v* /ˌbi: 'sɪk/
bill (pay the bill) *n* /bɪl/
bookcase *n* /'bʊkkeɪs/
boss *n* /bɒs/

career *n* /kə'rɪə/
chilly *adj* /'tʃɪli/
cigarette lighter *n* /sɪgə'ret ˌlaɪtə/
company *n* /'kʌmpəni/
cruel *adj* /'kru:əl/

decorator *n* /'dekəreɪtə/
dentist *n* /'dentɪst/
detective *n* /dɪ'tektɪv/
diarrhoea *n* /daɪə'rɪə/
document *n* /'dɒkjʊment/
dramatically *adv* /drə'mætɪkli/
drop out of (school) *v* /ˌdrɒp 'aʊt/
drugs (take drugs) *n pl* /drʌgz/

earring *n* /'ɪərɪŋ/
earthquake *n* /'ɜ:θkweɪk/
examine *v* /ɪg'zæmɪn/
exploit *v* /ɪk'splɔɪt/

farmer *n* /'fɑ:mə/
firefighter *n* /'faɪəˌfaɪtə/
flu *n* /flu:/
food poisoning *n* /'fu:d ˌpɔɪzənɪŋ/

get one free /ˌget wʌn 'fri:/
give up *v* /ˌgɪv 'ʌp/
glands *n pl* /glændz/
go on a diet *v* /ˌgəʊ ɒn ə 'daɪət/

hairdrier *n* /'heədraɪə/
have a word with (sb) *v* /ˌhæv ə 'wɔ:d wɪð/
headache *n* /'hedeɪk/
health *n* /helθ/
horse-race *n* /'hɔ:sˌreɪs/
housewife *n* /'haʊswaɪf/

in public /ˌɪn 'pʌblɪk/
infection *n* /ɪn'fekʃn/
invention *n* /ɪn'venʃn/
invisible *adj* /ɪn'vɪsəbl/

keep fit *v* /ˌki:p 'fɪt/
kill (= hurt: *My back's killing me.*) *v* /kɪl/

lawyer *n* /'lɔ:jə/
liquid *n* /'lɪkwɪd/
local *adj* /'ləʊkl/

mechanic *n* /mɪ'kænɪk/
miner *n* /'maɪnə/

overweight *adj* /ˌəʊvə'weɪt/

plumber *n* /'plʌmə/
poetry *n* /'pəʊətri/
prescribe *v* /prɪ'skraɪb/
prescription *n* /prɪ'skrɪpʃn/
prison *n* /'prɪzn/

qualifications *n pl* /ˌkwɒlɪfɪ'keɪʃnz/

raincoat *n* /'reɪnkəʊt/
receptionist *n* /rɪ'sepʃənɪst/
recommend *v* /ˌrekə'mend/
regular hours *n pl* /ˌregjələ(r) 'aʊəz/
responsibilty *n* /rɪˌspɒnsə'bɪləti/
rude *adj* /ru:d/
runny nose /ˌrʌni 'nəʊz/
rush hour *n* /'rʌʃ ˌaʊə/

satisfied *adj* /'sætɪsfaɪd/
scary *adj* /'skeəri/
shop assistant *n* /'ʃɒp əˌsɪstənt/
signpost *n* /'saɪnpəʊst/
silly *adj* /'sɪli/
slave *n* /sleɪv/
sneeze *v* /sni:z/
soldier *n* /'səʊldʒə/
sore throat *n* /ˌsɔ: 'θrəʊt/
speciality *n* /speʃi'æləti/
stomach ache *n* /'stʌməkˌeɪk/
strict *adj* /strɪkt/
support *n* /sə'pɔ:t/
surgery *n* /'sɜ:dʒəri/
swallow *v* /'swɒləʊ/
swollen *pp* /'swəʊlən/
sympathy *n* /'sɪmpəθi/
symptom *n* /'sɪmptəm/

tape recorder *n* /'teɪp rɪˌkɔ:də/
timetable *n* /'taɪmˌteɪbl/
tin opener *n* /'tɪn ˌəʊpənə/
tough (with sb) *adj* /tʌf/
traffic lights *n pl* /'træfɪk ˌlaɪts/
twisted *adj* /'twɪstɪd/

uniform *n* /'ju:nɪfɔ:m/
unsocial *adj* /ˌʌn'səʊʃl/

vet *n* /vet/
visa *n* /'vi:zə/

Unit 9

air-conditioned *adj* /ˌeə kən'dɪʃnd/
airline *n* /'eəlaɪn/
airport *n* /'eəpɔ:t/
answerphone *n* /'ɑ:nsəˌfəʊn/
available *adj* /ə'veɪləbl/

basement *n* /'beɪsmənt/
behaviour *n* /bɪ'heɪvɪə/
bite *v* /baɪt/
boundary *n* /'baʊndəri/
building site *n* /'bɪldɪŋ ˌsaɪt/

capitalism *n* /'kæpɪtəlɪzm/
century *n* /'sentʃəri/
communist *n* /'kɒmjʊnɪst/
commute *v* /kə'mju:t/
concrete *adj* /'kɒnkri:t/
conference centre *n* /'kɒnfərəns ˌsentə/
corner of the world /'kɔ:nə(r) əv ðə ˌwɜ:ld/
cousin *n* /'kʌzən/
crew *n pl* /kru:/
cruel *adj* /'kru:əl/

developer *n* /dɪ'veləpə/
disappear *v* /'dɪsəˌpɪə/
DNA *n* /ˌdi: en 'eɪ/
do me a favour /ˌdu: mi: ə 'feɪvə/
double room *n* /ˌdʌbl 'ru:m/
dramatic *adj* /drə'mætɪk/

earthquake *n* /'ɜ:θkweɪk/
energy *n* /'enədʒi/
environment *n* /ɪn'vaɪrənmənt/
exist *v* /ɪg'zɪst/

fight a war *v* /ˌfaɪt ə 'wɔ:/
flight (on a plane) *n* /flaɪt/
forest *n* /'fɒrɪst/
fundamentally *adv* /ˌfʌndə'mentəli/

gap year *n* /'gæp ˌyɪə/
get ill *v* /ˌget 'ɪl/
get on well with (sb) *v* /ˌget ɒn 'wel wɪð/
glorious *adj* /'glɔ:rɪəs/
ground floor *n* /'graʊnd 'flɔ:/

health care *n* /'helθ ˌkeə/
heart *n* /hɑ:t/
highway *n US* /'haɪweɪ/
hurt yourself *v* /'hɜ:t jəˌself/

incredible *adj* /ɪn'kredəbl/

keep in touch *v* /ˌki:p ɪn 'tʌtʃ/
kidney *n* /'kɪdni/

leader *n* /'li:də/
liver (= body organ) *n* /'lɪvə/
locked *pp* /lɒkt/
lung *n* /lʌŋ/

main road *n* /ˌmeɪn 'rəʊd/
make a complaint *v* /ˌmeɪk ə kəm'pleɪnt/
make a reservation *v* /ˌmeɪk ə rezə'veɪʃn/
make sure *v* /ˌmeɪk 'ʃɔ:,'ʃʊə/
make up your mind *v* /ˌmeɪk ʌp jə'maɪnd/

medicine *n* /'medsn, medɪsn/
megalopolis *n* /ˌmegə'lɒpəlɪs/
mess *n* /mes/
message *n* /'mesɪdʒ/
microchip *n* /'maɪkrəʊˌtʃɪp/

north *n* /nɔ:θ/

ocean *n* /'əʊʃn/
office block *n* /'ɒfɪs ˌblɒk/
optimistic *adj* /ˌɒptɪ'mɪstɪk/

pass exams *v* /ˌpɑ:s ɪg'zæmz/
pessimism *n* /'pesɪmɪzm/
pick (sb) up (= meet in a car) *v* /ˌpɪk 'ʌp/
pillow *n* /'pɪləʊ/
pilot *n* /'paɪlət/
plant *n* /plɑ:nt/
poster *n* /'pəʊstə/
power *n* /'paʊə/

race of people *n* /ˌreɪs əv 'pi:pl/
reaction *n* /ri'ækʃn/
religion *n* /rɪ'lɪdʒən/
remarkable *adj* /rɪ'mɑ:kəbl/
resources *n pl* /rɪ'zɔ:sɪz/
revolutionize *v* /revə'lu:ʃənaɪz/
room service *n* /'ru:m ˌsɜ:vɪs/

safari *n* /sə'fɑ:ri/
salary *n* /'sæləri/
save (money) *v* /seɪv/
scuba dive *v* /'sku:bə ˌdaɪv/
shocking *adj* /'ʃɒkɪŋ/
significant *adj* /sɪg'nɪfɪkənt/
single room *n* /ˌsɪŋgl 'ru:m/
skyscraper *n* /'skaɪskreɪpə/
snow storm *v* /'snəʊ ˌstɔ:m/
spare part *n* /ˌspeə 'pɑ:t/
speed *n* /spi:d/
spread *v* /spred/
state (= government) *n* /steɪt/
statistics *n pl* /stə'tɪstɪks/
stupidity *n* /stju:'pɪdəti/

tablets *n pl* /'tæblɪts/
take care *v* /ˌteɪk 'keə/
to our advantage /tu: ˌaʊə(r) əd'vɑ:ntɪdʒ/
top floor *n* /ˌtɒp 'flɔ:/
touch *v* /tʌtʃ/
towards *prep* /tə'wɔ:dz/
traditional *adj* /trə'dɪʃənl/
trip (= visit) *n* /trɪp/

ugly *adj* /'ʌgli/

visa *n* /'vi:sə/
vision *n* /'vɪʒn/
volcano *n* /vɒl'keɪnəʊ/

wake-up call *n* /'weɪk ʌp ˌkɔ:l/
water *v* /'wɔ:tə/
wealth *n* /welθ/

Unit 10

ache *v* /eɪk/
adventure *n* /əd'ventʃə/
alive *adj* /ə'laɪv/
alone *adj* /ə'ləʊn/
amazing *adj* /ə'meɪzɪŋ/
armed police *n pl* /ˌɑ:md pə'li:s/
at peace *adj* /ət 'pi:s/
background *n* /'bækgraʊnd/
balaclava *n* /bælə'klɑ:və/
beans *n pl* /bi:nz/
beg *v* /beg/
berries *n pl* /'beriz/
blindfold *n* /'blaɪndfəʊld/
brave *adj* /breɪv/
burn *n* /bɜ:n/
bush *n* /bʊʃ/
cake *n* /keɪk/
can't stand (sth) (= hate) *v* /ˌkɑ:nt 'stænd/
cartoon (on TV) *n* /ˌkɑ:'tu:n/
circumstances *n pl* /'sɜ:kəmstænsɪz/
confess *v* /kən'fes/
comedy *n* /'kɒmədi/
comfortable *adj* /'kʌmftəbl/
concentrate *v* /'kɒnsəntreɪt/
confession *n* /kən'feʃn/
contact *v* /'kɒntækt/
contain *v* /kən'teɪn/
covered in sweat /ˌkʌvəd ɪn 'swet/
crawl *v* /krɔ:l/
crazy *adj* /'kreɪzi/
dark (at night) *adj* /dɑ:k/
diary *n* /'daɪəri/
duck *n* /dʌk/
efficiently *adv* /ɪ'fɪʃəntli/
emergency services *n pl* /ɪ'mɜ:dʒənsi 'sɜ:vɪsɪz/
ending (of a book) *n* /'endɪŋ/
exhausted *adj* /ɪg'zɔ:stɪd/
fail an exam *v* /ˌfeɪl ən ɪg'zæm/
fall down (= break) *v* /ˌfɔ:l 'daʊn/
feel sorry *v* /ˌfi:l 'sɒri/
film star *n* /'fɪlm ˌstɑ:/
fizzy drink *n* /ˌfɪzi 'drɪŋk/
food poisoning *n* /'fu:d ˌpɔɪzənɪŋ/
footpath *n* /'fʊtpɑ:θ/
for a while /ˌfər ə 'waɪl/
forgive *v* /fə'gɪv/
freedom *n* /'fri:dəm/
frightened *pp* /'fraɪtənd/
get rid of (sth) *v* /get 'rɪd əv/
go climbing *v* /ˌgəʊ 'klaɪmɪŋ/
go on hands and knees *v* /gəʊ ɒn 'hændz ən(d) 'ni:z/
God bless all /ˌgɒd ˌbles 'ɔ:l/
graduate *v* /'grædjʊeɪt/
ground (= the floor) *n* /graʊnd/
haircut *n* /'heəkʌt/
hairdresser *n* /'heədresə/
handrail *n* /'hændreɪl/
hear from (sb) *v* /'hɪə frəm/
helicopter *n* /'helɪkɒptə/
high *adj* /haɪ/
hitchhike *v* /'hɪtʃˌhaɪk/
hobby *n* /'hɒbi/
hole *n* /həʊl/
horror film *n* /'hɒrə ˌfɪlm/
hunter *n* /'hʌntə/
instructor *n* /ɪn'strʌktə/
invent *v* /ɪn'vent/
investigate *v* /ɪn'vestɪgeɪt/
joke *n* /dʒəʊk/
kidnap *v* /'kɪdnæp/
let (sb) go (= release) *v* /ˌlet 'gəʊ/
library *n* /'laɪbrəri/, /'laɪbri/
lose consciousness *v* /ˌlu:z 'kɒnʃəsnəs/
lose weight *v* /ˌlu:z 'weɪt/
manage to do (sth) *v* /'mænɪdʒ tə 'du:/
manual *n* /'mænjʊəl/
meat *n* /mi:t/
moose *n* /mu:s/
narrow *adj* /'nærəʊ/
nature *n* /'neɪtʃə/
petrol station *n* /'petrəl ˌsteɪʃn/
plan *v* /plæn/
poisonous *adj* /'pɔɪzənəs/
posh *adj* /pɒʃ/
possessions *n pl* /pə'zeʃnz/
recipe *n* /'resəpi/
report (from school) *n* /rɪ'pɔ:t/
roller coaster *n* /'rəʊləˌkəʊstə/
row (= argument) *n* /raʊ/
scared *adj* /skeəd/
scream *v* /skri:m/
seed (of a plant) *n* /si:d/
shake *v* /ʃeɪk/
shelter *n* /'ʃeltə/
simple life /'sɪmpl ˌlaɪf/
sleeping bag *n* /'sli:pɪŋ ˌbæg/
spider *n* /'spaɪdə/
spy novel *n* /'spaɪ ˌnɒvəl/
squirrel *n* /'skwɪrəl/
starve *v* /stɑ:v/
steep *adj* /sti:p/
stove *n* /stəʊv/
strength *n* /streŋθ/
stuck in a lift /ˌstʌk ɪn ə 'lɪft/
survive *v* /sə'vaɪv/
sweat *n* /swet/
take (sb) to court *v* /ˌteɪk tə 'kɔ:t/
terrifed *adj* /'terɪfaɪd/
terrorist *n* /'terərɪst/
thin *adj* /θɪn/
thrill *n* /θrɪl/
tie (sb) up *v* /ˌtaɪ 'ʌp/
total *n* /'təʊtl/
trapped *pp* /træpt/
view *n* /vju:/
village *n* /'vɪlɪdʒ/
weak *adj* /wi:k/
wild (place) *adj* /waɪld/
wild mushrooms *n pl* /ˌwaɪld 'mʌʃru:mz/
witness *n* /'wɪtnəs/
woods *n pl* /wʊdz/

Unit 11

addict *n* /'ædɪkt/
addictive *adj* /ə'dɪktɪv/
advertise *v* /'ædvətaɪz/
advertisement *n* /əd'vɜ:tɪsmənt/
American Indians *n pl* /əˌmerɪkən 'ɪndɪənz/
ancient *adj* /'eɪnʃənt/
Arctic Circle *n* /ˌɑ:ktɪk 'sɜ:kl/
ban *v* /bæn/
banana *n* /bə'nɑ:nə/
beard *n* /bɪəd/
billboard *n US* /'bɪlbɔ:d/
bottle *n* /bɒtl/
briefcase *n* /'bri:fkeɪs/
can *n* /kæn/
cargo *n* /kɑ:gəʊ/
chain-smoke *v* /'tʃeɪnˌsməʊk/
chef *n* /ʃef/
chew *v* /tʃu:/
chewing gum *n* /'tʃu:ɪŋ ˌgʌm/
commercially *adv* /kə'mɜ:ʃəli/
complaint *n* /kəm'pleɪnt/
cotton *n* /'kɒtən/
cry (= call/shout) *v* /kraɪ/
death *n* /deθ/
drive-in restaurant *n* /ˌdraɪvɪn 'restrɒnt/
empty *adj* /'empti/
export *v* /ɪk'spɔ:t/
fabric *n* /'fæbrɪk/
factory *n* /'fæktri/
feed *v* /fi:d/
freshen *v* /'freʃn/
gallon *n* /'gælən/
genius *n* /'dʒi:nɪəs/
grass *n* /grɑ:s/
harm *v* /hɑ:m/
harvest *n* /'hɑ:vɪst/
hire *v* /haɪə/
history *n* /'hɪstri/
honey *n* /'hʌni/
ill-effect *n* /ˌɪl ɪ'fekt/
industrial *adj* /ɪn'dʌstrɪəl/
industry *n* /'ɪndəstri/
inhale *v* /ɪn'heɪl/
invent *n* /ɪn'vent/
joke *n* /dʒəʊk/
keep off *v* /ˌki:p 'ɒf/
leaves *n pl* /li:vz/
lie *n* /laɪ/
lift (give a lift to sb) *n* /lɪft/
lose weight *v* /ˌlu:z 'weɪt/
lung cancer *n* /'lʌŋ ˌkænsə/
luxury *n* /'lʌkʃeri/
match (sport) *n* /mætʃ/
motorway *n* /'məʊtəweɪ/
mouth *n* /maʊθ/
out of order /ˌaʊt əv 'ɔ:də/
overseas *adv* /ˌəʊvə'si:z/
packet *n* /'pækɪt/
partner *n* /'pɑ:tnə/
passenger *n* /'pæsɪndʒə/
pineapple *n* /'paɪnæpl/
plantation *n* /plɑ:n'teɪʃn/
popularity *n* /ˌpɒpjʊ'lærɪti/
produce *v* /prə'dju:s/
product *n* /'prɒdʌkt/
promise *v* /'prɒmɪs/
quantity *n* /'kwɒntɪti/
queue *n* /kju:/
rare *adj* /reə/
refine *v* /rɪ'faɪn/
revolution *n* /revə'lu:ʃn/
rice *n* /raɪs/
sailor *n* /'seɪlə/
secret *n* /'si:krət/
seed *n* /si:d/
serve *v* /sɜ:v/
services (on a motorway) *n pl* /'sɜ:vɪsɪz/
ship (to ship across the Atlantic) *v* /ʃɪp/
silk *n* /sɪlk/
skeleton *n* /'skelɪtən/
slave *n* /sleɪv/
slavery *n* /'sleɪvəri/
smelly *adj* /'smeli/
soil *n* /sɔɪl/
southbound *adj* /'saʊθbaʊnd/
space (go into space) *n* /speɪs/
stock exchange *n* /'stɒk ɪksˌtʃeɪndʒ/
sugar cane *n* /'ʃʊgə ˌkeɪn/
sweeten *v* /'swi:tən/
technology *n* /tek'nɒlədʒi/
tobacco *n* /tə'bækəʊ/
top secret *adj* /ˌtɒp 'si:krət/
train track *n* /'treɪn ˌtræk/
tree sap *n* /'tri: ˌsæp/
truth *n* /tru:θ/
unattended *adj* /ʌnə'tendɪd/
war *n* /wɔ:/
watch *n* /wɒtʃ/
wrap *v* /ræp/
zoo *n* /zu:/

Unit 12

apparent *adj* /ə'pærənt/
brain scan department *n* /'breɪn ˌskæn dɪˌpɑ:tmənt/
brain tumour *n* /'breɪn ˌtju:mə/
budgie *n* /'bʌdʒi/
cap (= hat) n /kæp/
consultant (in a hospital) *n* /kən'sʌltənt/
corridor *n* /'kɒrɪdɔ:/
criminal *n* /'krɪmɪnəl/
dizzy *adj* /'dɪzi/
dress *n* /dres/
fall in love *v* /ˌfɔ:l ɪn 'lʌv/
fill in (a form) *v* /ˌfɪl 'ɪn/
firmly *adv* /'fɜ:mli/
ghost *n* /gəʊst/
ghostbuster *n* /'gəʊstbʌstə/
give (sb) a lift (in a car) *v* /ˌgɪv ə 'lɪft/
grandmother *n* /'græn(d)mʌðə/
grey *adj* /greɪ/
haunt *v* /hɔ:nt/
hurry up *v* /ˌhʌri 'ʌp/
in my way /ˌɪn maɪ 'weɪ/
invisible *adj* /ɪn'vɪzəbl/
kick (sb) out *v* /ˌkɪk 'aʊt/
leave (sb) alone *v* /ˌli:v ə'ləʊn/
look forward to (doing sth) *v* /ˌlʊk 'fɔ:wəd tu:/
look out! /lʊk 'aʊt/
mind (= consciousness) *n* /maɪnd/
miss the train *v* /ˌmɪs ðə 'treɪn/
nasty *adj* /'nɑ:sti/
operation *n* /ɒpə'reɪʃn/
palace *n* /'pæləs/
pass on (a message) *v* /ˌpɑ:s 'ɒn/
portrait *n* /'pɔ:treɪt/
princess *n* /prɪn'ses/
put out (a cigarette) *v* /ˌpʊt 'aʊt/
run out of (sth) *v* /ˌrʌn 'aʊt əv/
servant *n* /'sɜ:vənt/
shoplifting *n* /'ʃɒplɪftɪŋ/
social worker *n* /'səʊʃl ˌwɜ:kə/
sort out (a problem) *v* /ˌsɔ:t 'aʊt/
spirit (= ghost) *n* /'spɪrɪt/
terrible *adj* /'terəbl/
toothache *n* /'tu:θeɪk/
transparent *adj* /ˌtræns'pærənt/
trouble *v* /'trʌbl/
typical *adj* /'tɪpɪkl/
uniform *n* /'ju:nɪfɔ:m/
unpleasant *adj* /ʌn'pleznt/
vicar *n* /'vɪkə/
victim *n* /'vɪktɪm/
voices *n pl* /'vɔɪsɪz/
wallet *n* /'wɒlɪt/
wedding *n* /'wedɪŋ/

Unit 13

advertisement *n* /əd'vɜ:tɪsmənt/
attack *v* /ə'tæk/
authoritative *adj* /ɔ:'θɒrɪtətɪv/
barrel of beer *n* /ˌbærəl əv 'bɪə/
barter *v* /'bɑ:tə/
beach *n* /bi:tʃ/
beachcomber *n* /'bi:tʃˌkəʊmə/
calm *adj* /kɑ:m/
checkout till *n* /'tʃekaʊt ˌtɪl/
connect (sb to sb on the phone) *v* /kə'nekt/
deer *n* /dɪə/
earn a living *v* /ˌɜ:n ə 'lɪvɪŋ/
employ *v* /ɪm'plɔɪ/
exactly *adv* /ɪg'zæktli/
fetch *v* /fetʃ/
filmmaker *n* /'fɪlmmeɪkə/
fluently *adv* /'flu:əntli/
fly a hot air balloon *v* /ˌflaɪ ə ˌhɒt ˌeə bə'lu:n/
get used to (sth) *v* /ˌget 'ju:st tu:/
get wet *v* /ˌget 'wet/
go out with (sb) (as boyfriend and girlfriend) *v* /ˌgəʊ 'aʊt wɪð/
heaven *n* /'hevn/
heavy *adj* /'hevi/
hold on (= wait) *v* /weɪt/
homeless *adj* /'həʊmləs/
honest *adj* /'ɒnɪst/
income *n* /'ɪnkəm/
indoors *adv* /ɪn'dɔ:z/
land (a plane) *v* /lænd/
lively *adj* /'laɪvli/
mainly *adv* /'meɪnli/
movie director *n* /'mu:vi dəˌrektə/
mystery tour *n* /'mɪstəri ˌtʊə/
outdoors *adv* /ˌaʊt'dɔ:z/
passion *n* /'pæʃn/
pension *n* /'penʃn/
philosophy *n* /fɪ'lɒsəfi/
pie *n* /paɪ/
plumber *n* /'plʌmə/
poor visibility /ˌpɔ:,pʊə vɪzə'bɪləti/
professionally *adv* /prə'feʃənəli/
put (sb) off (= make sb dislike sth) *v* /ˌpʊt 'ɒf/
realize *v* /'rɪəlaɪz/
regular job /ˌregjʊlə 'dʒɒb/
reply *n* /rɪ'plaɪ/
roller skates *n pl* /'rəʊlə ˌskeɪts/
routines *n pl* /ru:'ti:nz/
salary *n* /'sæləri/
seriously *adv* /'sɪərɪəsli/
skate *v* /skeɪt/
sunset *n* /'sʌnset/
tin *n* /tɪn/
waste *n* /weɪst/
wind (in the air) *n* /wɪnd/
windy *adj* /'wɪndi/

Unit 14

afterwards *adv* /'ɑ:ftəwədz/
bachelor *n* /'bætʃələ/
behave *v* /bɪ'heɪv/
character *n* /'kærəktə/
coin *n* /kɔɪn/
communicate *v* /kə'mju:nɪkeɪt/
cruel *adj* /'kru:əl/
delighted *adj* /dɪ'laɪtɪd/
desperate *adj* /'despərət/
fall in love *v* /ˌfɔ:l ɪn 'lʌv/
fall over *v* /ˌfɔ:l 'əʊvə/
fiction *n* /'fɪkʃn/
forever *adv* /fə'revə/
forgive *v* /fə'gɪv/
furious *adj* /'fjʊəriəs/
get in touch *v* /ˌget ɪn 'tʌtʃ/
heads or tails /'hedz ɔ: 'teɪlz/
hurt *v* /hɜ:t/
in a mess /ɪn ə 'mes/
knock *n* /nɒk/
make a will *v* /ˌmeɪk ə 'wɪl/
make up (after a quarrel) *v* /ˌmeɪk 'ʌp/
marriage *n* /'mærɪdʒ/
note (write a note) *n* /nəʊt/
novelist *n* /'nɒvəlɪst/
on condition /ˌɒn kən'dɪʃn/
pay *n* /peɪ/
politician *n* /pɒlə'tɪʃn/
quarrel *n, v* /'kwɒrəl/
remarry *v* /ˌri:'mæri/
revenge *n* /rɪ'vendʒ/
rubbish bin *n* /'rʌbɪʃ ˌbɪn/
shadow *n* /'ʃædəʊ/
silhouette *n* /ˌsɪlʊ'et/
sin *n* /sɪn/
single (= one, a single word) *adj* /'sɪŋgl/
soft (noise) *adj* /sɒft/
solicitor *n* /sə'lɪsɪtə/
suitcase *n* /'su:tkeɪs/
sway *v* /sweɪ/
toss (toss a coin) *v* /tɒs/
unfair *adj* /ˌʌn'feə/
unmarried *adj* /ˌʌn'mærɪd/
violent *adj* /'vaɪələnt/
water *v* /'wɔ:tə/
wedding *n* /'wedɪŋ/